Evolution and Path Dependence in Economic Ideas

EUROPEAN ASSOCIATION FOR EVOLUTIONARY POLITICAL ECONOMY

General Editor: Geoffrey M. Hodgson, *University of Hertfordshire Business School, UK*

Mixed Economies in Europe: An Evolutionary Perspective on their Emergence, Transition and Regulation
Edited by Wolfgang Blaas and John Foster

The Political Economy of Diversity: Evolutionary Perspectives on Economic Order and Disorder
Edited by Robert Delorme and Kurt Dopfer

On Economic Institutions: Theory and Applications
Edited by John Groenewegen, Christos Pitelis and Sven-Erik Sjöstrand

Rethinking Economics: Markets, Technology and Economic Evolution
Edited by Geoffrey M. Hodgson and Ernesto Screpanti

Environment, Technology and Economic Growth: The Challenge to Sustainable Development
Edited by Andrew Tylecote and Jan van der Straaten

Institutions and Economic Change: New Perspectives on Markets, Firms and Technology
Edited by Klaus Nielsen and Björn Johnson

Pluralism in Economics: New Perspectives in History and Methodology
Edited by Andrea Salanti and Ernesto Screpanti

Beyond Market and Hierarchy: Interactive Governance and Social Complexity
Edited by Ash Amin and Jerzy Hausner

Employment, Technology and Economic Needs: Theory, Evidence and Public Policy
Edited by Jonathan Michie and Angelo Reati

Institutions and the Evolution of Capitalism: Implications of Evolutionary Economics
Edited by John Groenewegen and Jack Vromen

Is Economics an Evolutionary Science? The Legacy of Thorstein Veblen
Edited by Francisco Louçã and Mark Perlman

Technology and Knowledge: From the Firm to Innovation Systems
Edited by Pier Paolo Saviotti and Bart Nooteboom

Evolution and Path Dependence in Economic Ideas: Past and Present
Edited by Pierre Garrouste and Stavros Ioannides

Evolution and Path Dependence in Economic Ideas

Past and Present

Edited by

Pierre Garrouste

Professor of Economics, Groupe d'Analysis et de Théorie Economique (GATE), France

Stavros Ioannides

Assistant Professor of Economics, Department of Political Science and History, Panteion University, Greece

EUROPEAN ASSOCIATION FOR EVOLUTIONARY POLITICAL ECONOMY

Edward Elgar

Cheltenham, UK • Northampton, MA, USA

Published by
Edward Elgar Publishing Limited
Glensanda House
Montpellier Parade
Cheltenham
Glos GL50 1UA
UK

Edward Elgar Publishing, Inc.
136 West Street
Suite 202
Northampton
Massachusetts 01060
USA

A catalog record for this book is available from the British Library

Library of Congress Cataloging in Publication Data

Evolution and path dependence in economic ideas : past and present / edited by Pierre Garrouste, Stavros Ioannides.
   "In association with the European Association of Evolutionary Political Economy."
   Includes bibliographical references and index.
   1. Evolutionary economics—History. I. Garrouste, Pierre, 1954– II. Ioannides, Stavros.
III. European Association for Evolutionary Political Economy.

  HB97.3 .E886 2001
  330.1—dc21

                                00–055118

ISBN 1 84064 081 2
Printed and bound in Great Britain by MPG Books Ltd, Bodmin, Cornwall

Contents

List of Contributors   vii

1   Evolution and path dependence in economic ideas: past and present   1
    Pierre Garrouste and Stavros Ioannides
2   Path dependence, its critics, and the quest for 'historical economics'   15
    Paul A. David
3   The meaning of market: comparing Austrian and Institutional
    economics   41
    Philippe Dulbecco and Veronique Dutraive
4   Schumpeter and the pendulum: how evolution was whipped out in
    the construction of canonical economics   71
    Francisco Louçã
5   Veblen and Commons on private property: an institutionalist
    discussion around a capitalist foundation   91
    Philippe Broda
6   Competition, competitive selection and economic evolution   107
    John Foster
7   Evolutionary themes in the Austrian tradition: Menger,
    Wieser and Schumpeter on institutions and rationality   133
    Richard Arena and Sandye Gloria-Palermo
8   Reading Edith Penrose's *The Theory of the Growth of the Firm*
    forty years on (1959–1999)   148
    Margherita Turvani
9   Economic analysis of human effort in organizations: a historical
    and critical perspective   179
    Bénédicte Berthe and Michel Renault
10 Path dependence in scientific evolution   205
    Albert Jolink and Jack J. Vromen
11 Reflections on the progress of heterodox economics   225
    A.W. Coats

Index   239

Contributors

Richard Arena
LATAPSES (CNRS)
University of Nice-Sophia Antipolis

Bénédicte Berthe
CEREO
Université de Bretagne Sud

Philippe Broda
Institut Commercial
de Nancy (ICN-Nancy)

A.W. Bob Coats
Department of Economics
University of Nottingham

Paul A. David
All Souls College, Oxford
and Stanford University

Philippe Dulbecco
CERDI (Centre d'Etudes et de Recherches sur le Développement International),
Université d'Auvergne Clermont 1, Clermont Ferrand

Veronique Dutraive
GATE (Groupe d'Analyse et de Théorie Economique)
Université Lumière Lyon 2

John Foster
University of Queensland
Brisbane, Queensland

Sandye Gloria-Palermo
GREUSET
University of Saint-Etienne

Albert Jolink
*Netherlands Institute for Advanced Study in the Humanities and Social Sciences
and Center for History in Management and Economics Studies
Erasmus University
Rotterdam*

Francisco Louçã
*Instituto Superior de Economia e Gestão
Universidade Técnica de Lisboa*

Michel Renault
*CREREG/IREIMAR
Université de Rennes 1*

Margherita Turvani
*DAEST-IUAV
University of Venice*

Jack J. Vromen
*Erasmus University
Rotterdam*

1. Evolution and path dependence in economic ideas: past and present

Pierre Garrouste and Stavros Ioannides

1 INTRODUCTION

One hundred years ago Thorstein Veblen (1898) asked 'Why is economics not an evolutionary science?', Alfred Marshall, ([1920] 1949, p. xii) declared that 'the Mecca of the economist lies in economic biology', and Carl Menger (1985) proposed his 'organic' account of the evolution of social institutions. And yet, mainstream 20th century economics has on the whole neglected such appeals and has carried on as if its subject matter could be safely assumed to be independent of history and essentially timeless. Time was thus relegated to the interval between two equilibrium states that follows an exogenous disturbance of the original market configuration. The axiom of rationality ensured that the optimum and, with it, efficiency will be attained, thus making this interval irrelevant for theoretical purposes. More importantly, in this account, time is not only theoretically irrelevant but also entirely reversible, since the 'former' and the 'latter' equilibrium states are determined solely by the sequence of change in external conditions.

Given this view of mainstream economics about its subject matter, it can only be expected that it holds a similar view about the history of economics itself. This history was and still is generally perceived as a sequence of successive refinements of the analytical tools of the discipline, a view that reconfirmed the optimizing outlook of the dominant paradigm. Of course, more sophisticated approaches to the history of the discipline always understood that economic ideas are not created in a vacuum, that an understanding of their evolution has to take into account the development of ideas in other social sciences, and even some natural sciences, the general intellectual climate in the context of which they emerged and the concrete economic problems that they were striving to address. However, even sophisticated historians of economic thought treated such influences on the development of economics little differently from the constraints under which, according to standard neoclassical theory, individual agents are supposed to maximize their utilities. Again, therefore, the history of the field was perceived as a process inevitably leading to an optimum.[1]

2   ON PATH DEPENDENCE...

Since the 1980s, however, there has been a renewed interest in attempts to introduce historicity in economic theory. There is now a growing literature that is characterized by an important concern for the analysis of the evolution of economic phenomena. Indeed, notions such as 'hysteresis' and 'path dependence' have already become familiar theoretical concepts. The basic idea behind this literature is that it is not possible to explain a state of the world without analysing the process that tends to lead to that state. As an example, Arthur (1985) shows that the competition between technologies, standards or conventions, can be conceived as a self-enforcing and reinforcing process that possibly ends in a lock-in, with the outcome of this process not necessarily being the optimal solution.

The argument rests on the realization that, under some specific conditions such as network positive externalities, there is an incentive for individuals to adopt a certain sort of behaviour, only due to the fact that a considerable number of others adopt it also. Indeed the incentive will be greater as more individuals adopt the specific behaviour. Thus, Paul David (1985, 1986) shows that the initial adoption of the standard keyboard layout QWERTY, made its further adoption look like a rational decision, thus reinforcing it. This process of positive 'feedback' continues until one solution is selected. What has made this line of analysis especially interesting in recent years is the realization that positive externalities as well as increasing returns are much more ubiquitous in economics than was usually assumed.

Therefore, recent interest in this mode of 'evolutionary' analysis stems from the realization that many economic phenomena can perhaps be understood as effects of path dependent processes. Although the issue is currently hotly debated,[2] Paul David's analysis of the way a standard is selected has had an important impact on the way economists are now dealing with the way an outcome emerges. This impact can be explained by three major implications of the analysis:

First, it is impossible to know *ex ante* what will be the outcome of such a process of competition among standards, because the future value of a stochastic variable cannot be predicted on the basis of its present and past values. In other words, it is impossible to predict what the future is going to look like. We thus come close to the evolutionary metaphor that sees the outcome of a selection process as unpredictable, due to possible mutations.

Second, the process is sensitive to very small variations of the variables or parameters that define it. Thus, Baumol and Benhabib (1989) show that a very small modification of a parameter may produce a switch from a cyclical trajectory to a chaotic one. Such phenomena resemble those Schelling considers in his *Micromotives and Macrobehavior* (1978), when he argues that it is possible to obtain what is known as a punctuated equilibrium (Young, 1996). Considering two societies where initial conditions are the same 'there is a positive probability that at any given future time they will be operating different conventions' as Young, (1996, p. 111) puts it.

Third, at the end of the selection process, that is to say, when the lock-in effect is taking place, the outcome becomes irreversible. Indeed, the only possibility to escape from a lock-in is through some sort of organized collective action. Young (1996) explains that a modification of a convention can only be realized under specific conditions. The inertia of the lock-in effect is perfectly illustrated by Egidi's work dealing with the emergence and evolution of routines of coordination (Egidi and Narduzzo, 1996).

3   ...AND THE HISTORY OF THOUGHT

The ideas of path dependence and hysteresis are not new when we look at economics in a historical perspective. In fact, the idea of path dependence was already present in the work of theorists who viewed economic processes in an evolutionary framework. Two examples can be presented: Menger's analysis of 'organic' institutions and Veblen's concept of 'cumulative causation'.

When dealing with the emergence of money, Menger was actually offering an explanation which is very close to the way modern economists analyse phenomena such as lock-in effects in technological competition (Arthur), the selection of standards (David), or the emergence of conventions. Menger thought that the best way for individuals to realize their own interests is to imitate those who have been most successful in the past. According to him, some individuals discover that the best solution for them is not to exchange directly a good they want with the good they have, but to exchange the good they have with a good that can be exchanged with many other goods. In this way, they can get an outcome that is much more advantageous than one obtained by direct bartering. In time, other individuals progressively come to imitate this kind of behaviour. The goods that are more exchangeable on the market are becoming more marketable and through a self-reinforced process, a good is progressively selected to become exchangeable with all others.

Veblen's evolutionism is based on the notion of 'cumulative causation', a cumulative process which explains why habits of thought are reinforced just because they have been shaped in the past. Therefore, Hodgson (1992, pp. 292–3) is correct in noting that 'it would seem that the cumulative and self-reinforced aspect of institutions and routines relates to some kind of process of positive feedback [...] Such locked-in phenomena can thus be regarded as sufficiently stable units of selection in an evolutionary process'.

These two conceptions of the emergence (Menger) and evolution (Veblen) of institutions, even though they are inspired by two different methodological principles (individualism vs. holism) are, for one, complementary rather than mutually exclusive (Garrouste, 1995). In addition, they are based on the same tool, the idea of path dependence or, more precisely, a process of self-reinforcement.

However, it is not only that institutions are important for the study of economic processes, for it can also be argued that the history of economic ideas is itself characterized by path dependence. Therefore, the institutional framework within which these ideas are produced, applied and reproduced must be as important as in the realm of actual economic processes. In this context, the institutional framework in the very general sense that encompasses both the formal institutions within which economists work – university departments, professional associations, academic journals, and so on – as well the dominant modes of thought about their field, must have profound implications for the kind of theory that comes to be produced. In other words, in every historical period it is precisely this institutional framework that determines what is generally perceived as the 'orthodoxy' or the 'mainstream'.

That this is indeed the case is evident from the fact that ideas like the ones we have presented above were not entirely forgotten after the hints of Veblen, Menger and Marshall, with which we opened this chapter. However, for 20th century economics, such ideas have always remained heterodox. Yet, it is remarkable that, even in this adverse intellectual climate, different schools of thought, different theorists, and different contexts kept reviving them. For after all, it was these ideas that came to the forefront when theorists stressed the importance of increasing returns (Sraffa, 1926), or expressed scepticism and reservations concerning the principle of rationality (Alchian, 1950), or questioned the timeless character of the concept of equilibrium (Kaldor, 1972; Robinson, 1978).

Of course, the above should not be taken to mean that modern work on evolutionary ideas and path dependence constitutes merely a rediscovery of the ideas of past masters. However, we believe that a blending of modern work with an exploration of how similar ideas have emerged in the history of economic thought may lead contemporary economists to two fruitful realizations.

The first concerns the importance of the history of economic thought. However, our focus here is not upon the history of thought *per se*. It seems to us important to consider the way economists of the past have dealt with problems very similar to our own, for this may help us address in a more sophisticated manner the theoretical riddles of our time. Indeed, we have noted that Menger and Veblen were trying to solve the problem of the emergence and evolution of institutions in a way which closely resembles the one we are now employing in trying to explain these phenomena. As an example, Schotter (1994, p. 557) writes that Von Neumann and Morgenstern's book was the only analytical solution to the Mengerian problem of 'organic' institution because 'Game Theory was to be the tool with which to realise Menger's program'.

Second, we wish to make the point that, in every historical phase, what is thought of as 'heterodoxy' often constitutes a kind of inspiration for the so-called 'orthodoxy'.[3] In other words, as institutionalism (old and new) as well as evolutionism are progressively introduced into economics, the notion of path dependence is bound to become more and more accepted. The idea that institutions matter, and that it is possible to explain their emergence and evolution, is now something that 'standard economics' is beginning to take into account. As we saw, Young is an example of such an evolution; using game theory he explains how conventions emerge and evolve. In the same way, evolutionary game theory shows that, due to a process of selection and mutation, it is possible for a population (that is to say, for a set of strategies) to converge to an evolutionary stable trajectory which is very close to a locked-in outcome.

In sum, we argue that an essential dimension of the conceptual development of the discipline must necessarily involve an examination of the history of its own concepts and a recognition that the process of conceptual development is itself characterized by path dependence and locked-in outcomes. Therefore, what characterizes the contributions collected in this volume is a critical stance towards the timeless and ahistorical theorizing – as well as self-perception – of mainstream economics. The twin ideas around which these contributions revolve are the *historicity* both of economic processes and of economic thought. Of course, the mere reference to the concept of historicity implies that these ideas have a past and a present. Hopefully, the contents of this volume will convince the reader that they also have a future.

4   AN OVERVIEW OF THE VOLUME

All contributions to this book stem from papers read at an international conference of the European Association for Evolutionary Political Economy that was held in Athens, in November 1997. They were selected for this thematic volume after a review process and an elaboration as well as revision of original presentations.

In Chapter 2, 'Path dependence, its critics, and the quest for "historical economics"', Paul David attempts to set the theoretical framework within which economics could genuinely acquire the character of a historical science, thus giving substantive content to the assertion that 'history matters'. David maintains that *path dependence* constitutes the central concept for such an approach. However, the ahistorical character of mainstream economics makes the adoption of the concept difficult, while, additionally, the sunk costs that most economists have incurred in their training in static analysis hinders that adoption. Moreover, it is precisely these sunk costs that often lead mainstream theorists to an unwarranted rejection of the concept of path dependence.

David thus attempts to explicate the theory of path dependent phenomena by explicitly addressing the critiques that the concept has attracted. First of all, he shows that path dependence is only relevant to *stochastic* processes, which allows him to juxtapose it to chaos theory. In the latter, small variations in initial conditions may have profound implications for future outcomes. However, the deterministic nature of chaos theory cannot capture the significance of small historical events, which is precisely where the relevance of path dependence for historical social science lies. Secondly, David addresses the concept of lock-in and especially its rejection by the critics of path dependence. The latter base their critique on the coupling of the notion of lock-in to that of market failure. In their view, the persistence of an inefficient outcome may simply mean that agents don't switch to the more efficient configuration because of prohibitive switching costs. Contrary to this view, Paul David argues that even in such a case agents still end up in a trajectory that is not as efficient as another that was readily available at the moment the choice was made. Therefore, path dependent processes may, though not necessarily, lead to inefficient outcomes, albeit of a kind that is not tractable through static welfare analysis.

Finally, Paul David addresses some of the policy implications that the idea of path dependence entails. Far from favouring a comprehensive public inter-vention – of the kind that standard welfare analysis recommended for cases of market failure and that the critics of path dependence usually assume to follow from this idea – it sheds new light on how public policy can help the private sphere to cope with the uncertainty that any decision over standards entails. It therefore helps not by replacing markets but by assisting private agents to make decisions that are less myopic and less prone to disregard the wider implications of their decisions.

In Chapter 3, 'The meaning of market: comparing Austrian and Institutional economics', Philippe Dulbecco and Veronique Dutraive take another look at historicity, by attempting to trace the concept in the work of two schools of thought that are usually thought of as theoretically incompatible: Austrian and Institutional economics. In fact, the authors claim that it is precisely the view of economic processes as essentially irreversible in time that constitutes a major, and hitherto overlooked, common ground between the two schools.

Dulbecco and Dutraive base their analysis on the conception of the institution of the market that they extract from representative works of the two theoretical camps. The main idea that bridges, as it were, the two schools of thought is that market and more generally economic phenomena must be thought of as processes. In turn, the notion of process leads to two important ideas, that are shared by the two schools and that set them apart from the view of the market espoused by the standard neoclassical mainstream: *endogeneity* and *time*. Unlike the mainstream view of agency as passive, for example 'price taking' behaviour, for Institutionalists and Austrians the idea of endogeneity presupposes a creative view of agency. On the other hand, the idea that economic processes unfold in real time means that the order in which specific events occur determines future outcomes. Therefore, in both schools we find, albeit in a rudimentary form, the idea of path dependence.

Of course, Austrian economics and the Institutionalists differ in important methodological respects. The former views the individual agent as the ultimate unit of analysis, and thus individual behaviour as the basis for any explanation of social phenomena. By contrast, Institutionalists treat the 'institution' as the basic unit of analysis, and thus see human agency as conditioned by the institutional framework within which action takes place. However, the authors argue that, even in the issue of institutions, Austrian and Institutionalist views can be reconciled. They show that Austrians place emphasis on the creation of institutions through individual action, while the latter focus on how institutions change through time. For both schools of thought, however, the institution is a central concept, for only through institutions is knowledge, which is necessary for action, disseminated through the system. On these grounds, the authors argue that a dialogue between Austrians and Institutionalists may prove especially fruitful.

We argued above that the problem of the historicity of economic phenomena and processes has always plagued economic theory. Therefore, the history of thought can designate instances in which the issue came to the forefront of debates. The way it was actually settled, at each phase of the history of the discipline, can provide important insights for the ways we can theorize about the ideas of evolution and path dependence today. Francisco Louçã writes about such an exciting exchange of ideas between Joseph Schumpeter and Ragnar Frisch, in Chapter 4, 'Schumpeter and the pendulum: how evolution was whipped out in the contruction of canonical economics'.

Louçã describes the exchange that took place in the summer of 1931, through the private correspondence of the protagonists, on the correct way of modelling and analysing econometrically the phenomenon of business cycles. Frisch, who was a pioneer in the field and one of the most important figures in the early development of econometrics, sought to model cycles as the outcome of a propagation mechanism and random exogenous impulses. Schumpeter, by contrast, thought that an adequate understanding of cycles had to take into account the endogenous creation of novelty by economic agents, that is, innovation. Both theorists resorted to metaphors in their arguments. However, whereas the former sought a metaphor from physics – hence the prominent place of the pendulum in the exchange – the latter's inspiration came from the historicity, that is, the irreversibility, of biological evolution.

The incident analysed by Louçã constitutes one of the earliest examples of a debate on the questions of evolution and path dependence. Of course, as is evident from most of contemporary mainstream economics too, it was the mechanical metaphor that was to acquire a prominent place in the toolbox of the economics profession. Thus the exchange between Schumpeter and Frisch offers an example of path dependence not just in the sphere of economic processes but also in the evolution of the conceptualizations and the tools of economics. We thus have here a small historical event *à la* Arthur that shapes the future development of a science.

The excursion into the history of thought continues in Chapter 5, 'Veblen and Commons on private property: an institutionalist discussion around a capitalist foundation'. Here Philippe Broda compares the views on private property of two major figures of early institutionalism: Thorstein Veblen and John R. Commons. On the normative side, the views of the two theorists are entirely contrasting. The 'radical' Veblen considers private property as a relic of the 'barbarian' phase of social development and a hindrance to the development of the benefits of modern technology, while Commons considers it a major coordinating institution of modern society.

Despite their differences in the evaluation of private property, however, both theorists base their analyses on a historical explanation of how this institution emerged and came to dominate modern capitalist society. For Veblen, this analysis is grounded on a periodization of human history that emphasizes either the conflictual or the cooperative elements in each stage, thus elevating the latter to the ideal towards which human society must strive. Commons, on the other hand, thought that competition is a constitutive element even of early societies, thus considering private property as a *sine qua non* for the effective governance of interpersonal conflicts and for the coordination of human activities towards progress and growth. Both authors, therefore, attempt to ground their views on the role of private property in contemporary society on a historical explanation of how this institution emerged in the course of human history.

But the analyses of both theorists are not only grounded in history, as they also provide important insights on institutional change. By considering private property as an institutional relic of a previous stage of social development, Veblen views institutional change as the outcome of a struggle between the ethos of the 'capitalist' and that of the 'engineer'. In that framework, the outcome of this struggle will have major implications for the ethos – that is, the new configuration of institutions, norms and habits of thought – that will emerge. Commons, by contrast, does not see private property as an institution that may hinder development but rather as one that has to be regulated in order to continue to play its coordinating role in the context of ever novel historical phases. Consequently, his focus is on the institutions of justice, which, in his view, tend to shape and reconfigure property rights as human society evolves.

In Chapter 6, 'Competition, competitive selection and economic evolution', John Foster embarks upon an exploration of how biological concepts have found their way into various strands of economic theorizing. The analysis focuses on one such concept, natural selection, and its linking to one of the central ideas in economics, that of competition. The author shows that the diminution of theoretical interest in the concept of perfect competition since the 1970s has gone parallel with a rediscovery by economists of the idea of natural selection in its neo-Darwinian interpretation. However, for most of mainstream economics, natural selection has been taken as synonymous with the 'survival of the fittest' idea, that Foster maintains is closer to Spencer than Darwin. Although the author asserts that this outlook is related to wider developments in the discipline itself, he maintains that the political philosophy of the New Right has provided the necessary ideological foundation for the unquestioned acceptance of the benign effects of competition.

A major implication of the analysis is that we can't be too careful when attempting to employ the biological metaphor in economics. Foster stresses that the mainstream and neo-Darwinism share one important aspect: an espousal of the Newtonian physical analogy. In that context, they neglect the analysis of processes in favour of a focus on final outcomes, that is, the results of competition or natural selection. Interestingly, the author extends his criticism towards evolutionary economists who consider competition among firms as the major force of evolutionary economic change. In his view, the insistence on the implementation of a neo-Darwinian metaphor in economics is bound to keep the discipline trapped in a Newtonian impasse, which blinds it to the social, political and psychological context of economic evolution.

John Foster is not critical of all attempts to transfer biological analogies to economics. He insists, however, that these analogies should not be sought in neo-Darwinism and the idea of natural selection. Instead, they should be sought in the notion of economic 'self organization'. The idea is that natural selection can only operate upon a collection of traits that are characterized by variety. But in that case, variety itself has to be explained. The notion of self-organization aims precisely at explaining how variety is constantly created, that is, through the novelty created by agents. The author stresses the Lamarckian quality of this notion. At the same time, he shows that self-organization, rather than competition, constitutes one of the pivots of classical political economy – at least in Adam Smith's version. Therefore, the history of thought can again provide us with important insights for contemporary research in economics.

Richard Arena and Sandye Gloria-Palermo offer a further exploration of the origins of evolutionary ideas in the history of thought. In their 'Evolutionary themes in the Austrian tradition: Menger, Wieser and Schumpeter on institutions and rationality' (Chapter 7), they trace these ideas in the work of the founders of the Austrian school of economics. In their view, a common concern for the emergence and the evolution of institutions runs through the work of the three authors that they focus their analysis on, which, as they argue, indicates some kind of continuity in their thought.

According to Arena and Gloria-Palermo, there is first of all a strong 'evolutionary line' of thought running from Menger, to Wieser and Schumpeter. This is an important assertion because, while the evolutionary element in Menger is generally acknowledged, the other two authors are usually taken to have moved the Austrian tradition towards marginalist neoclassicism; a process that ends with Schumpeter's endorsement of Walras. Second, the authors of the chapter argue that the three thinkers, true to their Austrian origins, are trying to explain how social institutions emerge. The point of departure for this argument is the now well-identified Mengerian distinction of social institutions into organic and pragmatic ones.

As we have already mentioned, the argument for continuity in the thought of Menger, Wieser and Schumpeter regarding the emergence and evolution of institutions, is an original and thought-provoking idea. However, equally important is the central idea on which Arena and Gloria-Palermo base their argument. In their view, this continuity is premised on the attempt of all three authors to analyse the emergence and evolution of institutions as the outcome of the interaction between two social groups; those that initiate change and those that follow primarily by imitating the innovations of the former. This conceptualization is best illustrated in Wieser's distinction between the *leaders* and the *masses*. However, it is equally present in Menger's 'organic' account of the development of social institutions and, of course, in Schumpeter's ideas on entrepreneurial innovation. Nonetheless, Arena and Gloria-Palermo are well aware that their three authors should not be thought of as sharing a unique evolutionary schema. As they show, the ideas of Menger and Wieser were closer to biological evolution, whereas Schumpeter was closer to Marshall in adopting a more historical view of economic change. Still, the common thread in their thought may prove useful today in helping us overcome this dichotomy.

In Chapter 8, 'Reading Edith Penrose's *The Theory of the Growth of the Firm* forty years on (1959–1999)', Margherita Turvani undertakes to re-evaluate this famous classic from the vantage point of today. Implicit in Turvani's analysis is the question of whether the book should be considered a classic merely because of its position in the history of theories of the firm in the 1950s, or because of its current relevance both for the theory of the firm and for its wider contribution to economics. She maintains that the second contribution is the essential one.

Turvani argues that the most fundamental concept that Penrose introduced into the theory of the firm is the distinction between the resources employed by the firm and the services obtainable from these resources. This distinction implies that the growth of the firm does not only depend on the resources that it commands but, most importantly, on the services that its management can extract from them. Two important implications follow. The first is that the growth of the firm depends crucially on the way the capabilities of the firm's resources grow, thus being able to provide new and improved services. Second, the firm's most important resource is managerial services, for it is management that restructures the firm's resources towards growth, acting entrepreneurially.

Turvani's interpretation is important and not just for the theory of the firm. Indeed the 'knowledge-based economics' put to the point those theories that are able to take this kind of phenomenon into account. What is then important to explain is the ways in which individual, and, much more importantly, collective knowledge evolves. Such a point of view is interesting inasmuch as the recent developments of the theories of the firm are based on the existence of asymmetries of information and the dispersion of knowledge among individuals.

In Chapter 9, 'Economic analysis of human effort in organizations: an historical and critical perspective', Bénédicte Berthe and Michel Renault challenge the theoretical way in which human effort within organizations is usually analysed. Human effort is usually conceived of as a cost–benefit problem, even though some theorists take benefits (the wages) to determine the agent's costs (the effort). What Berthe and Renault are trying to show is that the problem is much more complex than simple cost–benefit analysis maintains.

As they put it, 'Conventions, cognitive frameworks and the social behaviour of the group all figure as important variables that need to be taken into account'. Following insights from the Old Institutional Economics, they show that if the employees are not only hedonist agents, the way they behave cannot be reduced to a simple cost–benefit calculation. This makes necessary the introduction of new assumptions in order to understand agents' behaviour. According to Berthe and Renault, the fact that employees are embedded in social relations means that their behaviour – i.e. the provision of effort – cannot be explained by recourse to a simple wage–effort trade off.

Berthe and Renault first appraise the theories based on the 'principle of least effort'. The 'canonical' Jevons' model constitutes a perfect example of the mechanistic conception of human effort. What characterizes those theories is a reductionist point of view concerning human effort. The authors then proceed to propose an alternative conceptualization, rooted in Old Institutionalism and evolutionary ideas. Contrary to the mechanistic view, they maintain that effort depends on the logic of trust as much as it does on the logic of self-interest.

Moreover, the fact that effort is displayed in organizations implies the necessity of taking into account the sociological factors that explain group behaviour.

In 'Path dependence in scientific evolution', (Chapter 10), Albert Jolink and Jack Vromen undertake an original re-examination of the history of economics as a science. In contrast to the Kuhnian conception of scientific development as a series of revolutions, each marking the transition to a new paradigm, the authors maintain that the history of economics should better be thought of as a path-dependent evolutionary process. Therefore, they juxtapose the idea of 'conventional' science to Kuhn's notion of 'normal' science, i.e. the paradigm that comes to be established after a scientific revolution. As they argue, 'the evolution of science can be described in terms of a path-dependent process, in the course of which it may become locked-in to a steady state of what we shall call a conventional science'.

According to Jolink and Vromen, this path dependence is characterized by three main attributes: it is a *process,* which has *transition probabilities* and is influenced by *historical factors.* They illustrate their conception with two examples. First they explain the evolution of general equilibrium theory from Walras to Debreu, and show some crucial, albeit 'small', switches of conventions, vocabulary, agenda and standards, that occurred during that process. Second they analyse game theory and its evolution from the early con- tributions due to Von Neumann and Morgenstern to the Nash equilibrium concept. As an example, they note that during this process of selection, cooperative game theory progressively disappeared as an important aspect of game theory, and non-cooperative game theory became the 'convention'.

The conception of the history of economics as a path-dependent process has, of course, important implications for the way we think about the development of this science and especially about the development of the tools, methods and ideas that economists employ in their research today. If transition probabilities and historical factors have indeed shaped the science as it is today – and as the authors show – then the study of the institutional context in which these historical factors appeared has profound implications for the way the discipline evolved. It is precisely the importance of this line of research that Jolink and Vromen's contribution brings to the fore.

The Athens conference, from which all papers collected in this volume have been selected, ended with a lecture by A.W. Coats, which is reproduced here as Chapter 11, 'Reflections on the progress of heterodox economics'. Bob Coats focuses his attention on the relation between orthodoxy and heterodoxy in economics. He discusses, first of all, the difficulties that heterodoxy faces when it attempts to 'organize' itself. How does a heterodox association manage, for example, its resemblance to other heterodox economic associations? But the much more important problem concerns its relation with the mainstream, 'whether to chip away at mainstream economics or work constructively towards a *rapprochement*'.

In fact, this problem is linked to one's definitions of heterodoxy as well as orthodoxy. Much more importantly, Coats shows, to begin with, that the boundaries between orthodoxy and heterodoxy are sometimes fuzzy. He also analyses the comparative evolution of heterodoxy and orthodoxy, in fact arguing that there is something we can call a co-evolution of the two. He exemplifies his arguments with a comparison between the Old and the New Institutional Economics and argues, after Rutherford, that the internal homogeneity of those two streams is not watertight. In fact, Coats maintains that there are conflicts and complementarities within as well as between the two schools. In order to explain that orthodoxy is evolving and answering its critics he writes that 'nowadays these and related concepts such as path dependency, hysteresis, and the irreversibility of historical time are the subject of fruitful discussion and analysis among economists of many different doctrinal persuasions'.

According to Bob Coats, therefore, the willingness of economists to consider ideas nurtured in theoretical traditions other than their own as well as their openness to constructive argument with these traditions, constitutes an important condition for the development of our science. As editors of this volume, we could not end this introduction without noting our full agreement with this appeal.

NOTES

1. Schumpeter (1954) can be treated as a good example of this trend. For a more recent restatement of this, see J. Niehans (1990).
2. See especially the essays of Liebowitz and Margolis collected in their 1999 work and Paul David in this volume.
3. In fact 'orthodoxy' as well as 'heterodoxy' is facing the same kinds of problem and it seems more interesting for them to debate on the way it is possible to solve them than to consider themselves as two 'churches'.

REFERENCES

Alchian, A.A. (1950), 'Uncertainty, evolution, and economic theory', *Journal of Political Economy*, **58** (3): 211–21.
Arthur, B. (1985), 'Competing technologies and lock-in by historical events: The dynamics of allocation under increasing returns', CEPR discussion paper, Stanford University.
Baumol W.J. and J. Benhabib (1989), 'Chaos: significance, mechanism, and economic applications', *Journal of Economic Perspectives*, **3** (1): 77–105.
David, P.A. (1985), 'Clio and the economics of QWERTY', *American Economic Review*, **75** (2): 332–7.

David, P.A. (1986), 'Understanding the economics of QWERTY: the necessity of history', in W.N. Parker (ed.), *Economics, History and the Modern Economist*, Oxford: Basil Blackwell.

Egidi, M. and A. Narduzzo (1996), 'The emergence of path-dependent behaviors in cooperative contexts', CEEL Working Papers WP-3–1996, University of Trento.

Garrouste, P. (1995), 'L'origine et l'évolution des institutions, pour un dialogue entre C.Menger et T.Veblen', in M. Baslé, D. Dufourt, J.A. Héraud and J. Perrin (eds), *Changement institutionnel et changement technologique; évaluation, droits de propriété intellectuelle, système national d'innovation*, Paris: Editions du CNRS.

Hodgson, G. (1992), 'Thorstein Veblen and post-Darwinian economics', *Cambridge Journal of Economics*, **16**: 285–302.

Kaldor, N. (1972), 'The irrelevance of equilibrium economics', *Economic Journal*, **82**, December: 1237–55.

Liebowitz, S.J. and S.E. Margolis (1999), *Winners, Losers and Microsoft: Competition and Antitrust in High Technology*, Oakland, CA: Independent Institute.

Marshall, A. (1920), 'Preface to the eighth edition', in *Principles of Political Economy*, (1949), London: Macmillan.

Menger, C. (1985), *Investigation into the Method of the Social Sciences*, New York: New York University Press.

Niehans, J. (1990), *A History of Economic Theory: Classic Contributions, 1720–1980*, Baltimore and London: Johns Hopkins University Press.

Robinson, J. (1978), 'History versus equilibrium', in *Contributions to Modern Economics*, Oxford: Basil Blackwell.

Schelling, T.C. (1978), *Micromotives and Macrobehavior*, New York: Norton.

Schotter, A. (1994), 'Social institutions and game theory', in P.J. Boettke (ed.) *The Elgar Companion to Austrian Economics*, Aldershot, UK and Brookfield, US: Edward Elgar.

Schumpeter, J.A. (1954), *History of Economic Analysis*, London: George Allen & Unwin.

Sraffa, P. (1926), 'The laws of returns under competitive conditions', *Economic Journal*, **36**: 535–50.

Veblen, T.B. (1898), 'Why is economics not an evolutionary science?', *Quarterly Journal of Economics*, **12**: 373–97.

Young, H.P. (1996), 'The economics of conventions', *Journal of Economic Perspectives*, **10**: 105–22.

2. Path dependence, its critics and the quest for 'historical economics'

Paul A. David

1 INTRODUCTION

Contemporary research and writing being undertaken in the genre of evolutionary economics can be viewed as part of a broader, more catholic intellectual movement, one that I would characterize as a quest for *historical social science*. Yet, a decade after it began to be trendy among economists to say that 'history matters', some things remain less than entirely clear about the possible meanings attached to that phrase, if indeed it is taken to carry any substantive content at all. For me, at least, the expression 'history matters' does carry a quite precise set of connotations, namely those associated closely with the concept of *path dependence*. The latter refers to a property of contingent, non-reversible dynamic processes, including a wide array of processes that can properly be described as 'evolutionary'. The set of ideas associated with path dependence consquently must occupy a central place in the future, historical social science that economics should become.

However, by now you may well have begun to wonder whether the matter of history mattering really has been greatly clarified by my tying it to a second catchy expression that, unfortunately like the first, has come to be invoked more frequently than it is defined. What *is* 'path dependence' anyway? Does it have a meaning more precise than the slogan: 'history matters'? Is it about 'the economics of QWERTY' or about something more general? If we were to conduct a systematic survey, even one confined to the academic economics profession, it probably would confirm my casual impression that the rising popularity of the term 'path dependence' has spawned a variety of usages, a perceptible measure of confusion, and even some outright misinformation.[1] If there are few who are prepared to dissent from the assertion that 'history matters', there are more who wonder whether history matters in ways that are important for economists to think about, and, there are many more who hold diverse and sometimes contradictory notions of how it comes about that history matters.

My immediate task on this occasion, therefore, is to try to clarify the meaning and amplify the economic significance of 'path dependence'. My hope is that the results of such an undertaking will enable others to appreciate better some of the salient implications for our discipline of recovering a conceptualization of change as a process that is *historical*, including implications for the way economic policy analysis is approached. A task so simple to describe, however, is not necessarily so easy to perform. For one thing, much of the training of the modern economist tends to weaken the recipients' natural, intuitive understanding of historical causation. Consequently, some remedial work is required in addressing an audience of academic economists, many of whose members' advanced education will have left them severely incapacitated in this particular regard.

To put this differently, most of us have been well-schooled in working with mathematical economic models whose dynamics admit perfect reversibility and lack any strong sense of genetic causation. It strikes me that neither those economists who casually assign to the influence of 'history' the things for which their analysis does not adequately account, nor those sceptics who say 'Sure, history matters, but not for much', are adequately responding to the challenges posed by the quite different class of dynamic processes that generate sequences of causally related *events*. One of the things about 'events' that our everyday experience of change seems to confirm, is that they happen – and never 'un-happen'. By contrast with the realities of the world around us, recognition of which forces itself implicitly and often only incompletely into the consciousness of practising economic advisors, much of the formal teaching of economic analysis refers to a very different and special class of dynamic processes in which all motion in the long run is 'continuous locomotion'. In the context of analytical structures of that kind, which are familiar enough to students of classical mechanics, 'change' may be said to occur without there being any specific, individual events that have causal significance.

To abandon the learned habits of peering at the world of economics automatically and exclusively from the peculiar vantage point afforded by a certain and now certainly antiquated branch of physics, and to be able therefore to take up another and contrary perspective, cannot be simply a matter of un-learning. Something additional, and for many, something new has to be learned. That 'something' can stand alongside neoclassical economic analysis, and so enhance one's appreciation of the special features distinguishing that paradigm from what may be called *historical economics*.

In asserting that 'history matters' I do not maintain that in economic processes history always matters in the same ways. Nor would I contend that economic processes have worked in the same way throughout history. The issue of how much importance should be attached to the particular category of path dependent dynamical processes, in the sense of what proportion of the changes occurring in the economy around us can best be understood in such terms, remains for me one that can must be addressed by empirical enquiries. But, like virtually all interesting empirical questions, this one cannot be resolved in an analytical vacuum. The very nature of the evidence that would be required to address it is prescribed by reference to alternative, analytical and statistical models that admit of historical changes that are path dependent, and changes that are path independent. Data acquire meaning only in the context of economic theory: as T.S. Ashton, the British economic historian, said long ago: 'the facts do not wear their hearts on their sleeves'.

To say that is not to diminish the value of 'mere facts', nor to dilute the force of the imperative to get details of the story straight. Examination of particular cases may serve to illustrate the phenomenon of path dependence, to exemplify one or another methodology of studying historical economics, and to identify and explore unresolved problems. The writing of a piece of economic history in this way may also be good fun, and, when it is well done it typically manages both to provide entertainment and to satisfy particular points of curiosity. To do it well, however, we must begin with some grasp of the conceptual issues and the theoretical framework that endows observations with meaning and import.

Therefore, on this occasion I am not going to delve into the details of selected historical cases, whether illustrative of the evolution of technologies, or of institutions and organizational forms, or of cultural beliefs. Historical economics needs greater investment in suitable theory, and the kind of theory that is required is harder than that upon which ahistorical economics has been able to rest. So I must ask that you forgo for the present the enjoyment of another excursion into economic history, and, instead, attend more closely to the conceptual foundations that serve to underpin further researches into path dependence in the economy. There will be an ancillary benefit in following this course: by anchoring our discussions firmly on these foundations with the aid of some precise definitions of path dependence (in section 2), it is quite straightforward to dispose of the misleading presentations of the concept by sceptics and critics.[2] I can then proceed (in section 3) to try clearing up the confusion that has developed in the literature over the connection between path dependence and economic inefficiency, before turning (in section 4) to take up the meaning and economic significance of the widely used term 'lock-in'.

After this necessary clearing of obscuring 'undergrowth' it will be seen (in section 5) that once we enter an explicitly dynamic framework, the questions of static welfare 'efficiency' and the meaning of 'market failure' become more complicated and involve subtle issues that the critics of path dependence have thus far failed to take on board. Moreover, the implications of path dependence for economic policy studies are in reality quite far-reaching, in arguing for the abandonment of static welfare-analytic approaches to the problem of where government should intervene in the economy, and its replacement by explicitly dynamic analysis that asks whether 'now' is the time in this or that specific market. Moreover, the general thrust of the recommendations regarding issues of technology policy that emerge from considerations of path dependence, will more often than not turn out to be entirely opposite in nature to those that seem to be most worrisome to the concept's *laissez-faire* critics.

In sum, I am unable to find any compelling reasons why economic analysis should remain 'locked in' to an ahistorical conceptual framework, apart from the unfortunate hysteresis effects of 'intellectual sunk costs'. But those effects are real, and must be countered. Therefore, drawing upon the analogy offered by field models of physical systems that have multiple basins of attraction, I suggest (in section 6) that some injection of further, intellectual 'energy' is likely to be necessary in order for our discipline to free itself from the local region of 'low potential' in which it has too long remained trapped.

2   ALMOST EVERYTHING YOU WANTED TO KNOW ABOUT 'PATH DEPENDENCE' – BUT WERE AFRAID TO ASK

Path dependence, as I wish to use the term, refers to a dynamic property of allocative processes. It may be defined either with regard to the relationship between the process dynamics and the outcome(s) to which it converges, or the limiting probability distribution of the stochastic process under consideration.

At the most intuitive level we may draw a distinction between dynamic processes that are path dependent, and the rest. The latter, path-*independent* processes, may be said to include those whose dynamics guarantee convergence to a unique, globally stable equilibrium configuration; or, in the case of stochastic systems, those for which there exists an invariant (stationary) asymptotic probability distribution that is continuous over the entire feasible space of outcomes, that is, a limiting distribution that is continuous over all the states that are compatible with the energy of the system (see, for example, Liggett, 1985).

Stochastic systems possessing the latter properties are said to be *ergodic*, and have the ability eventually to shake free from the influence of their past state(s). In physics, ergodic systems are said to be connected, in the sense that it is possible to transit directly or indirectly between any arbitrarily chosen pair of states, and hence, eventually, to reach all the states from any one of them.

Path dependent processes thus may be defined negatively, as belonging to the class of exceptions from the foregoing set of processes, in which the details of the history of the systems' motion do not matter – because they cannot affect its asymptotic distribution among the states. This leads us immediately to

A negative definition: *Processes that are non-ergodic, and thus unable to shake free of their history, are said to yield path dependent outcomes.*

In this connection, it may be worthwhile to notice that the familiar homogeneous Markov chain invoked in many applications in economics – models of population migration and spatial distribution, of income and wealth, and occupational and social status distributions, firm size distribution, and so forth – is characterized by an invariant set of state-dependent transition probabilities that are finite (positive), and for convenience in many applications contexts, are specified so as to ensure that the process is *ergodic*. The distributions of the individuals or firms whose motions among the states are governed by Markov chains of this kind will each converge to their respective, invariant asymptotic probability distribution – a distribution that is continuous over the entire feasible state space. (This unique limiting distribution is the one that emerges as the transition matrix operator is repeatedly iterated.) When there is an absorbing state or subset of connected states (from which the probability of escape to the subset of transient states is zero), the system will converge weakly to that single attractor. Obviously, such a system's behaviour is not deterministic, but it may be said to be 'pre-destined' in the sense of being governed from the outset by a unique asymptotic probability distribution.

However, when a state-dependent process has two or more absorbing subsets (that is, distinct regions of equilibria that are locally stable), the homogeneous Markov process becomes *non-ergodic, and its outcomes can be said to be path dependent.* In the trivial case in which the initial condition of the system was one or the other of the absorbing states, it is plain that whatever governed that selection would fix the limiting position of the system. Further, it is no less self-evident that if there is at least one transient (non-absorbing) state from which the multiplicity of absorbing states can be reached, directly or indirectly, then the realization of the random process at that point in the system's history (on its path) will select one rather than the other outcome(s) to which the system eventually must converge.

For many purposes, however, we would like to say what a path dependent process *is*, rather than what it is not. Help from the probability theorists can be invoked in order to do so in a precise way. Focusing upon the limiting patterns generated by a random process (thus characterizing a dynamic system), we have

A positive definition: *A path dependent stochastic process is one whose asymptotic distribution evolves as a consequence (function of) the process's own history.*

This broader definition explicitly takes in processes that possess a *multiplicity* of asymptotic distributions, as generally is the case for *branching processes* – where the prevailing probabilities of transitions among states are functions of the sequence of past transient states that the system has visited. Branching processes that are subject to local irreversibilities share the property of non-ergodicity. The latter therefore characterizes the processes of biological evolution, because speciation constitutes a non-reversible event.

Transition probabilities that are not invariant functions of the current state are also the characteristic feature of so-called non-homogeneous Markov chains. Rather confusingly, however, probability theorists sometimes refer to the latter as having *path dependent transition probabilities*, thereby contrasting them with the more familiar class of homogeneous (or first order) Markov chains whose transition probabilities are (current) *state* dependent.[3] But, as has been seen from the negative definition discussed above, path dependence of the transition probabilities is not a necessary condition for a process that generates path dependent outcomes.

The foregoing account of what the term 'path dependence' means may now be compared with the rather different ways in which it has come to be explicitly and implicitly defined in some parts of the economics literature. For the moment we may put aside all of the many instances in which the phrases 'history matters' and 'path dependence' are simply interchanged, so that some loose and general connotations are suggested without actually defining either term. Unfortunately much of the non-technical literature seems bent upon avoiding explicit definitions, resorting either to analogies, or to the description of a syndrome – the phenomenon with whose occurrences the writers associate path dependence. Rather than telling you what path dependence *is*, they tell you some of the symptomology – things that may, or must happen when the condition is present. It is rather like saying that the common cold *is* sneezing, watering eyes and a runny nose. I can illustrate this with the following two passages:

> Path dependence is the application to economic systems of an intellectual movement that has lately come into fashion in several academic disciplines. In physics and mathematics, the related idea is called chaos – sensitive dependence on initial conditions. As chaos theory has it, a hurricane off the coast of Florida may be the fault of a butterfly flapping its wings in the Sahara. In biology the related idea is called contingency – the irreversible character of natural selection. Contingency implies that fitness is only a relative notion: survival is not of the fittest possible, but only of the fittest that happen to be around at the time. (Liebowitz and Margolis, 1995c, p. 33)

Elsewhere, the same authors propose a kindred explanation, albeit one that is slightly more formal:

> The use of path dependence in economics is, for the most part, loosely analogous to this mathematical construction: Allocations chosen today exhibit memory; they are conditioned on past decisions. It is where such a mathematical process exhibits

'sensitive dependence on initial conditions', where past allocations exhibit a controlling influence, that it corresponds most closely to the concerns that economists and others have raised as problems of path dependency [sic]. In such a case, 'insignificant events' or very small differences among conditions are magnified, bringing about very different outcomes. It is that circumstance that yields both the 'non-predictability' and 'potential inefficiency'. (Liebowitz and Margolis, 1995b, p. 210)

Much could be said about the inaccuracies in the texts just quoted. For the present, however, it will be sufficient to notice one thing that they do not say, and three things that they do say.

That path dependence is a property of *stochastic* sequential processes is *not* mentioned, and only the allusion to 'contingency' provides any hint of the subject's probabilistic context. Of course, in order to pick up this clue, one would need to suppress the extraneous and misleading surmise that 'contingency' has a meaning that is specific to (evolutionary) biology, where it 'implies' something about the nature of selections made on criteria of inclusive fitness.[4] Even that slender clue, however, is disguised by the statements that would have us associate path dependence with *deterministic* chaos, and the property of 'sensitive dependence on initial conditions' which characterizes that class of dynamic systems (see, for example, Stewart 1990, Ruelle 1991). The coupling of path dependence with chaos constitutes the first of the three positive assertions to which I previously referred, and it is incorrect. What it reflects is a too common predilection among mainstream economic writers for transposing concepts and arguments that are probabilistic in nature into simple deterministic models.[5] This habit is often seriously misleading, and must be especially so where neither certainty equivalence nor the operation of the central limit theorem of probability can legitimately be presupposed.

The second and third assertions disclose the authors' reasons why path dependence should be denounced as a problematic departure from the economic mainstream. They allege that a dynamic system in which there is 'memory' will be unpredictable, and worse, that it will be characterized by a potential for generating inefficient resource allocations. Like the first of the triad of assertions, these too are simply incorrect. There are some classes of non-ergodic stochastic processes whose outcomes are predictable, and I have said a great deal about these on previous occasions (David 1988a, 1993a, 1998b). Further, it is vitally important to insist on logically distinguishing between systems that have the general property of path dependence, and that special sub-category of non-ergodic dynamic systems that may display (as an additional attribute) a susceptibility to one or another form of market failure.

The latter condition, of course, is the one that adherents of strict neoclassical orthodoxy seem to find especially troublesome. Although I partake in the interest that most modern economists show regarding the efficiency of economic resource allocation, an obsession with the spectre of inefficiency was not what motivated me to inject the notion of path dependence into wide economic discourse, or to associate it with the application of insights from formal models of non-ergodic stochastic processes. This confession ought not to come as a surprise, especially to those who have encountered material that I have published before and since the pair of essays in which Clio, the muse of History, was coupled with the emergence of QWERTY as the *de facto* standard for typewriter keyboards (David 1985, and 1986).

The concept of path dependence and the associated framework of analysis is anchored in my long-standing quest to integrate *historicity* into economics. I think it important to distinguish between that peculiar aim, and the broader objectives of the 'new economic history' movement during the 1960s and 1970s, which saw the wholesale importation of the apparatus of modern economic analysis and econometric techniques, into the study of economic history (see, for example, McCloskey 1976). Although the use of the economist's preferred methods of study of the past, undoubtedly has proved extremely illuminating in many contexts, it had become evident to some within the field that new constraints and analytical contradictions had been created by trying to understand economic history – which is to say 'economic dynamics' – through the assiduous application of *ahistorical* concepts and tools. It was the prospect of resolving those problems within the framework of path dependence that made the latter attractive from my vantage point. Imagine, then, my utter surprise to find this approach being attacked as a rival paradigm of economic analysis, whose only relevance consisted in the degree to which it could be held to represent a direct rejection of the normative, *laissez-faire* message of neo-classical microeconomics!

3   SIGNIFICANCE: DOES PATH DEPENDENCE MEAN THERE WILL BE INEXTRICABLE INEFFICIENCIES?

> Welcome to the world of path dependence, a world governed not by our stars, not by ourselves, but by insignificant accidents of history. In this unpredictable world, small seemingly inconsequential decisions lead inexorably to uncontrollable conse-quences....In the world of path dependence...our expectations for market outcomes are turned upside down. The Invisible Hand does not work in the world of path dependence. (Liebowitz and Margolis (1995c, p. 33)

This passage, from the article 'Policy and path dependence – from QWERTY to Windows 95' published in the Cato Institute's journal *Regulation*, ironically describes what is purported to be the essential message of those propounding the concept of path dependence. It is the authors' general contention that path dependence really cannot hold much interest for economists, because the world of market economies does not conform to the one that they construe the concept to be describing, because remedies for unsatisfactory situations generally will be available, and found quickly by profit-hungry entrepreneurs attracted by the potential 'surplus' that is implicit in any seriously inefficient state of affairs. Hence, on this reasoning, the only sorts of path dependent phenomena which would warrant the attention of economists must be extremely rare occurrences.

But, as has been seen, the core content of the concept of path dependence as a dynamic property refers to the idea of history as an irreversible branching process. One must logically distinguish from this the idea that it is possible that some branchings are 'regrettable' because they created inextricable inefficiencies that, in some counter-factual but equally feasible world, could have been avoided. Moreover, it is plainly a mistake to impute to the economic theory of path dependence *as such* the set of propositions that underlie the second of these ideas, for the notion of market failure has been long established in the literature of welfare economics.

Actually, it is within the context of static general equilibrium analysis that economists developed the concept of 'market failure', namely, that the Pareto optimality of allocations arrived at via atomistically competitive markets is not guaranteed *except* under a stringent set of convexity conditions on production and preference sets, and, further, it requires the existence of markets for all extant and contingent commodities. One may or may not accept the usefulness for pragmatic policy purposes of defining ''market failure' in a way that takes those conditions as a reference ideal. Analytically, however, it remains a total *non sequitur* to assert that the essence of path dependence – a property defined for analyses of dynamical and stochastic processes – consists in asserting propositions regarding the possibility of 'market failure' that were proved first in the context of purely static and deterministic models.

Quite the contrary proposition holds: under full convexity conditions a nontatonnement general equilibrium process can be shown to converge in a strictly path dependent manner on one among the continuum of valid 'core' solutions which satisfy the criterion of Pareto optimality (see Fisher 1983, and David 1997b). This should be sufficient to expose the logical error of claiming that the essential difference between models of path dependence and standard neoclassical analysis must be the former's insistence on the presence of 'market failure.' To be sure, there are some underlying connections between the existence of conditions that give rise to path dependence in economic processes, and the possibility that the workings of competitive markets in those circumstances would result in allocations that are inefficient (see, for example, Föllmer 1974). But the circumstances in which competitive markets will not yield Pareto efficient outcomes are not in themselves either new, or arcane.

It might then be noticed that the taxonomy of path dependence proposed by Liebowitz and Margolis (1995b), and curiously described as 'definitions of path dependence', embraces a classificatory principle that is based entirely on static optimality criteria. Inasmuch as such criteria remain conceptually orthogonal to the nature of the dynamical processes under consideration, it is perhaps not surprising to observe that the definitions offered by Liebowitz and Margolis for 'first-degree' and 'second-degree' path dependence do not actually serve to distinguish between dynamic systems that are path independent and those that are path dependent. The first-degree form describes a situation in which all the outcomes among which selections might be made are not Pareto-ranked, such as would exist for the Nash equilbria in a pure coordination game; the second-degree situation is one in which the outcome realized is dominated by a feasible alternative, yet represents the unavoidable *ex post* consequence of having taken an action that *ex ante* represented the 'best' strategy.[6]

In discussing the conceptualization of third-degree path dependence in which there is market failure leading to inefficiencies of an 'irremediable' kind, Liebowitz and Margolis (1995b) make reference to the test of 'remediability' suggested by Oliver E. Williamson. But, they entirely omit mention of the important distinction that Williamson's (1993) work drew between remedia-bility through 'private ordering' and through 'public ordering'. Nowhere in the literature dealing with theoretical and empirical aspects of path dependent economic phenomena have I found it said that this property leads to outcomes for which remediation via public ordering is wholly *infeasible*. For the state to undertake to 'correct' a market outcome might become socially inefficient. But that is a different proposition from its being simply infeasible. So, it is not open to the critics to claim that path dependence would have empirical or policy substance for economists if only it did not exclude the possibility of remediation by public ordering in those circumstances where private ordering was unworkable.[7]

One certainly must agree that among economists at large most of the interest in path dependence results from the possibilities that sub-optimal equilibria will be 'selected' by a dynamic process. So it is understandable (and certainly to be expected) that brief treatments of points of controversy concerning theoretical contentions and empirical 'evidence' would tend to focus upon that question to the exclusion of everything else. Nevertheless, there is more to economic life than the possibility of welfare losses due to static inefficiencies. The identities of winners and losers in market rivalries are of interest to the owners and employees of the enterprises involved. The structure of industry itself may be of significance for dynamic efficiency through innovation and entrepreneurship. Indeed, the intense recent interest of the business press (and the Justice Department) in the positions of Microsoft and its present and future rivals in the market for web-browsers and related software, makes it plain that something more is perceived to be at stake than the comparative social rates of return on further incremental investment in their respective product lines.

More generally, all manner of political and social sequelae, as well as questions of equity, are attached to the dynamics governing the evolution of income and wealth distributions, and processes of socio-economic stratification. If analysis of positive feedback mechanisms that affect those aspects of life would significantly enhance economists' abilities to understand and predict the path dependent phenomena arising therein, does that not warrant at least some notice in assessment of the conceptual framework's significance?

4   THE MEANING OF 'LOCK-IN' IN THE HISTORICAL CONTEXT OF PATH DEPENDENCE

The current state of imprecision and confusion in discussions of the meaning and significance of the term 'lock-in' has not been alleviated by the use of 'lock in' as one among the taxonomic criteria applied to classify path dependent processes in the recent work of Professors Liebowitz and Margolis. Quite the reverse. I must begin by reiterating some doubts as to the coherence of creating a taxonomy for path dependent economic processes that turns upon whether or not it is possible to imagine a system being inextricably 'locked in' to a state that is locally and globally dominated by other allocative arrangements. Yet the latter would appear to be the very condition that is indicated, when the term is taken by Liebowitz and Margolis (1994, 1995b, 1995c) to refer to a situation where all the participating agents know they would derive a *net* gain by arranging by whatever means were necessary, collectively to exchange the status quo for some other available configuration.

By 'net gain', in this definition, is meant a surplus over and above the full costs of organizing and implementing the move to another state. *Ex hypothesis* there will be sufficient surplus in the new state to compensate everyone and leave someone better off after absorbing all the costs of negotiation, mechanism design, and insuring credible commitment that may be required to implement a collective escape. Therefore, in the circumstances thus posited, one would be hard put indeed to see how, if the agents involved were economically rational individuals, the status quo could have persisted long enough to be of interest. What is there in the imagined situation that would serve to lock in anyone to so unstable an attractor? Either we accept that people behave rationally and that such situations will be as scarce as hens' teeth, or this is a rendering of the notion of lock-in that would oblige economists to acknowledge that sometimes history that really matters is a result of the workings of the mysterious, the irrational, or the wildly improbable forces in economic life – or possibly all three.

By contrast, as the term 'lock-in' has been used in my work and that of Arthur (1989), it simply is a vivid way to describe the entry of a system into a trapping region – the basin of attraction that surrounds a locally (or globally) stable equilibrium. When a dynamic economic system enters such a region, it cannot escape except through the intervention of some external force, or shock, that alters its configuration or transforms the underlying structural relationships among the agents. Path dependent systems – which have a multiplicity of possible equilibria among which event-contingent selections can occur – may thus become locked in to attractors that are optimal, or that are just as good as any others in the feasible set, or that take paths leading to places everyone would wish to have been able to avoid, once they have arrived there.

From this vantage point, Arthur's (1989) phrase 'lock-in by small historical events' is evidently a gloss that should not be read too literally; it is a convenient contraction of the foregoing reference to the way in which trapping regions may be entered – although somewhat unfortunate, in allowing a hasty reader to suppose that the antecedent events somehow have *created* the local stability, or locked-in state. To be more precise, albeit more cumbersome, one should say that such configurations are self-sustaining (Nash) equilibria; that in the case of a path dependent process some particular historical event caused, that is, initiated the sequence of transitions that effectively selected one rather than another among such configurations to be realized as the system's emergent property.

In some circumstances, as in the case of pure coordination games (where there are strategic complementarities in the dynamic interactions among agents) there is no Pareto-ranking of a multiplicity of available equilibria from amongst which a path dependent, branching process can make a selection. *Which* coordination point is reached is a matter of welfare indifference to the parties involved. A coordination equilibrium, thus, provides us with the paradigmatic situation in which individuals are content to remain doing something, even though they would be happier doing something else if everybody would also do that other thing too. The reason they don't change what they are doing is, generically, that there are information imperfections that make it unlikely that a decentralized process can get everyone coordinated to move elsewhere, collectively.[8] Now notice that while incomplete information may be critical in blocking spontaneous escapes from dominated coordination equilibria, it is not a necessary condition for decentralized market processes to select such states. This is another reason why presenting 'lock-in' as a particular (pernicious, and supposedly uncommon) form of path dependence is an invitation to further analytical confusions.

This last, important point can be elaborated on by observing that the generic problems of escaping from lock-in of the system to a globally inferior (but locally stable) attractor are rooted in 'pure' coordination costs. Such costs may be very high, however, especially if the individual agents are expected to act spontaneously under conditions of incomplete information. Hence, the nature of the *ex post* coordination problem generally is not the same as the problem of arranging coordination with agents who do not yet exist, or who have yet to recognize the complementarities between their interests and capabilities and those initiating the action. The sources of *ex ante* market failure that allow the system to be led into a globally inferior equilibrium are not necessarily the ones that make it very hard to get out.

Of course, if and when the structure of economic incentives and constraints bearing upon the process under study is altered by events that, for the purposes of the analysis may reasonably be regarded as 'exogenous innovations' (in the state of relevant knowledge, or in the regulatory institutional regime), the previous attractor(s) may be destroyed, freeing the system to endogenously begin to evolve some new configurations. Thus, the advent of microwave transmission technologies in the 1950s may be seen to have undermined the prevailing regulatory regime governing the US telecommunications industry (which had itself emerged through a path dependent process); and the denouement, in the event of the AT&T divestiture, brought into being a liberalized regulatory regime and new market structure that may be said to have formed new 'attractive paths' for the evolution of digital telecommunications technologies. But, to claim that the evidence of change itself is sufficient to dispose of the notion of a persisting inefficient lock-in is tantamount to supposing that Schumpeter's gale of 'creative destruction' is blowing continuously at full force, through every niche, nook and cranny of the economy. Indeed, it is a way of losing one's sense of the variations in the flow of events through time that makes it interesting to read histories.

Strategic re-definitions, playing with words to avoid the force of the concepts with which they were originally associated, is a form of rhetoric that is essentially obscurantist. By the purely semantic trick of re-defining path dependence to come in various degrees of 'seriousness', and by associating the most 'serious' form to be not a process, but a particular outcome state gauged in terms of allocational efficiency, it is possible to give superficial plausibility to the claim that no serious economic consequences are associated with the phenomenon of path dependence. This has been the taxonomic gambit tried by Professors Liebowitz and Margolis, who reserve their 'most serious' form of path dependence (third-degree) to be the state in which the status quo is Pareto-dominated *even after all transition and adjustment costs are considered*. They then can ask, rhetorically, why should one suppose that we would ever find a situation of 'serious path dependence', where people refused to make themselves individually and collectively better off, after paying all the bargaining, transactions and information costs of arranging their escape from a bad situation? Why indeed? If one insists that the only sort of sub-optimality worth worrying about is the kind so wasteful as to justify escaping at any finite cost, then one is implicitly accepting the actual or equivalent loss of all the remedial expenditures (the costs of undoing the effects of outcomes we collectively prefer not to live with). Yet, those remedial expenditures might not have been unavoidable *ex ante*. Is it not pertinent for economists advising private and public agencies to consider the likelihood that some substantial portion of those costs were consequences of the path dependence of the dynamic process through which 'regrettable' outcomes were 'selected'?

Suppose, for the moment, that the significant economic question to be addressed in regard to the possibility of lock-in is this: How can we identify situations in which it is likely that at some future time individuals really would be better off had another equilibrium been selected *ab initio*? By that we must mean that an alternative outcome would be preferred in some collective sense (perhaps by application of a compensation test) to the one that they are now in, and that they also (collectively) should be ready to incur some substantial costs to rectify the situation – assuming it was feasible to do so. Were it possible to answer that question by saying that such conditions will never obtain, then economists could well afford not to bother with the distinction between dynamic processes whose outcomes were path dependent and those which were path independent. It would be a distinction that might interest students of history, but would otherwise be inconsequential for economic policy. But such would be true only if multiple equilibria could be shown never to exist outside the context of pure coordination games (that is, where none are Pareto-dominated); or if it could be shown that it would never be possible to identify the structural conditions that give rise to other multiple equilibrium situations. We have no impossibility theorems of this sort, and neither of these propositions is likely to be established empirically.

5   PATH-CONSTRAINED MELIORATION, THE BURDENS OF COUNTERFACTUAL HISTORICAL ANALYSIS, AND SOME POLICY IMPLICATIONS

There is, however, another way to look at the question. It may be that the selection of Pareto-dominated equilibria in positive feedback systems is never allowed to become serious enough (in the Liebowitz–Margolis sense) to impress the contemporary observer who can imagine clever, if costly, mechanisms for organizing collective escapes from locally sub-optimal situations. This, indeed, is a cogent point, and deserves closer attention than it usually receives from economists who challenge the champions of historical economics to look around and find a 'really important' example – by which they seem to mean, a case of path dependent dynamics leading to a grossly inefficient equilibrium. Instead of imagining that history is played out without anybody noticing what is happening, and then, when an equilibrium appears to be reached people gather round and assess its optimality, we must allow for the process to encompass possibilities and consequences of incremental *path-constrained meliorating actions* being taken by observant, intelligent agents.

The static framework of welfare analysis within which too many economists are still being taught to do their thinking tends to suppress the natural disposition to conceptualize the whole flow of current economic life as contingent upon the results of antecedent choices. Seen in truly historical perspective, a great deal of human ingenuity, especially the sort that is said to be 'mothered by necessity', is devoted to trying to cope with 'mistakes' that are threatening to become 'serious' in their economic consequences; to assuring, somehow, that their more pernicious effects will be moderated, if not abated altogether. This is done *ex post*, by contriving technological 'fixes' and 'patches', by commandeering temporary task forces to handle emergencies that established organizational structures are discovered to be handling badly, by sustained efforts at 'reforming' (not reinventing) long-standing institutions, and, yes, by concerted educational campaigns to untrain people who have acquired dysfunctional habits of one sort or another.

We like to refer to all of that activity as 'progress' and, in a historically local sense, that is just what it is: melioration. But the meliorative options are more often than not quite tightly bounded by the existing critical situation: it was the existing software code that threatened to malfunction badly when the year 2000 dawned, not some other programs and data formats that were not implemented, although they might well have been trivial to modify. The resources spent in such perceived loss-avoidance activities are part of what we are happy to consider productive investments, adding to the net product, whereas some part of it could equally well be thought of as the deferred costs of regrettable decisions made in haste to be remedied at leisure, and sometimes for great profit. They might equally be called regrettable economic opportunities for 'learning' (see David, Maude-Griffin and Rothwell 1996; 1999).

Most of the situations in which the discomforts of remaining in a bad coordination equilibrium could be really large are those in which the institution, or technology, or behavioural norm has become highly elaborated and deeply embedded in numerous activities throughout the economy. One must then contemplate a counter-factual world in which the whole general equilibrium course of evolution would have been very different. Consideration of the implications of general purpose technologies is one of the ways in which economists today are coming to grips with this sort of systems analysis. Little wonder that economic historians have been and should be concerned primarily with such questions.

In considering the nature of the policy lessons that might be drawn from the foregoing view of the incremental evolutionary development of complex technological systems, some remarks on the putative role played by 'historical accidents' in path dependent processes are now very much in order. Unfortunately, the use of that phrase itself is prone to cause misunderstandings. It is quite misleading to take it to suggest that some original economic irrationality, or implementation error (accident) must be implicated whenever we find that positive network externalities have given rise to a sequence that turned out to be other than a globally optimal path. Indeed, only those who are hostile to the very idea of path dependence would repeatedly insist upon a literal interpretation of the phrase 'accidents of history'. Doing so suggests that the essential feature of such processes is that the original actors in the drama – whether as contributors to the design of a technical system, or an institutional rule structure, or a particular form of business organization, or as the initial adopters of such innovations – had to have been acting arbitrarily, or irrationally in the context of their economic circumstances. Such an interpretation is not only logically unwarranted; it obfuscates an important but widely overlooked feature common to the histories of many network technologies, and one that has some bearing upon the way public policy might be approached in that area.

The facts of all the technological instances recently under re-examination – QWERTY, 64K lower memory in the IMB PC, AC vs. DC electrical current, light–water reactors, and VCR formats too – are quite consistent with the view that the behaviour of the initiating actors of the drama, generally, was quite deliberate (not at all random in the sense of remaining inexplicable to the historian); and furthermore reasonably conformable to the urgings of the profit motive. Yet, generally, their actions were also bounded by a parochial and myopic conception of the process in which they were engaging – in the sense that these decision agents were not concerned with whether the larger system that might (and was) being built around what they were doing would be optimized by their choice.[9] In most cases they can be held to have failed entirely to foresee the complementary innovations and investments that would be influenced by their initial commitment to one rather than another course of action. In other words, their failure of imagination took the form of not thinking *systemically* about the technological and industrial structures that they were engaged in developing. Thomas Edison, of course, being a systems inventor *par excellence*, was an exception in that particular regard; yet, as has been shown by David (1991), Edison's business strategy in the context of the 'Battle of the Systems' – including his sudden decision to withdraw from the flourishing electrical supply systems industry altogether – appears to have been driven by quite different, rather myopic, but nonetheless rational economic considerations.

In general, what was difficult for the pioneers in any area to foresee were the complementaries that would emerge subsequently, and in so doing open the possibilities of developing a more complex, distributed system whose components were not produced or purchased integrally. The Remington Co. engineers who put the finishing touches on the first commercially successful typewriters to carry QWERTY into the world did not dream of the possibility of touch-typing manuals; Edison had not anticipated that anyone would devise an efficient and economical converter to link DC electrical supply facilities with distant users, by way of polyphase AC networks. Similarly, in more modern times, neither of the rival vendor groups behind the Sony Betamax and VHS cassette formats in the early VCR market had anticipated the commercial importance of pre-recorded movies and video rental stores.[10] Nor were the IBM engineers in Texas, as they rushed to create a readily producible personal computer, concerned with the amount of random access memory that would be needed to load a word processing program like WordPerfect whilst keeping an Excel spreadsheet and a LAN-modem open and running in the background.

The point here is not that these folks ought to have seen the shape of the future. Rather it is that the shape of the larger systems that evolved was built upon their work, and thus in each case preserved, and was in some respects much constrained by it – even in the way that they coped with the legacies of those initial decisions, taken quite deliberately, but with quite other and in some measure more evanescent considerations in mind.

From the foregoing it may be seen that a proper understanding of path dependence, and of the possibilities of externalities leading to market failure, is not without interesting implications for economic policy. But those are not at all the sorts of glib conclusions that some critics have alleged must follow if one believes that history really matters – namely, that government should try to pick winners rather than let markets make mistakes. Quite the contrary, as I began trying to make clear more than a decade ago.[11] One thing that public policy could do is to try to delay the market from committing to the future inextricably, before enough information has been obtained about the likely technical or organizational and legal implications, of an early, precedent-setting decision.

In other words, preserving open options, for a longer period than impatient market agents would wish, is the generic wisdom that history has to offer to public policy makers in all the applications areas where positive feedback processes are likely to be preponderant over negative feedbacks. Numerous dynamic strategies can and have been suggested as ways of implementing this approach in various, specific contexts where public sector action is readily feasible. Still more sensible and practical approaches will be found if economists cease their exclusive obsession with traditional questions of static welfare analysis and, instead of pronouncing on the issue of where state intervention would be justified in the economy, start to ask what kind of public actions would be most appropriate to take at different points in the evolution of a given market process.

The 'first best' public policy role in these matters, therefore, is not necessarily the making of positive choices, but instead the improvement of the informational state in which choices can be made by private parties and government agencies. In the context of the recent literature on sunk cost hysteresis and options theory, one may see that the more history matters – because complementaries create irreversibilities in resource commitments – the more worthwhile it is to invest in being better informed prior to leaping. There is an evident opportunity cost in giving priority to investments in further information acquisition; quite standard economics can be relied on to balance the expected value of waiting (searching) for further 'news', against the anticipated costs to the current generation(s) of not allowing markets to make choices on the basis of the knowledge that is presently available. Obviously, some assessment of the rate at which the relevant information states are capable of evolving will turn out to be of critical importance in determining when a stage has been reached where it no longer is best to defer irreversible resource commitments.

6   OVERCOMING 'INTELLECTUAL SUNK COST HYSTERESIS' AND ESCAPING FROM DISCIPLINARY 'LOCK-IN' TO AHISTORICISM

The cluster of ideas that are now identified with the concept of path dependence in economic and other social processes probably would not excite such attention, nor require so much explication, were it not for the extended prior investment of intellectual resources in developing economics as an ahistorical system of thought. For many economists, their own costs sunk in mastering that discipline have produced a facility for reasoning that suppresses natural, human intuitions about historical causation. They thus have a 'learned incapacity' (in Thorstein Veblen's apt phrase) to see how historical events could exert a causal influence upon subsequent outcomes that would be economically important. Perhaps unknowingly, such folk have fully internalized Aristotle's teleological principle of explanation, which rejected the method of reference to antecedents, and so escaped infinite explanatory regress by substituting forward-looking functionalism (as we would describe it). This was undoubtedly useful, even though it has had the intellectual side-effect, in many disciplines, of encouraging the formal suppression of the intuitive impulse to refer to pre-existing states and intervening 'events' when asked to account for the way things are today.

Mainstream economics is not alone among the social sciences in providing a way to explain an existing state of the world by reference to the purpose or end (*telos*) that it serves, rather than to the conditions from which it may have evolved.[12] This has proved a source of deep insights into many matters, but not into all matters of concern to economists and students of broader cultural phenomena, such as the spread of languages and social communication norms.[13] Nor, for that matter, does it suffice to provide good accounts of biological phenomena. In modern Darwinian evolutionary theory there is a beautiful, productive tension between the teleological principle of natural selection according to inclusive fitness, and the antecedents principle, namely, that the possibilities of evolution are tightly constrained at every moment by the current contents of the gene pool, which is the product of species' history. Perhaps that is why we might be drawn towards evolutionary biology as 'the Mecca for economics'.

Modern economics in its ahistorical, convergence model formulation serves some intellectual purposes very well, and the perpetuation of the methodological status quo can be seen to serve still other rational private ends. Nevertheless, if that style of explanation was entirely satisfactory in accounting for all economic and social phenomena without reference to legacies from the past, some of us would not presently be so exercised by trying to adjust contemporary economic thinking to the notion that history matters – nor would others be strenuously resisting that adjustment. Path dependence is a concept requiring explication for many today, simply because so much of economics committed itself to theories that would make the results of choice behaviours consistent in the sense of being path independent. But there is no compelling reason to regard that as an exclusive commitment.

Path dependence, at least to my way of thinking, is therefore about much more than the processes of technological change, or institutional evolution, or hysteresis effects and unit roots in macroeconomic growth. The concepts associated with this term have implications for epistemology, for the sociology of knowledge, and cognitive science as well.[14] Nevertheless, it would be quite wrong to imagine that positive feedback dominates all aspects of economic life (let alone 'life'), just as it is unwarranted to proceed on the supposition that economic dynamics everywhere are intrinsically characterized by the operation of stabilizing, negative feedback systems. Considering the possibility that the former framework is the one most relevant in a particular context, does not rule out the opposite conclusion, nor preclude appropriate resort to the latter framework – the familiar convergence models of neoclassical economics. These really are not necessarily mutually exclusive tool-sets, or incompatible standards, that cannot be integrated into a larger intellectual system. Even though we should be aware of the workings of strong social processes, 'familiar in the sociology of knowledge', that can turn normal science procedures into exclusionary dogmas, it is not necessary for social and behavioural scientists to adopt positions that exacerbate and amplify those tendencies.

Once the concept and the ideas surrounding path dependence are properly understood, there can be no reason to construe them as necessarily corrupting the discipline of economics, or to fear that once admitted they would be subversive of all *laissez-faire* policies. There simply are no good grounds to go on actively resisting these ideas, which if accepted will lead us into previously little-explored regions of theoretical and empirical enquiry. Nor is there even a sound precautionary case for seeking to contain their spread until it can be determined what would become of the grand edifice of economic analysis as we know it, once the assumed global dominance of negative feedback processes were discarded. The logic of sunk cost hysteresis has a legitimate place in the conventional theory of optimal investment behaviour. Yet, when it is carried over and applied to the field of *intellectual* investments in new tools of economic analysis, the result is a self-defeating orthodoxy of thought and surely not the optimal progress of our discipline.

ACKNOWLEDGEMENTS

I am grateful for the pithy comments that I received on a related earlier paper (David 1997b), from Avner Greif, Frank Hahn, Joel Mokyr, Robert Solow, Edward Steinmueller and Gavin Wright. Stavros Ioannides contributed very helpful editorial corrections. None among them should be held responsible for the deficiencies or excesses that remain in the present text.

NOTES

1. I hestitate to write 'dis-information' at this point, as that connotes intentions rather than consequences. I prefer to proceed on the supposition that those who have repeatedly misrepresented the meaning of the term in the course of criticizing 'path dependence' as an erroneous economic theory, and those who have deemed it to be an empty concept (in the sense that it is essentially devoid of empirical relevance for economists), simply are confused about its meaning.
2. For this purpose it is best that I confront the critical treatment of path dependence by Professors Stanley Liebowitz and Stephen Margolis (1995b, 1995c). I therefore put to one side a rebuttal of the specific factual allegations that have been adduced in Liebowitz and Margolis's (1990) riposte to the story of QWERTY as related in David (1985, 1986). That attack has recently been cited by Ruttan (1997), who refers to the emblematic tale of QWERTY as 'the *founding myth* of the path dependence literature' (emphasis added). Although Liebowitz and Margolis fail to substantiate their contention that QWERTY simply is 'a fable', their rhetorical strategy of attacking that case as though it constituted the only economically interesting exemplar of path dependence, managed to raise a small cloud of doubt regarding the empirical significance of the more general phenomenon. On the later issue, however, see David (1999) for another view.
3. Liebowitz and Margolis (1995b: pp. 209–10) fall into just this confusion on the one occasion on which they offer a formal definition of the meaning of 'path dependence'. They say, correctly: 'The meaning closest to current use in economics is that of stochastic processes that incorporate some concept of memory.' But, thereupon they draw from the *Encyclopedic Dictionary of Mathematics* (Cambridge, MA: MIT Press, 1987) the following definition of 'path dependence': Letting $P(n)$ be the probability of event $E(n) = A(1)$ on the n-th trial, and $(1–P(n))$ be the probability of $E(n) = A(2)$, then the general 'response probability' for the sequential process is: $P(n+1) = f\{P(n), E(n), E(n–1),...,E(1)\}$. When the function $f = f\{P(n), E(n), E(n–1),..., E(n–d)\}$, the response probability is said to be 'd-trial path dependent'. In the special case where $d = 0$ it is 'path independent'.

   The text in Liebowitz and Margolis (1995b: p. 210) then goes on to assert, quite erroneously: 'The use of path dependence in economics is, for the most part, loosely analogous to this mathematical construction: Allocations chosen today exhibit memory; they are conditioned on past decisions.' One should notice that if 'allocations' are associated with 'events', $E(i)$, and (probabilistic) decisions at moment n are characterized by the pairs $[P(n); 1-P(n)]$, then the foregoing statement does not correspond to the mathematical construction of d-trial path dependence, any more than the latter corresponds to the generic usage of path dependence by David (1985, 1986, 1989, et seq), or by Arthur (1988, 1989, 1990, 1994), by Cowan (1991, 1996), by Durlauf (1990, 1996), Krugman (1991, 1994), and others contributing to the economics literature.

4. The reference in the passage quoted to 'contingency' as the conceptual counterpart in biology of the idea of path dependence is followed by Liebowitz and Margolis's (1995b, p. 33) statement that 'In *Wonderful Life*, Stephen J. Gould applies this intellectual revolution to paleontology.' But, it should be shiningly clear from that work by Gould (1989, pp. 282ff, esp.), and really no less from his earlier writings, that he is not drawing upon a recent intellectual revolution: 'I regard Charles Darwin as the greatest of all historical scientists. Not only did he develop convincing evidence for evolution as the coordinating principle of life's history, but he also chose as a conscious theme for all his writings...the development of a different but equally rigorous methodology for historical science....Historical explanations take the form of narrative: E, the phenomenon to be explained, arose because D came before, preceded by C, B, and A. If any of these earlier stages had not occurred, or had transpired in a different way, then E would not exist (or would be present in a substantially altered form, E', requiring a different explanation....I am not speaking of randomness (for E had to arise, as a consequence of A through D), but of the central principle of all history – *contingency*.' (Gould, 1989, pp. 282–3). Further on, Gould (1989, pp. 283–4) writes of the universal psychological appeal of the notion of historical contingency, in terms that leave no doubt that this is not a concept specific to evolutionary biology: 'Historical explanations are endlessly fascinating in themselves, in many ways more intriguing to the human psyche than the inexorable consequences of nature's laws....Contingency is the affirmation of control by immediate events over destiny....Contingency is a license to participate in history, and our psyche responds. The theme of contingency, so poorly understood and explored by science, has long been a mainstay of literature....Tolstoy's theme in all his great novels.' What Gould provides in *Wonderful Life* is a new interpretation of the record of life left in the Burgess Shale, but, as he takes pains to acknowledge, this interpretation 'is rooted in contingency' – a very old and far from revolutionary idea. See also Teggart (1977), Eldridge (1985).

5. The practice can be employed with potent rhetorical effect on an unsophisticated audience, because the deterministic reformulation may then be subjected to criticisms from which the original analysis would be immune. A striking instance of such a switch is to be found in Liebowitz and Margolis's (1995b, pp. 214–15) reproduction and critique of a deterministic payoff tableau, used by Arthur (1989) purely *as a heuristic device* – to convey the possibility that a sequence of myopic adoption decisions under increasing returns to adoption could result in the commitment of the ensemble of adopters to a dominated outcome. In the course of pointing out that the payoff tableau may be read in a way that is inconsistent with the results reported for Arthur's stochastic model, there appears the following commendably candid footnote (pp. 214–15, n. 15): 'Actually, Arthur states that this example does not exhibit any "non-ergodicity", meaning that it is not path dependent in the sense that small differences in historical sequences play a role in the final equilibrium. In this example the end result is the same no matter the order of initial participants. But it illustrates lock-in very well.' I might note that this footnote is the only place I have found in Liebowitz and Margolis's publications on path dependence where the concept is explicitly defined with reference to non-ergodicity, and even so the passage omits explicit reference to probability.

6. Furthermore, Liebowitz and Margolis (1995b) offer a description of 'third-degree' path dependence that would apply equally to deterministic chaos – which, as was noted above, the authors correctly acknowledged to be not really the same thing as path dependence.

7. This, however, would seem to leave Liebowitz and Margolis in the position of having to insist that economists should not attach real importance to path dependence because its 'third-degree' form ignores the reality that, even when remediation would not occur via 'private

ordering', it would most likely be achievable through 'public ordering'. That is hardly what one expects from defenders of *laissez-faire*.

8. For discussion of this in the context of technical compatibility standards, see, for example, David and Greenstein (1990b); on social conventions, organizational routines and formal institutions, David (1994c), and David (1994d).
9. See, for example, David (1987, 1990); David and Bunn (1988), Cowan (1991).
10. Compare the detailed analyses of the VHS market in Baba and Imai (1990), Cusumano, Mylonadis and Rosenbloom (1992) and Grindley (1992), none of which are noticed in Liebowitz and Margolis (1994), or the latter authors' subsequent references to this case.
11. Especially in David (1987), David and Bunn (1988), David and Greenstein (1990) and, most forthrightly in David (1992b).
12. See David (1993b) for more on the teleological mode of analysis in economics.
13. For further discussion of the latter topics, see, for example, David (1993a, 1994c), David and Foray (1993d, 1994d).
14. On these epistemological topics, see, for example, the stochastic models developed in David (1997), and David and Sanderson (1997) and David (1998b, 2000).

REFERENCES

Works by Paul A. David
A chronological listing of publications dealing explicitly with conceptual and methodological aspects of path dependence, macro-level irreversibilities and hysteresis in economic processes. **Co-authors' names** appear in boldface.

(1969), 'Transport innovation and economic growth: Professor Fogel on and off the rails', *Economic History Review*, **22**, (3), December: 506–25.
(1971), 'The landscape and the machine: technical interrelatedness, land tenure and the mechanization of the corn harvest in Victorian Britain', in D.N. McCloskey (ed.), *Essays on a Mature Economy*, London: Methuen, pp. 145–205.
(1975), *Technical Choice, Innovation and Economic Growth: Essays on American and British Experience in the Nineteenth Century*, Cambridge: Cambridge University Press.
(1985), 'Clio and the economics of QWERTY', *American Economic Review*, **75** (2), May.
(1986), 'Understanding the economics of QWERTY: The necessity of history', in W.N. Parker (ed.), *Economic History and the Modern Economist*, London: Basil Blackwell.
(1987), 'Some new standards for the economics of standardization in the information age', in P. Dasgupta and P.L. Stoneman (eds), *The Economics of Technology Policy*, London: Cambridge University Press.
(1988a), 'Path dependence: putting the past into the future of economics', *Institute for Mathematical Studies in the Social Sciences Technical Report 533*, Stanford University, November.
(1988b), 'The economics of gateway technologies and network evolution: lessons from electricity supply history', (with **Julie A. Bunn**), *Information Economics and Policy*, **3**, Winter: 165–202.
(1989), 'When and why does history really matter?', *A Presidential Address to the Economic History Association*, Delivered at the Smithsonian Museum of Science and Technology, Washington DC, September. [Department of Economics Working Paper, Stanford University, October 1989.]

(1990), 'The economics of compatibility standards: an introduction to recent research', (with **S. Greenstein**), in *Economics of Innovation and New Technology*, **1** (1 & 2), Fall: 3–42.

(1991), 'The hero and the herd: reflections on Thomas Edison and the "Battle of the Systems"', in P. Higonnet, D.S. Landes and H. Rosovsky (eds), *Favorites of Fortune: Technology, Growth, and Economic Development Since the Industrial Revolution*, Cambridge, MA: Harvard University Press.

(1992a) ''Path dependence and economics', The 1991–1992 Marshall Lectures delivered at the University of Cambridge, April 28–29. Lecture I: 'The invisible hand in the grip of the past'; Lecture II: 'Models of non-ergodic economic dynamics, and their implications for policy'. (Center for Economic Policy Research Working Paper, Stanford University, August, 1992).

(1992b) 'Path dependence in economic processes: implications for policy analysis in dynamical system contexts', *Background Paper – Rosselli Foundation Workshop on Path Dependence*, Turin, Italy, 29–30 May. (Center for Economic Policy Research Working Paper, Stanford University, August, 1992).

(1992c) 'Heroes, herds and hysteresis in technological history', *Journal of Industrial and Corporate Change*, **1** (1): 129–80.

(1993a) 'Path dependence and predictability in dynamic systems with local network externalities: a paradigm for historical economics', in D. Foray and C. Freeman (eds), *Technology and the Wealth of Nations*, London: Pinter Publishers.

(1993b) 'Historical economics in the long run: some implications of path dependence, in G.D. Snooks (ed.), *Historical Analysis in Economics*, London: Routledge.

(1993c) 'Intellectual property institutions and the panda's thumb: patents, copyrights, and trade secrets in economic theory and history', in M. Wallerstein, *et al.*, (eds), *Global Dimensions of Intellectual Property Protection in Science and Technology*, Washington, DC: National Academy Press.

(1993d) 'Percolation structures, Markov random fields and the economics of EDI standards diffusion', (with **Dominique Foray**), in G. Pogorel (ed.), *Global Telecommunication Strategies and Technological Change*, Amsterdam: Elsevier Science Publishers.

(1994a) 'Dynamics of technology diffusion through local network structures', (with **Dominique Foray**), in L. Leydesdorff (ed.), *Evolutionary Economics and Chaos Theory: New Developments in Technology Studies*, London: Pinter Publishers.

(1994b) 'Positive feedbacks and research productivity in science: reopening another black box', in O. Grandstrand and P. Jacobson (eds), *Technology and Economic Change*, Amsterdam: Elsevier, chapter 8.

(1994c), 'Les standards des technologies de l'information, les normes de communication et l'état: un problème de biens publics', in A. Orleans, (ed.), *L'Analyse économique des conventions*, Paris: Presses Universitaires, chapter 10.

(1994d), 'Why are institutions the "carriers of history"? Path dependence and the evolution of conventions, organizations and institutions', *Structural Change and Economic Dynamics*, **5** (2): 205–20.

(1995), 'Dépendence du sentier et économie de l'innovation: Un rapide tour d'horizon', (with **Dominique Foray**), *Revue d'Economie Industrielle*: Special edition: 'Economie industrielle – développements récents', 1st trimester, 1995: 27–51.

(1997a), 'Making use of treacherous advice: cognitive progress, Bayesian adaptation and the tenacity of unreliable knowledge', (with **Warren C. Sanderson**), in J.V. Nye and J. Drobak (eds), *Frontiers of the New Institutional Economics*, San Diego, CA: Academic Press, chapter 12.

(1997b), 'Path dependence and the quest for historical economics: one more chorus of the ballad of QWERTY', University of Oxford Discussion Papers in Economic and Social History, No. 20, (November) (www.nuff.ox.ac.uk/ukeconomics/history/pap20).

(1998a), 'Marshallian externalities and the emergence and spatial stability of techno-logical enclaves', (with **Dominique Foray** and **Jean-Michel Dalle**), *Economics of Innovation and New Technologies*, (Special issue on Economics of Localized Technical Change, ed. C. Antonelli), **4**(2&3): 147–82.

(1998b), 'Communication norms and the collective cognitive performance of "invisible colleges",' in G.B. Navaretti, P. Dasgupta, K.-G. Maier and D. Siniscalco (eds), *Creation and Transfer of Knowledge: Institutions and Incentives* London: Springer.

(1998c), 'From the economics of QWERTY to the millenium bug', *Stanford University Economics Department Newsletter*, Stanford CA, Fall 1998/99.

(1999), 'At last, a remedy for chronic QWERTY-skepticism!', Discussion Paper for the European Summer School in Industrial Dynamics (ESSID), held at l'Institute d'Etudes Scientifiques de Cargèse (Corse), France, September.

(2000), 'Path dependence and varieties of learning in the evolution of technological practice', in John Ziman (ed.), *Technological Innovation as an Evolutionary Process*, Cambridge; Cambridge University Press, chapter 10.

Other Works

Arthur, W.B. (1988), ' Self-reinforcing mechanisms in economics', in *The Economy as an Evolving Complex System* (Santa Fe Institute Studies in the Science of Complexity, **5**), Redwood City, CA: Addison-Wesley.

Arthur, W. Brian (1989), 'Competing technologies and lock-in by historical small events', *Economic Journal*, **99** (March): 116–31.

Arthur, W. Brian (1990), 'Industry location patterns and the importance of history', *Mathematical Social Sciences*, **19**: 235–51.

Arthur, W. Brian (1994), *Increasing Returns and Path Dependence in the Economy*, Ann Arbor: University of Michigan Press.

Arthur, W. B, Yu. M. Ermoliev, and Yu. M. Kaniovski, (1983), 'A generalized urn problem and its applications', *Kibernetika*, **19**: 49–57 (in Russian). Translated in *Cybernetics*, **19**: 61–71.

Arthur, W. B, Yu. M. Ermoliev, and Yu. M Kaniovski, (1986), 'Strong laws for a class of path-dependent urn processes', *Proceedings of the International Conference on Stochastic Optimization, Kiev 1984*, Arkin, Shiryayev and Wets (eds), New York: Springer (Springer Lecture Notes in Control and Information Sciences, p. 81).

Baba, Y. and K. Imai (1990), 'Systemic innovation and cross-border networks: the case of the evolution of the VCR systems', Paper presented to the Schumpeter Society Conference on Entrepreneurship, Technological Innovation and Economic Growth, held at Airlie House, VA, June 3–5.

Cowan, R. (1990), 'Nuclear power reactors: a study in technological lock-in', *Journal of Economic History*, **50** (3), September: 541–67.

Cowan, R. (1991), 'Tortoises and hares: choice among technologies of unknown merit', *Economic Journal*, **101** (407), July: 801–14.

Cowan, R. and P. Gunby (1996), 'Sprayed to death: path dependence, lock-in and pest control strategies', *Economic Journal*, **106** (436), May: 521–42.

Cusumano, M. A., Y. Mylonadis and R.S. Rosenbloom (1992), 'Strategic maneuvering and mass-market dynamics: the triumph of VHS over Beta', *Business History Review*, 66 (Spring): 51–94.

David, P.A., R.C. Maude-Griffin and G.S. Rothwell (1996), 'Learning by accident? Reductions in the risk of unplanned outages in US nuclear power plants after Three Mile Island', *Journal of Risk and Uncertainty*, **12**: 175–98.

Durlauf, S. (1990), 'Non-ergodic economic growth and fluctuations in aggregate output', *American Economic Review*, **80** (3).

Durlauf, S. (1996), 'Neighborhood feedbacks, endogenous stratification, and income inequality', in *Dynamic Disequilibrium Modelling*, Cambridge: Cambridge University Press.

Eldridge, N. (1985), *Time Frames: The Rethinking of Darwinian Evolution and the Theory of Punctuated Equilibria,* New York: Simon and Schuster.

Fisher, F.M. (1983), *The Disequilibrium Foundations of Equilibrium Economics*, New York: Cambridge University Press.

Föllmer, H. (1974), 'Random economies with many interacting agents', *Journal of Mathematical Economics*, **1**: 51–62.

Gould, S. J. (1989), *Wonderful Life: The Burgess Shale and the Nature of History*, New York: W. W. Norton and Company.

Grindley, P. (1992), *Standards, Business Strategy and Policy: A Casebook*, London: London Business School.

Krugman, P. (1991), *Geography and Trade*, Cambridge, MA: MIT Press.

Krugman, P. (1994), *Peddling Prosperity*, New York: W.W. Norton and Company.

Liebowitz, S.J., and Stephen E. Margolis (1990), 'The fable of the keys', *Journal of Law and Economics*, **33** (1), April: 1–25.

Liebowitz, S.J., and Stephen E. Margolis (1994), 'Network externality: an uncommon tragedy', *Journal of Economic Perspectives*, **8** (2), Spring: 133–50.

Liebowitz, S.J., and Stephen E. Margolis (1995a), 'Are network externalities a new source of market failure?', *Research in Law and Economics*, **17** (0):1–22.

Liebowitz, S.J., and Stephen E. Margolis (1995b), 'Path dependence, lock-in, and history', *Journal of Law, Economics, and Organization*, **11** (1), April: 205–26.

Liebowitz, S. and Stephen E. Margolis (1995c), 'Policy and path dependence: from QWERTY to Windows 95', *Regulation: The Cato Review of Business & Government*, number 3: 33–41.

Liggett, T. M. (1985), *Interacting Particle Systems (Grundlehren der mathematischen Wissenschaftern* **276**), Berlin: Springer-Verlag.

McCloskey, D.N. (1976), 'Does the past have useful economics?', *Journal of Economic Literature*, **14** (2), June: 434–61.

Ruelle, D. (1991), *Chance and Chaos*, Princeton: Princeton University Press.

Ruttan, V.W. (1997), 'Induced innovation, evolutionary theory and path dependence: sources of technological change', *Economic Journal*, **107** (444), September: pp. 1520–47.

Solow, R.M. (1986), 'Economics: is something missing?', in William N. Parker (ed.), *Economic History and the Modern Economist*, Oxford: Basil Blackwell: pp. 21–9.

Steward, I. (1990), *Does God Play Dice? The New Mathematics of Chaos*, London: Penguin.

Teggart, F.J. (1977), *Theory and Processes of History* (second paperback printing of the 1941 edition of *Theory of History* (1925) and *The Processes of History* (1918), published in one volume), Berkeley: University of California Press.

Williamson, O.E. (1993), 'Transaction cost economics and organization theory', *Industrial and Corporate Change*, **2** (2): pp. 107–56.

3. The meaning of market: comparing Austrian and Institutional economics

Philippe Dulbecco and Veronique Dutraive

1 INTRODUCTION

Economics has long concentrated almost exclusively on the analysis of purely competitive market structures, in which the institutional framework is exogenously determined and very weakly specified. But although it is more and more recognized that this model falls short of characterizing market economies in which the price system operates with costs, and necessitates specific institutions, and in which firms are more than purely rhetorical devices, an alternative unified market economy theory is still missing. The main reason is that, outside the structuralist tradition, the market appears as a polysemic concept (Hodgson, 1988) associated with various theoretical levels and dealing with extremely specific economic problems.

However, both the New Institutional Economics (NIE) (Langlois, 1986) and the Industrial Dynamics approaches (Carlsson, 1989) aim at identifying some common themes which represent new directions in economic theory. The market theme constitutes of course one of the most discussed subjects, especially (not surprisingly) in an Austrian perspective. But while it is well known that the Austrian analysis of the market process represents (if we may paraphrase F. Hahn) a real 'base camp' for an alternative theory of the coordination of economic activities, a growing number of works are nowadays underlining the potential fruitful connections between Austrian and Institutional works on markets (O'Driscoll and Rizzo, 1996; Boettke and Prychitko, 1994; Wynarczyk, 1992).

Our contribution aims precisely at revealing the terms of a confrontation between these two schools concerning the nature and the role of markets. In this perspective, we exhibit not only the common features, but also the possible complementarity of the market approaches contained in both theories.

The attempts to bring together two approaches traditionally considered as being antinomic are very recent. Though such difficult but fruitful confrontation has produced numerous publications,[1] the question of the nature and the role of the market do not appear to have been systematically treated. After stressing the obstacles, the difficulties and the broad lines of a dialogue between two rival theories (section 2), we will show that these two traditions converge in offering a processual market representation in an economic world characterized by strong uncertainty and historical influence (section 3). The institutional element plays in this context a very ambiguous role: not only do institutions constitute an external framework (one that removes uncertainty) for market transactions (Commons, 1934), they also appear to be internal to individual transactions, those leading to their adjustment and evolution. Following Lachmann (1994) the problem thus becomes to provide a joint analysis of the *permanency* and *flexibility* of institutions. Such analysis, based on a combination of elements stemming from both traditions,[2] gives the opportunity to build an alternative framework which offers an approach to individual and group problem-solving activity within institutional-knowledge constraints (section 4).[3]

2   AUSTRIAN AND OLD INSTITUTIONAL ECONOMICS: FROM RIVALRY TO DIALOGUE

Why is there a confrontation between Austrians and Institutionalists on market process? The New Institutional Economics (NIE) (Langlois, 1986) programme intends to draw one's inspiration from old Austrian economics rather than from Old Institutional Economics (OIE), which is regarded generally as theoretically inconsistent. Nevertheless, the contemporary debate on the evolutionary nature of the firm and market, and on economics as a process leads to a revival of the OIE way of analysing economics as an evolutionary science (Hodgson 1994; 1996). In some comparisons, OIE and NIE are seen as alternative or complementary programmes (Hodgson, 1989; Langlois, 1986, 1989; Leathers, 1989; Rutherford, 1989b, 1994; Vanberg, 1989). If we consider, after Langlois, that NIE is torn between a neoclassical and an Austrian approach, we can say that OIE is surely an alternative programme to the neoclassical one, but the relation is not so clear when it comes to the Austrian approach.

It is the problematic confrontation of Austrian and Old Institutional Economics that we briefly discuss now.

2.1   A Missed Appointment

The story begins with a missed appointment, a large mutual ignorance and a misconception of the respective contributions of OIE and Austrians to economics.

It is a well-known episode in the history of economic thought that Veblen failed to de-homogenize Jevons', Walras' and Menger's conceptions of economic behaviour when examining the marginalist preconception of human nature[4] (Langlois, 1989). Veblen[5] was unaware of Menger's contribution to an economic theory of social institutions and ignored the famous distinction between pragmatic and organic institutions.

However, Veblen's works shared Menger's attacks against the German Historical School's argument that the historical and social diversity of institutions prohibits a theoretical generalization. They also both stress the importance of ridding social theory of teleological elements of explanation. In distinguishing between pragmatic and organic institutions, Menger emphasizes the necessity for social science to analyse how organic institutions evolved without a 'common will directed toward establishing them' (Menger, 1963, p. 146). Using the biological metaphor of the evolutionary framework of explanation along a Darwinian perspective, Veblen saw institutions as the product of 'blind cumulative causation'. But along the 'compositive method' of Menger's approach, the stress is put on individuals pursuing their own interests and on an invisible-hand explanation of the formation of complex social phenomena. For Veblen, on the other hand, there is a self-reinforcing causality between individuals and culture, neither of them being exclusive for social explanation.[6]

The same way that Veblen failed to take into account Menger's work, Hayek failed to take into account Veblen's.

Hayek's comments on Institutional economics in general are negative and grounded on very few arguments. According to him, Institutionalism is an American heir of German historicism and thus shares the same critique: they didn't produce a theory of institutions but a simple description, that is monographs without scientific economic analysis. While Hayek called for a study of evolutionary process of social phenomena similar to biological selection, he surprisingly didn't refer at all to Veblen's evolutionism, even as an opponent of his own. As Leathers shows, Hayek has nevertheless developed a theory of cultural evolution grounded on an instinctual conception of human nature with numerous interesting parallels to Veblen's[7] (Leathers, 1990).

Neither has Commons taken into account the Austrian theory of institutions and evolution: Menger's works are evaluated in the light of their affinity with Marginalism or *Methodenstreit*. So despite some strong common elements in the Austrian and the OIE thought, the founders have never held a dialogue.[8]

2.2   Austrian and OIE as Antithetic

The main reason for this lack of dialogue is that Austrian is a market focus tradition while OIE is an institutional focus tradition. As Samuels clearly states: 'Austrians stress the markets as the allocative mechanism, Institutionalists stress the institutions and power structure which form and operate through the market as the real allocative mechanism' (1989, pp. 59–60). Austrians didn't ignore the existence of organization and state regulation, they also significantly contributed to an evolutionary conception of the economic system. But they are mainly interested in abstracting the function and essence of the market as a system of order from the historical specificity of economic systems. By contrast, OIE do not see specific market structures as inherently 'normal' or 'natural' (Miller, 1989) and do not agree that markets can be analysed *qua* market forces. The concept of 'market' is seen as a metaphor for the institutions, which form its structure and operate through it (Samuels, 1995). Old Institutionalists did not take the actual legal basis of the capitalist system for granted, rather they questioned the formation and consequences of property rights. Moreover, according to OIE, government, legal foundations and politics inextricably intertwine with the operation of markets (Samuels, 1989) and cannot be 'exogenized'.

A consequence is that while Austrians emphasize non-deliberative decision making, OIE emphasizes deliberative decision making or, put in Menger's dichotomy, Austrians are focused on organic institutions while Institutionalists are focused on pragmatic institutions. For OIE, the 20th century economic system cannot be understood with a pure market analysis. This anticipates the contemporary interest in the theoretical status of the firm, stressing the economic study on the 'major institution of capitalism', the business enterprise. The corporation cannot be reduced to the idea of the entrepreneur, because it results from the joint action of many groups. Veblen initiated the managerial conception of the firm and the corporate control problem that the interaction of bankers, shareholders and managers carries (Veblen, 1904). For Commons, the collective action in going concerns is the main characteristic of the actual economic system. He particularly insisted on the dual agency relationship (workers/employers) torn between cooperation and conflict and on the legal working rules supporting the system (Commons, 1934). A corollary of this so-called 'decision making' point of view is that Institutionalists consider analysis of power structure and of government agency in the formation and performance of markets to be necessary (Samuels, 1995).

This great difference leads to a strong ideological opposition: Austrians are pro-market while Institutionalists think that the market system needs social control and reform. According to the former, the scope of government activity must be limited in the defence of freedom (stated in political terms), or contractual liberty (stated in economics terms), and legislation must conform to the market order. Institutionalists emphasize that the free market economy is itself a system of social control, and that specific markets are what they are, and perform as they do, because institutions operate as a social control (Samuels,

1995). They deny that markets are automatically efficient and suggest that a democratic economic government can improve existing arrangements. They do not see market and government as the two terms of an analytical opposition, but as Polanyi says, 'the road to the free market was opened and kept open by an enormous increase in continuous, centrally organised and controlled interventionism' (1994, p. 141).

Austrian and Institutionalist are also seen as two strong and durable dissenting traditions in the light of economic methodology.

OIE is often misconceived as the American Historical School. Consequently, Austrians and OIE are seen as representative opponents in the *Methodenstreit*.[9] The first principle of the opposition is the duality: theory versus history. According to Austrians, the nature of the economic problem is the discovery and description of general laws that are present in any economic system. OIE denies the universality of economic laws that are considered, conversely, as embedded in institutional or historical circumstances.[10] A consequence of these opposite views is that Austrians are supposed to adopt an *a priori* deductive reasoning while Institutionalists are rather empiricists and pragmatists. The latter cannot accept the logical consistence of assumptions as a criterion of scientificity but rather that economic propositions are heuristics for social design (Miller, 1989; Gordon, 1989; Samuels, 1989).

A last notable methodological opposition can be noticed: the explanatory variables in economic theory are individuals for the first, and institutions for the latter. The Austrian subjectivism is the foundation of its methodological individualism in contrast with the so-called Institutionalist's holism. According to Austrians, social structures are the unintentional result of the individuals' self-seeking interests whereas for OIE, institutions mould individual preferences and choices.

While many issues seem to divide the two traditions, Samuels and Boettke (neo-Institutionalist and neo-Austrian respectively) nevertheless defend the idea that there 'seemed to be significant common subject-matter and much parallel substantive content' (Samuels, 1989, p. 49).

The chief point of convergence is that they are outsiders *vis-à-vis* neoclassicism. As we shall explain in the next section, they both object to atemporal equilibrium analysis. The economy is rather viewed as a dynamic process in an evolutionary perspective. They also contest the neoclassical conception of economic behaviour seen as passive and predetermined. They share emphasis on economics as a praxeological science in an uncertain environment, with imperfect knowledge and a radically indeterminate future. For both approaches, time is a major issue in the necessary acquisition of knowledge governing human action, and institutions are a medium for learning and for complex social interactions.

3   THE MARKET AS AN ECONOMIC PROCESS: AN ECUMENICAL POINT OF VIEW

Presenting the intent of his 1986 book, *The Market as an Economic Process*, Lachmann explains:

> The central idea of this book is the market regarded as an economic process, that is, an ongoing process, impelled by the diversity of aims and resources and the divergence of expectations, ever changing in a world of unexpected change. *It is my hope that this idea may also gain some sympathy from those whose inspiration flows from other than Austrian sources.* (1986, p. x)[11]

A few years later, authors such as Boettke and Prychitko (1994) echoed this will by stressing the relevance of exchanges with the Institutional work for the future trends of the Austrian theory of market processes. The question is then to determine the terms of such an exchange, which can only be done after singling out a minimum number of features common to both approaches.

3.1   The Processual Nature of Economic Phenomena

The first feature, at the core of our project, relates to the dismissal of the notion of atemporal equilibrium that is 'an equilibrium in which economic actions at a particular point in time are co-ordinated independent of what transpired just before that instant and what may transpire just after' (Garrison, 1986, p. 89).

Such dismissal represents, as everyone knows, one of the most obvious features of Austrian economics. By rejecting the concept of atemporal equilibrium, the Austrian school rejects the possibility of an objective knowledge of economic phenomena. The outcomes of the running of the market system cannot be objectively known, the adjustment process being likely to take on various forms which reflect the modes of interaction between individual plans. Markets are then best regarded as processes and the market economy is defined as 'a network of markets in each of which, and between which, phenomena that may be described in terms of processes are occurring' (Lachmann, 1986, p. 3).

The concept of process consists of two distinct elements (Ioannides, 1992): (1) the principle of endogeneity which states that all economic processes are endogenously mobilized, and (2) time, underlining the fact that 'the sequence of events becomes an issue of fundamental importance, as each event really constitutes the cause of the one succeeding it' (ibid., p. 9). Finally 'the outcomes of market depend on what happens at their various stages and on the order in which events happen. This means in particular that antecedents will influence subsequent events *in so far as acting men attribute significance to them* and that therefore the order in which events happen matters' (Lachmann, 1986, p. 4).

However, the rejection of the state of equilibrium doesn't necessarily mean the rejection of the concept of equilibrium itself. First of all, because the idea of an individual equilibrium which implies that all aspects of an individual plan are compatible with each other is assumed, in the Austrian tradition, to hold *a priori*, even if the maintenance of such equilibrium over time requires that the data generated by the economy do not disrupt the agent's expectations. Second, because the traditional Austrian theory of market processes[12] does not rule out the idea of a trend towards a market equilibrium. On the other hand, there exists between Lachmann's view of the fundamental indeterminateness of the market process and Mises's belief in the *a priori* nature of the tendency toward equilibrium, a wide range of positions, which are not really inconsistent with the notion of equilibrium.[13] The Hayekian and the Kirznerian stands are, in this point of view, representative of the place and the role assigned by this traditional Austrian theory to the notion of equilibrium. Whereas for Hayek (1937), the degree of indeterminateness of the market equilibrium viewed as the outcome of the interaction of several minds functioning independently from each other is removed by the empirical convergence of expectations, the entrepreneur is the one who, according to Kirzner (1973, 1979, 1985, 1992), acts as the stabilizing force and leads to the adjustment of the market process towards equilibrium, by discovering and cancelling market errors, that is by exploiting profit opportunities.

Nowadays, the idea of a trend towards equilibrium is, however, widely criticized within the Austrian family itself. Following O'Driscoll and Rizzo it is possible to state that 'today many, if not all, Austrians accept the importance of disequilibrating tendencies in markets' (1996, p. xviii).[14] Indeed, it appears more and more clearly, from an Austrian point of view, that 'the equilibrium metaphor has proven misleading and that the time has come to seek a less mechanical metaphor, one that does not trivialise the incessant change of market processes' (Boettke, Horwitz and Prychitko 1994, p. 65). In particular, the question is to oppose the Hayekian argument, which sees equilibrium as an empirical fact, with the idea that if the equilibrating tendencies of markets are an empirical regularity, then human society must be tending towards a state of affairs without money, firms, or market institutions.

The important point here is that the recognition of the importance of disequilibrating forces goes together with another feature of modern Austrian economics, that is with a greater attention given to the prerequisites for equilibrating behaviour. As soon as the disequilibrating tendencies in markets are not simply the result of changes in the exogenous data, but arise from the source of equilibrating behaviour (the indeterminate response to perceived profit opportunities), it becomes necessary to discover the cooperating conditions that are needed to make equilibration more or less likely (O'Driscoll and Rizzo, 1996, p. xxi). In other words, the problem is to determine the *ordering principles* which produce mutually reinforcing sets of expectations without denying that some expectations will be wrong (Boettke, Horwitz and Prychitko 1994).[15] Such ordering principles will assume different forms in different markets, depending on what Lachmann (1986) calls the *proximity of agents* and their range of action.

The concept of *pattern coordination* proposed by O'Driscoll and Rizzo (1996) makes it possible to incorporate this dynamic character of the notion of market process, thus providing a solution to the problem of identifying ordering principles. Based on the distinction between *typical* and *unique* events,[16] the pattern coordination analysis indicates that if the market is able to coordinate typical events and consequently to stabilize the economy, it is no more the case when the unique characteristics of human actions are taken into account. Indeed in this last case the market process becomes entirely indeterminate and the coordination of plans needs alternative coordination mechanisms. It is here important to notice that this analysis is general, insofar as it can deal with the numerous Austrian approaches of market process, the convergence towards equilibrium being a very particular occurrence in which identical events are repeated period after period.

Although Institutionalists didn't use the term 'market process', which is an Austrian 'copyright', they share the interest in the study of economic process. A distinctive characteristic of Institutional economics is its emphasis upon the concept of change. As Hamilton put it:

> The Institutionalist (...) considers change to be part of the economic process. Instead of viewing the economy as a fixed system periodically prodded into movement to a new point of non-motion, he holds that the economy is at all times undergoing a process of cumulative change, and that the study of economics is the study of process. (Hamilton, 1973, p. 17)

Institutionalism thus rejects, along with the Austrian approach, an atemporal equilibrium conception of the economy. 'The conception of the economy is of an evolving, open system in historical time, subject to processes of cumulative causation, instead of approaches to theorising that focus exclusively on mechanical equilibria' (Hodgson, 1994, pp. 68–9). With some notable differences, Veblen's and Commons' principal preoccupation was to analyse the process of change in the modern economy, and the neoclassical and marginalist conception of economic equilibrium was, according to them, inadequate for this theoretical purpose.

Veblen gave further grounds for developing an evolutionary economics, by stressing the processes of economic evolution and technological transformation. According to him, economics must break with its Newtonian preconceptions that make it no more than a 'taxonomic science', in order to become an evolutionary science (Veblen, 1898). His idea is that the economic system is not a self-balancing mechanism, but a 'cumulatively unfolding process'. For him, 'Modern science is becoming substantially a theory of the process of consecutive change, realized to be self-continuing or self-propagating and to have no final term'.[17] The economic change and evolution process is captured by the Veblenian concept of cumulative causation: the prevailing way of thinking and acting are cumulatively reinforced and lead to locked-in phenomena. Hodgson interprets Veblen's view as a positive feedback analysis, in opposition to the neoclassical negative feedback conception (Hodgson, 1994). In the latter the economic movement is stabilized and even broken, whereas in the former it is amplified and leads to a dynamic change with self-reinforcing property. These self-reinforcing attributes are a factor of continuity in this process of continuous change. For Veblen, the stability of the economic system depends on the coherence between the factors of continuity and the factors of change. But this form of equilibrium in the never-ending evolution can be disrupted when the factors of continuity fail to be coherent with the new circumstances. Hodgson (1994) thinks that Veblen's evolutionism fits the modern biological theory better than the gradualist conception. Particularly, the link between crisis and continual change in Veblen's explanation fits the idea of 'punctuated-equilibria' (Eldredge and Gould, 1977). There is something that is transmitted in the process of change and that constitutes the continuity and the identity of the economic system. But this form of equilibrium is not at all the same as in neoclassical economics.

In the same perspective, the central problem of economics is, according to Commons,[18] a classical one: how can an order exist out of the conflict of individual interests due to scarcity? Commons departs himself from the explanation in terms of automatic harmonization and unconscious cooperation generated by the price mechanism. The origin of order lies in what he called the working rules that specify what individuals can or cannot, must or must not, may or may not do in their transactions. 'The working rules regulate behaviour in such fashion that potential conflicts of interest do not undermine the security of expectations without which individuals will not be willing to enter into transactions' (Ramstad, 1990, p. 58). But the order grounded on the working rules of the society is neither natural nor immutable: it is an evolving order. The actual working rules always give rise to unanticipated consequences. Disputes and unregulated conflicts of interest are generated by new circumstances that lead to the rise of new working rules in a process of 'artificial selection' conducted by the authority figures that decide conflicts. Economic process is characterized by conflicting and cooperative transactions in many going concerns and by a permanent authoritative adjustment of the rules, aimed at maintaining the order. The equilibrium can be understood as the 'workable mutuality' and compromise brought by rules out of conflict. But it is, as for Veblen, an evolutionary perspective unsuitable to an atemporal equilibrium conceptualization.

With a very different state of mind, Institutionalists and Austrians thus converge on some very important points of view about economics. Market process (enlarged to economic process for Institutionalists) cannot be understood with an atemporal equilibrium analytical apparatus. The principle of 'endogeneity' and that of 'time', that characterize the concept of process, are significant in the Institutionalist perspective: change is a cumulative process with reinforcing properties for Veblen, while for Commons change is the joint effect of unintended results of transactions and the resolution of the conflicts that emerge; the process is historical because change never produces a return to a previous state of affairs (positive feedback).

However, the evolutionary point of view doesn't necessarily mean the rejection of the concept of equilibrium. Equilibrium is a matter of convergence of the ways of thinking and acting, that are transmitted by time and the current state of affairs in Veblen's view; whereas it is the workable mutuality and reasonableness of actual rules that regulate potential conflicts in economic life according to Commons. For both, as for the Austrians, the meaning of equilibrium is a question of ordering principle and pattern of coordination, both of which harmonize and secure the agents' expectations. In other words, equilibrium then does not primarily depend on prices, but on expectations, information systems, and the interpretative frameworks which are used by economic agents (Loasby, 1991). But this conception of equilibrium is far from the neoclassical perspective.

3.2   The Creative Character of Human Action

A second area of convergence for the Austrian and Institutional approaches, regarding the analysis of the operation of markets, lies in the fact that they both take into account the active behaviour of economic agents.[19] This point is related to the recognition of the ignorance and uncertainty faced by market agents as well as to the essential complexity of the market.

This is particularly blatant within the Austrian approach. Actually, one of the implications of considering the market as a spontaneous order is that no one has a particular knowledge of all relevant conditions on which economic action is based. The rejection of the price-taking behaviour and the conception of the market as a system in constant flux are based on the idea that the flow of information is the moving force of economic activity. Consequently, ignorance and uncertainty will surround most market decisions: 'when a person is ignorant of particular influences in his economic environment and therefore uncertain about the success of possible undertakings, he will be alert to new information, and he will mull over the information he does have in formulating his decisions' (High, 1994, p. 25).

The Austrian School's method of incorporating ignorance, uncertainty, and expectations into economic theory has been to stress the entrepreneurial element in human consciousness. Entrepreneurship theory indeed offers an answer to two important questions raised by the analysis of market processes (Ioannides, 1992): (1) the question of describing the motives that mobilize the use of knowledge, and (2) the question of the (exact) way this behaviour is expressed in the market process. More precisely, it is possible to distinguish two types of answers which refer to two types of active behaviours, each one referring to the distinction previously pointed out between equilibrium market processes and indeterminate market processes (Boettke, Horwitz and Prychitko 1994).

The first type of behaviour is more particularly associated with Kirzner's work (1973, 1979, 1985, 1992). Indeed as is well known, Kirzner defends the idea that the market economy opens up *arbitrage* possibilities because of the ignorance of individuals: finding a good that sells for different prices in the market is the most obvious example, but Kirzner believes that the *discovery* of factors of production that can be transformed into consumer goods can also be considered as an arbitrage if factor prices are lower than the price of the consumer good. The essence of the entrepreneurial behaviour is thus the discovery of profit opportunities. It is, however, important to notice that if such an entrepreneurial activity is a product of market disequilibrium, its character is by definition equilibrating, since taking advantage of a profit opportunity is equivalent to cancelling it. The *discovery–arbitrage* behaviour represents a force that constantly pushes the market toward equilibrium.

This first kind of active behaviour is, however, considered as too poor, that is too mechanical, by the Austrian analyses which would rather adopt a Lachmannian reasoning.[20] Boettke, Horwitz and Prychitko thus explain that: 'Austrians have traditionally postulated a world of Robbinsian maximisers, and allowed the entrepreneur to seek arbitrage opportunities which equilibrate the market. Such an entrepreneur need only exercise alertness to profit opportunities. *But entrepreneurship is also characterised by judgements about imagined future opportunities*' (1994, p. 65).[21] The problem is hence to focus on the Lachmannian *creative* dimension of entrepreneurial behaviour: 'the creative agent builds plans upon her imagination of the future[22] whereas the discoverer elaborates plans exclusively on the basis of the knowledge at her disposal' (Gloria, 1996, p. 8). However, when the role of judgement is added to alertness, expectations are granted full force and the satisfaction of some individuals' expectations can come only at the expense of the disappointment of others (Lachmann, 1986).[23] The consequence of this is that the market is now described as a process characterized by unexpected change and inconsistency of plans, incompatible with a systematic tendency toward equilibrium.

The conception of human action is a cornerstone of Institutional economics. The revision of the standard economic theory of behaviour was central to its understanding of social interactions in historical time. Institutionalists wanting to theorize foundations of economic order and its evolutionary process cannot be satisfied with the mainstream idea of rational choice, that takes individual behaviours as a given (Mitchell, 1935). On the contrary, they focus on the formation of preferences (Hodgson, 1985) in tight connection with the economic process itself. In contrast with the hedonist and optimizing point of view, the Institutionalist understanding of human behaviour outlines, on the one hand, the habits, routines, customs and rules that mould individual behaviour and constitute the larger agency of *ex ante* coordination of social relationships. On the other hand, individual action is cardinal in the process of change. Consequently, human nature is seen as an active and creative agency in the evolutionary course of the economic system.

Veblen underlined the paradox of the hedonistic and rationalist conception of the economic man: the individual is the first cause of economic phenomena but, at the same time, its psychology is exogenous and its choices are totally predetermined in the analysis. Human nature is, in this line, passive, inert and immutable.[24] In opposition to the calculating, optimizing agent of the neoclassical theory, Veblen puts forward a less competent but less determined and more purposeful individual. The concept of habits plays a central role in the Institutionalist picture of the economic man.[25] 'Habits are a form of nonreflexive behaviour that arises in repetitive situations; they are influenced by prior activity and have self-sustaining qualities' (Hodgson, 1996, p. 6). Veblen was inspired by pragmatist philosophers and social scientists such as James, Peirces and Dewey who considered that habits make it possible to solve the problems of uncertainty and complexity faced by human beings (Waller, 1988). But if habits repeat past practices in routines, they are not opposite to purposeful behaviour, free will and choice. Pragmatists say that habits are the primordial manifestation of human intelligence. Stated in contemporary terminology, they economize cognitive resources by reproduction of past actions in similar circumstances and permit a focal attention on new situations. According to Hodgson, modern economists (Becker, for example) regard habits as an appendage of rational choice (Hodgson, 1996). The pragmatist and Institutionalist perspective is the reverse: rational choice (economic calculus) is supported by habits, which authorize concentration on strategic factors whereas everyday existence is driven by routinized rules of action.

Habits are the link between past and future. At the same time, they are a factor of stability of behaviours, and authorize adaptative, innovative and creative scope of action in an evolutionary perspective (that is to say in an evolving environment).

Commons also stresses the habitual and 'volitional' dimensions of human behaviour. He shares the pragmatist analysis of the human being, as a 'creative agency' whose intelligence is grounded on rules and habits. But the originality of his point of view lies in the unit of economic analysis (long before Williamson and with very different implications): the transaction instead of the individual. According to him, the individual cannot be considered as an 'object of nature', but as a part of an ongoing social process or, in his terminology, as a participant in transactions. Transactions are joint actions (or collective actions) where individuals meet and where working rules control and expand individual action. Through collective action, working rules set limits to individual action and, at the same time, are 'a liberation of individual action from coercion, duress, discrimination, or unfair competition, by means of restraints placed on other individuals' (Commons, 1934, p. 17). A transaction is a situation of negotiation where rules are interpreted and adjusted and where preferences and wills are altered, where collective rules and individual choices are continually modified in the process of interaction (Bazzoli and Dutraive, 1996).

This transactional point of view implies putting forward social interactions and collective patterns in the conception of human psychology that he called 'negotiational psychology', that is a 'social psychology' because individuals are social beings and their actions are always transactions with others. Rules mould perceptions, representations and actions, and bring order out of conflicts and dependence between agents. But it is also a 'volitional psychology' which deals with human purposes and wills in a context of radical uncertainty. Commons considers the mind as 'a creative agency looking toward the future and manipulating the external world and other people in view of expected consequences' (Hodgson, 1996, p. 6). Will aims at exercising power over things and other humans, grounded on expectation of consequences in a context of uncertainty and complex social interactions. The fundamental 'law of human nature' is then the search for a security of expectations. Habits satisfy this fundamental need for reducing uncertainty and complexity. Commons calls activities which do not imply conscious deliberation or attention, 'routine transactions'. They support 'strategic transactions' focused on a 'limiting factor' in new situations where past rules or habits are inappropriate and need attention and deliberation.

Institutionalism thus defends the fact that individual action occurs in real time: present action is the result of expectations about the future and of a process of learning from past experience which transforms sense-data into information and knowledge and shapes individual choices in a context of radical uncertainty. In such a context, perfect knowledge of the consequences of actions and of possible alternatives is impossible. The neoclassical link between rationality and optimization is broken and replaced by a link between purposeful action and habitual behaviour. Habits are the condition of the creative activity of the individual mind, which concentrates on innovation.

It now seems obvious that Austrians and Institutionalists are closely linked according to the importance given to human behaviour: economics as a praxeologic science, as Ludwig von Mises would state.[26] The agent is seen as a true actor (Langlois, 1986) with an active and creative behaviour turned toward an uncertain, unpredictable and widely indeterminate future. It is now able, through market transactions, to exercise its intelligibility and economic understanding. This aptitude stems, in one case, from an extension of individualism to subjectivism, and in the other from the integration of social components into the formulation of market plans by individuals. Thus, and although the analytical figures proposed by each tradition are specific, reflecting both the issues and theoretical foundations of two distinctive paradigms, both approaches understand behaviour as dealing with learning, adapting and acquiring the knowledge needed to face the complexity and uncertainty linked to economic action.

3.3 Towards an Economics of Time and Ignorance

Finally, the Austrian and Institutional approaches converge in the exploration of the reality of the historical time, uncertainty, and ignorance in which market decisions and actions are taken. Doing so, they both contribute to the same dynamics of market mechanisms, which is the one at work in 'the economics of time and ignorance' (O'Driscoll and Rizzo, 1996).

The emphasis placed by the two traditions on the disequilibrium processes and novelty cannot make do with an analysis which takes place in a *logical time* framework, with no genuine causality, a time-span for which 'at any moment (...), the past is determined just as much as the future' (Robinson, 1962, p. 26). Both traditions 'take time seriously' and accept that the properties of time, more precisely of real time, characterize the sphere of economic activity.

The idea, shared by the two approaches, of a non-determined market process involves a *sequential causality* (Hicks, 1979), which seeks to identify prior cause and subsequent effect, rather than to consider that everything affects everything else simultaneously (Setterfield, 1997, p. 69). The behaviours are therefore constrained by a *strong history* (David, 1988), (the movement can only be forward, there is no scope for moving backwards through history) and the analysis is punctuated by *the time of intention* (Currie and Steedman, 1990), that is a time that, while connecting the experience from the past and the expectations about the future to the objectives aimed through current decisions, represents the main driving force behind individual behaviour.

The notions of short and long period lose their meaning in such a framework; the Austrian and Institutionalist analysis of the market and economic processes thus contribute to the elaboration of a historical time framework: 'In a historical model, causal relations have to be specified. Today is a break in time between an unknown future and an irrevocable past. What happens next will result from the interactions of the behaviour of human beings within the economy. Movement can only be forward' (Robinson, 1962, p. 26).

Until now, the institutional dimension of the Austrian and Institutionalist approaches has merely been stressed, whereas this dimension is essential in the view of linking together the Austrian and Institutionalist standpoints within an ecumenical analysis of market processes which takes place in the economics of time and ignorance (O'Driscoll and Rizzo, 1996). Indeed, when the future is unknowable, the expectations divergent and the discoordination forces as strong as the coordination ones, social institutions may enter the picture in order to align expectations and by so doing, they become part of a theory of plan coordination.

In this line, Boettke (1989) Garrouste (1995), Rutherford (1989a) and Vanberg (1989) state that the Austrian and the Institutionalist conceptions of institutions are more complementary than conflicting. Boettke shows a methodological common ground between Veblen and the modern Austrian theory of institutions.[27] Garrouste and Vanberg, comparing respectively Veblen's and Menger's conceptions of institutions – the former – and Commons' and Menger's conception of evolution – the latter – assert the complementarity thesis. According to Garrouste, the Austrian conception is about the institutional genesis, while Institutionalism is about institutional change. According to Vanberg, the Austrian conception is about spontaneous institutions, while Institutionalism is about designed institutions. Even the methodological dissension can be dislocated in a *via media* between individualistic and holistic points of view.[28]

Our point of view, although contributing to the complementarity thesis, is different in the sense that it analyses the nature and the role of institutions in reference to the theoretical issue of the market process. Indeed, if the economic analysis of institutions constitutes an essential link in the Austrian project of building an alternative theory of markets, it is probably also the weakest one. The benefit of the confrontation is thus no longer, in our point of view, to underline the similarities but the complementarities in order to draw up a theory of institutions compatible with an (Austrian) market process analysis.

4 MARKET PROCESSES AND INSTITUTIONAL CHANGE: THE FLEXIBILITY vs. PERMANENCY DILEMMA

It is unanimously recognized that institutions are, in an Austrian approach, of great influence in explaining the market process.[29] In this respect, Lachmann's argument is representative:

It would be wrong to think that a market economy, when faced with the problems just outlined, could, or in the ordinary course of events would, find no answer to them. History shows that whenever left sufficiently free from political interference to evolve its response to such challenges, the market economy has 'grown' the institutions necessary to deal with them. (Lachmann, 1978, p. 67).

4.1 Information, Knowledge and Coordination of Individual Plans: the Institutions as Points of Orientation

The whole set of formulating concepts used to deal with social institutions, relies basically on the notion of *rule-following behaviour* (Langlois, 1993, p. 166): institutions are roughly regularities of behaviour understandable in terms of rules, norms and routines (Nelson and Winter, 1982). According to Schotter, the definition of a social institution can be drawn from an Austrian perspective as 'a regularity in social behaviour that is agreed to by all members of society, specifies behaviour in specific recurrent situations and is either self-policed or policed by some external authority' (1981, p. 11). Institutions are the means by which agents are able to gather sufficient information in order to cooperate.

More precisely, institutions convey knowledge through at least three different channels.[30] As 'congealed social knowledge', they aim at reducing a set of possible options, which amounts to saying that they reduce the agents' uncertainty related to each other's actions. This involves a better coordination of each individual plan according to environment specificities (O'Driscoll and Rizzo, 1996). Moreover, institutions do not transmit knowledge itself, but rather the knowledge of how to make an effective use of skills that an individual will never possess. The idea is thus that, if people can rely on others in order to fulfil specific roles, then their expectations will be likely to be more coordinated. Finally, institutions transmit knowledge in the sense that the routine courses of action they embody are efficient adaptations to the environment.[31]

In a word, institutions save knowledge and information (Lachmann, 1970).[32] Institutions then consist of general or enduring pieces of knowledge (O'Driscoll and Rizzo, 1996, p. xxii) which provide 'points of orientation' likely to make actions and expectations relatively compatible (Lachmann, 1970).[33] Any practice that allows individual goals to be reached spreads until it becomes an institution.

The peculiar status granted to the institution within the Austrian framework seems clearer now: since institutions are used to explain the transmission of information and knowledge, which is integrated in the formation and revision of plans, they represent the 'key link' that makes it possible to complete the reasoning chain of the Austrian theory about market processes. O'Driscoll and Rizzo indeed indicate that:

Rules provide, as it were, safe bounds for behaviour in a relatively unbounded world. Institutions are the social crystallisation of rule-following behaviour or, in other words, the overall pattern of many individuals following a similar rule (...). Thus, the circle is closed. Time and genuine uncertainty promote the following of rules and the development of institutions. The latter, in turn, serve to reduce, but not eliminate, the unboundness of the economic system by providing the stable patterns of interaction. (1996, p. 6).

The validity of the proposition that there is (or is not) a tendency toward equilibrium, thus depends critically on the nature of the institutional arrangements (Garrison, 1986).[34] Of course, the overall demonstration supposes that the knowledge spread by institutions is stabilizing (in the sense that it constantly reaffirms the stability of the social framework) whereas the one dispersed by the price system is of a dynamic nature (in the sense that it leads individuals to a continuous revision of their plans) (Hayek, 1945).

An endogenous explanation about the dynamics of institutions is, however, required in order to loop the loop. Indeed, if institutions act as signposts in a world of uncertainty, what we need is a theory of plan coordination, which integrates the fact that, not only do social institutions serve to align expectations, they may also deal successfully with the forces of change. It would otherwise be difficult to concede that the institutional element achieving completion of the analysis of the dynamic functioning of market processes will be the only one outside these dynamics. It is then a matter of assessing the Austrian representation in relation to its capacity for producing an analysis of the evolution of institutions within a market economy.

4.2   Permanency and Flexibility of Institutions: an Austrian Dilemma

Such analysis must allow solving three types of problems (Lachmann, 1970, pp. 51–2). Firstly, there is the problem of institutional change and how to reconcile the idea of an institutional change with that of an institution as a 'point of orientation', which assumes its fixity. Secondly, the issue of the institutional order and its unity is formulated: if the complementarity of institutions builds the institutional order of a society, the purpose is then to identify the forces of integration as well as the circumstances under which these forces cease to work. Finally, there is the question of the rise of new institutions that is to underline the requirements needed for new institutions to fit into the existing structure. Solving these three kinds of problems comes down to providing a solution to what we have agreed to call the permanency–flexibility dilemma: 'If institutions are to remove uncertainty, they must be permanent. But if they are to be shaped by market forces they must be flexible. How, within the institutional order of modern market society, is this problem resolved?' (Lachmann, 1994, p. 50).

Although there is no place for the evolution of institutions within Menger's conception, the analysis of change is, on the contrary, an essential aspect of Hayek's approach to institutions (Garrouste, 1994, 1998). The latter holds in the idea mentioned above which implies that institutions embody efficient adaptation modes according to the environment. This means that institutions with inferior survival properties are removed by means of a selection mechanism. Besides the fact that in Hayek's analysis an imprecision is found through the definition of the selection criterion (Garrouste, 1994, p. 863), as well as through the explanation of those survival properties (O'Driscoll and Rizzo, 1996, p. 40), such discussion of the dynamics of institutions cannot hold if the existing complementarity[35] of institutions within an institutional order (Lachmann, 1970) is taken into consideration. The routine courses of action that comprise institutions are indeed not all independent. Some truly inferior routines must be maintained in order to permit the existence of those that are actually superior: 'The implication of these considerations is that, in the absence of a clear conception of the nature of survival properties, we cannot know whether any given institution or course of action is the most adaptative' (O'Driscoll and Rizzo, 1996, p. 40).

Lachmann's interpretation of the dynamics of institutions holds a distinctive place within the Austrian approach. Besides the fact that it claims to go back to a logic much more rooted in a Weberian discourse than in a Mengerian one, its main purpose consists in drawing the conditions for the attainment of both *coherence* and *permanence* of the institutional order, that is to deal with the accurate issue of complementarity.[36]

The overall demonstration is based on the distinction made by the author between 'legal norms' or 'designed institutions' which are 'the products of legislation and other manifestations of the "social will" ' (Lachmann, 1970, p. 69) and the 'recurrent patterns of conduct which we call institutions' (ibid., p. 75) or 'undesigned institutions'.[37] But, following Lachmann's logic, if, on the one hand, all institutions[38] do not take on the same status and function,[39] they share, on the other hand, the flexibility property linked to the permanency of a whole. Indeed, the permanence of the institutional order as well as the legal one does not indeed involve the permanence of each part: 'Institutions rise and fall, they move and change. An institution may last a long time, but during this time assume new functions or discard old ones' (ibid., p. 77–8). The matter that now arises is how to make institutional change and structural permanence compatible, since it is not so much the change *per se* which brings up problems here but rather unexpected change. Only the last type of change is likely to upset some plans in the course of actions. The issue is of course all the more important because the institutional change affects long-term plans. A much more harmful outcome from the occurrence of this kind of unpredictable change concerns the relationship between designed and undesigned institutions. Indeed, as institutions can only be designed to face specific well-known situations 'the unexpected change of undesigned institutions may not merely jeopardise the coherence of the institutional structure as a whole, but in addition may obviate the very design of the designed institutions' (ibid., p. 80).

The solution put forward by Lachmann in order to cope with this last kind of problem consists in setting up designed institutions which allow the integration change without altering the institutional structure as a whole. The notion of *interstices* within the legal order represents here a key component for the institutional dynamics: 'the undesigned institutions which evolve gradually as the unintended and unforeseeable result of the pursuit of individual interests accumulate in the *interstices* of the legal order' (ibid., p. 81). The function of those interstices is actually to lead to the accumulation of sediments coming from the evolution of undesigned institutions so that the coherence of the whole remains. Hence, according to Lachmann, if a society is fundamentally made of two types of institutions, the *external* ones which constitute the outer framework of the society and the *internal* ones, which gradually evolve as a result of market processes, the institutional dynamics, however, arise from the specificity of those interstices, shared by both kind of institutions.

Such understanding of the institutional dynamics therefore deserves various comments.[40] The proposed pattern stems from the assumption that only the undesigned institutions evolve. But designed institutions also change. The analysis of the institutional dynamics then requires us to consider two emerging issues: the first one is related to the structural change of designed institutions and the second is linked to the relationship existing between the changes in the legal order and the evolution of undesigned institutions. In other respects, it is possible that the coherence and permanence of the current social order would be jeopardized even without change in the legal system. It is particularly the case when the slow evolution of institutions extends beyond the interstices of an existing social and legal order, leading to what Lachmann has called 'deformation of social space' (ibid., p. 83). Although such relevant issues have substantial implications in formulating an overall representation based on the endogenous dynamics of institutions, they cannot be handled here. This stresses (if it was needed) all the difficulties faced by the Austrian theory in order to elaborate a theory concerned with the evolution of institutions.

The confrontation with the Institutionalist analysis is from this perspective decisive because the latter is precisely well known for being interested in the nature and the evolution of institutions.

4.3   OIE on the Evolution of Institutions

We want to stress here that even if the Lachmannian conception in terms of a permanency–flexibility dilemma is formulated well enough to embrace the institutional foundation of market process, the solution he proposed is not fully satisfactory. The point is that the historicity of the economic process and the role of individuals in the evolution process are not adequately thought about. The Austrian conception of the market as a natural order constitutes a major difficulty for building a complete institutional dynamics analysis, that is, an analysis which will consider the evolution of the legal order itself, in relation with the global process of change. We think that the old institutional school can bring elements to complete the unfulfilled Lachmannian framework.

The first point is that there is an originality of the general Institutionalist conception of institutions that cannot be reduced to the 'external' coordination function of institutions, even if some functional properties that Institutionalists associate with institutions fit the Austrians' conception. In a very uncertain environment, individuals with bounded rationality need a pattern of coordination; rules bring knowledge and information for plans and organize actions out of complexity. Veblen called 'Institution' the 'habits of thought common to the generality of men' (1919, p. 239) when Commons' definition was 'collective action in control, liberation and expansion of individual action' (1934, p. 73). Even if they seem very different, these quotations point out two important topics: action, choice and preference are not data but are moulded by institutional settings; individual action cannot be isolated from a process of social interaction. But this fundamental influence of institutions on human value, preferences and modality of choice is not a deterministic one. If institutional rules and norms mould individual actions and interactions, they never totally determine the result of the economic and social process.[41] As we have already said, the individual is a creative agency of change at any level of the institutional framework. The general principle of evolutionary dynamics results from the interaction between institutional rules and principles and human agency, that leads to an incremental and reinforcing change in the structures and in the pattern of preferences and behaviours.

The second point is that the process is not always an efficient one. The Institutionalist representation of evolution looks like the Hayekian 'smooth adaptation mechanism', but with notable differences. The incremental evolution of institutions and human behaviours can lead to crisis, disruption, bifurcation and finally to real innovation. The criterion of selection in the Austrian understanding of evolution is in accordance with the idea of efficiency of practices *vis-à-vis* the environment, that is, the behaviour of the most successful group is imitated and developed. There is no such reference to efficiency in the Institutional standpoint, which stresses that institutions do not necessarily serve the functional needs of the society, but 'vested interests'. Veblen points out the existence of long-lived 'imbecile institutions', 'archaic' and 'ceremonial' habits of thought that restrict the potential benefits of the spread of production and of technological innovations. Abandoning a reasoning in terms of efficiency, OIE is thus more likely to release the permanency–flexibility dilemma.

The third point, adopting Veblen's reasoning, is that the problem of evolution is less a question of adaptation according to a criterion of efficiency, than a problem of coherence out of the institutional diversity in a general institutional framework, and a problem of synchronization in historical time. This idea is closely akin to Lachmann's questioning about the genesis of novelty inside a stable institutional framework or, put in theoretical terms, the permanency *versus* flexibility dilemma. Yet, it departs from it in some fundamental points including, on the one hand, the historicity and the path dependence magnitude of the evolutionary process and, on the other hand, the idea that the economic process is a whole process of change, and not only a change of 'internal institutions'. The idea of Veblen is that human beings are the result of a combination of fundamental instincts[42] selected by the institutional configuration. Institutional patterns remove internal variation and stabilize individual behaviour. As Hodgson showed, in a self-reinforcing mechanism, institutions become locked in relatively stable and constrained paths of development (1994). In this line, there is a relative invariance and self-reinforcing character of institutions. For Veblen, this process can lead to an incompatibility or incoherence between predominant institutional principles and the material or technological state of the art. The instinctual human nature is an element of an endogenous tendency of evolution, because human action can generate novelty, diversity in the practices, and new routines, particularly in the technological area. In contrast, the stability of the institutional principle (the institutional lag) can bring conflict with the actual conditions of economic life. In other words, a disruption can emerge in the evolutionary process because of a temporal gap between, on the one hand, past and self enforcing routines and, on the other hand, new habits of thought stemming from human creativity. 'Institutional development and change in these terms can be linked to strata shifting slowly at different rates, but occasionally causing seismic disturbance and discontinuities' (Hodgson, 1994, p. 65).

The last point concerns the articulation between designed and undesigned aspects of institutional evolution. Precisely, Lachmann links together the stability property of the legal order (seen as a designed institution) and the dynamic property of market process (seen as undesigned) with his idea of interstices between internal and external institutions (see above). Underlying the legal order of the market, Lachmann shares Commons' interest in *The Legal Foundation of Capitalism* (1924) and the importance of the 'legal/economic nexus'[43] in the understanding of the logic of economic transactions, but Commons' conception is a more evolutionary analysis, that includes the change in legal order itself. According to Commons, evolution is a 'volitional process' submitted to an 'artificial selection' (Ramstad, 1990, 1994). This perspective is in radical opposition with the natural selection metaphor of economic evolution in as much as it relates to what is usually taken as undesigned institutions, like money. Commons gave a subtle demonstration that economic order itself is an artefact.[44] But this conception is not as deterministic as a superficial evaluation could conclude, because Institutional economics does not embrace a crude holistic viewpoint but rather a combination of institutional causation and individual causation for understanding social process. Working rules delimit and support the transactions, but transactions give rise to unanticipated consequences, new opportunities and conflict about the share of 'burdens and benefits' of the wealth created by collective action. The economic process includes a never-ending process of making new rules regulating conflicts of interests, because a procedural resolution of conflicts is a necessary support for transactions and order. This is an 'artificial selection' because the choice (if not the emergence) of new rules is the fact of, and the reflection of the purpose of authoritative figures. 'Commons understood the economic process to involve a circular causation in which the individual will and its objective expression, a choice, is at one consequence and cause of working rules' (Ramstad, 1990, p. 79).

The point is that legal order is not only, as in Lachmann's conception, an institutional matrix for market forces (that eventually impedes market forces from efficiency) or in Lachmann's terms, an external institution that evolves independently from economic process[45] and whose function is to support stability of fundamental principles of market and to correct market failures (uncertainty and information problems). Indeed in Commons' analysis, the legal order is (so to speak) inside each transaction[46] (intrinsically defined and ordered by working rules) and evolves in close articulation with the economic process itself. Evolution is an incremental process of change of rules and behaviours, and the diversity of practices is filtered by an 'artificial selection' of new rules promoted by authority figures. One consequence is that there is no such strict distinction between designed and undesigned institutions. All forms, at any level of the hierarchy of the institutional framework, are in part designed and in part spontaneously produced.

From this viewpoint, the figure of the market is not that of a natural order but that of a historical and social product of evolution, that is, a set of rules and arrangements purposefully selected out of conflicts.

The Austrian conception of institutional evolution fails to undertake the very nature of market process as an evolving set of institutions, because the market is understood as an immutable order (in its essence if not in its form) independent of the 'volitional' process of selection of rules that incarnates it. Austrians not only reject the idea of the authoritative choice at work in the market process (understood as a corruption of the well functioning of the system), but by so doing, they underestimate the real potential creativity of individuals. The market process is thus, *in fine*, an abstract constituting principle of people's interactions, not a historical product of creative agency, because people's actions never influence the form and principles of the market system. In contrast, Institutional economics understands the market system as a never-ending process of change in practices and rules; looking at it this way, the market never remains the same, but is a changing institutional configuration. The Austrian analysis explains the permanency in reference to the naturality of catallactic principles but at the same time this reference prevents it from satisfying an evolutionary conception. The flexibility of the market process is not evolution. In the reverse, the Institutionalist analysis is able to loop the loop of Lachmann's reasoning about the institutional dynamic. If institutions provide 'points of orientation' and 'patterns of coordination' for transactions, transactions induce a permanent and cumulative process of change in institutions themselves, and, at the highest level of the institutional structure, create an evolution of the legal order itself. The general order is, from this point of view, not set up as an abstract and permanent principle, but as a real product of human will in conflict/cooperation, and as a result of a cumulative and historical process.

5   CONCLUSION

The purpose of this chapter was to lay out the broad lines of a positive confrontation between the Austrian analysis and the Institutionalist one, founded on the market coordination theme. Such an approach, though being *a priori* heretical is justified by, on the one hand, the characteristics shared by both theoretical traditions, and on the other by the existence of complementarity, which founds a representation of market mechanisms in terms of process. The analysis thus obtained, which highlights the importance of the dynamics of institutions, builds a bridge between two traditions which have more to exchange than is usually thought, particularly in the perspective of the elaboration of an alternative theory of the market inside which time matters.

NOTES

1. In addition to the Symposium on *Austrian and Institutional Economics* (Samuels 1989), see Garrouste (1995), Wynarczyk (1992), Leathers (1990, 1989), Vanberg (1989), Gunning (1986).
2. The fact that both Austrian and Institutional economics are internally heterogeneous makes comparisons between these two research traditions difficult, since one has to identify 'representative' members for both. Our purpose is not to be exhaustive but to highlight some similarities and possible complementarities between the two schools regarding the notion of market process.
3. This project has been formulated by Wynarczyk (1992).

4. Jaffé (1976) has argued that Veblen's critique of the economic man fits Jevons' and Walras's theory better than Menger's.
5. Veblen also discussed Böhm Bawerk's theory of capital, but we do not examine here this analytical link between the Austrian and Institutional thinking. See Veblen (1891–92).
6. According to Garrouste, these approaches are more complementary than usually considered because Menger focuses on the institutional genesis, while Veblen focuses on institutional change (Garrouste, 1995).
7. Leathers' concluding statement is that 'a close inspection, (...) reveals substantial differences in their concepts of instincts. Veblen developed a more general theory of the types of instincts and how instinctive proclivities interact with acquired habits to shape human behaviour. Hayek's instincts of solidarity and altruism resemble in some respects Veblen's parental bent, but there are no Hayekian counterparts to the instincts of workmanship and idle curiosity' (Leathers, 1990, p. 175).
8. Mitchell wrote the introduction to an English version of Wieser's *Social Economics* and Hayek studied with him in the early 1920s.
9. We set out general principles for the methodological opposition between the two traditions that are inevitably somewhat exaggerated. A close examination, which is not the main object of this contribution, would show a great methodological diversity within both traditions.
10. Neither Veblen nor Commons, or even Mitchell defend an a-theoretical conception of economic science. Their works are rather attempts to fit the theory to the actual economic characteristics, as they considered that the classical and neoclassical theories fitted the 18th century's capitalist economic system, not the actual system.
11. Our emphasis.
12. The 'traditional' Austrian theory of the market process refers to the contributions of Hayek, Mises, Kirzner and Lachmann.
13. For an analysis of how Austrians have used the equilibrium construct, see Fink and Cowen (1985).
14. Of course, Kirzner does not share this position.
15. Let us remember that 'The concept of order (...) has the advantage that we can meaningfully speak about an order being approached to various degrees, and that order can be preserved throughout a process of change. While an economic equilibrium never really exists, there is some justification for asserting that the kind of order of which our theory describes an ideal type, is approached in a high degree' (Hayek, 1978, p. 184).
16. Typical events are events that an observer perceives as being repeated regularly, as long as the process itself is being repeated. Unique events are the ones that occur only once and are thus time dependent; they can never be discovered (O'Driscoll and Rizzo, 1996).
17. Quoted by Hodgson (1994, p. 66).
18. It is not our purpose to expose the very dense theoretical system of Commons, based on very interesting concepts such as transaction, going concern, working rules, sovereignty, negotiational psychology, institutionalized mind, reasonable value.... For a more complete exposition, see Ramstad (1990). Our purpose is just to connect Commons' approach to the question of equilibrium.
19. It is here impossible to pass over the Institutionalist criticism of the subjectivist approach. The main target of this criticism is the rational and hedonistic character of the 'Austrian subjectivist economic man'. However, it is possible to demonstrate, considering the works of Perlman (1986), Boettke (1989) and Wynarczyk (1992), that the praxeological approach not only dismissed the alleged rationality of the Benthamite calculus but also the hedonism which motivated it.
20. That is, a reasoning which tries to take into account the subjective character of both anticipations and knowledge (Lachmann, 1976).
21. Our emphasis.
22. 'Successive stages of market processes thus reflect nothing so much as successive modes of re-orientation as the mind of the actors fits means to ends in ever new forms prompted by new forms of knowledge and imagination' (Lachmann, 1986, p. 5).

23. 'In a competitive game there are winners and losers. By the same token, competitive market forces will cause discoordination as well as co-ordination of agents' plans. In fact they cannot do the latter without doing the former' (Lachmann, 1986, p. 5).

24. We cannot resist the pleasure of quoting Veblen's famous description of the so-called economic man: 'The hedonistic conception of man is that of a lighting calculator of pleasures and pains, who occilates like a homogeneous globule of desire of happiness under the impulse of stimuli that shift him about the area, but leave him intact. He has neither antecedent nor consequent. He is an isolated, definitive human datum, in stable equilibrium except for the buffets of impinging forces that displace him in one direction or another. Self-poised in elemental space, he spins symmetrically about his own spiritual axis until the parallelogram of forces bears down upon him, where-upon he follows the line of the resultant. When the force of the impact is spent, he comes to rest, a self-contained globule of desire as before' (Veblen, 1898, pp. 389–90).

25. Veblen's idea of human behaviour is also grounded on a few fundamental instincts, but we do not develop this aspect here.

26. Let us remember that 'praxeology rests on the fundamental axiom that individual human beings *act*, that is, on the primordial fact that individuals engage in conscious actions toward chosen goals. This concept of action contrasts to purely reflexive, or knee-jerk, behaviour, which is not directed toward goals' (Rothbard, 1976, p. 19).

27. 'The Austrian criticism of neo-classical economics is firmly ground in a Veblenian appreciation of institutional and historical factors in economics' (Boettke, 1989, p. 74).

28. According to Rutherford, mentioning Agassi's institutional individualism, 'At least a significant part of work of Institutionalists and Austrians is not as methodologically incompatible as is usually thought' (Rutherford, 1989a, p. 164).

29. See for example the new introduction of the second edition of O'Driscoll and Rizzo's book (1996, p. xxii); see also Garrouste (1994, 1995) and the contributions in Boettke and Prychitko (eds) (1994). It is the very same motive which induces Langlois to state that 'Menger has perhaps more claim to be the patron saint of the New Institutional Economics than has any of the original Institutionalists' (Langlois, 1986, p. 5).

30. Here, we still consider an overall Austrian point of view.

31. This last conception (from Hayek) is examined below.

32. The role of institutions in reducing information costs is outlined by the game-theory approach through such notions as 'convention' (coordination game) or 'norm' (prisoners' dilemma game) (Schotter, 1994).

33. 'An institution provides means of orientation to a large number of actors. It enables them to co-ordinate actions by means of orientation to a common signpost' (Lachmann, 1970, p. 45). The so-called concept of 'orientation points' expresses the idea of a decreasing instead of an elimination, of uncertainty (Lachmann, 1994).

34. Indeed 'so long as the arrangements are such that expectations consistent with underlying economic realities are rewarded and expectations consistent with those realities are penalised, the tendency can be expected to prevail' (Garrison, 1986, p. 97).

35. O'Driscoll and Rizzo use the term 'indivisibility' (1996).

36. We do not, however, introduce the analysis about coherence.

37. One may recognize here the Mengerian distinction between pragmatic and organic institutions.

38. In the broad sense of the term, that is, taking into account both designed and undesigned institutions.

39. Some are more fundamental than others in the sense that they are basic institutions of market society: 'They must exist before there can be markets which function smoothly' (Lachmann, 1994, p. 50).

40. Lachmann himself has first suggested these remarks.

41. Lachmann and more generally Austrian economics take these arguments into account, but they appear to be marginal when they constitute the heart of the Institutional analysis.

42. According to Veblen, the idea of instinct justifies the selection of institutionalized behaviours out of the diversity of conducts grounded on instinctual proclivity (workmanship instinct, parental bent, idle curiosity, and predatory instinct). This idea of instinctual proclivity in

human behaviour is not inconsistent with an evolutionary conception of human being; it is a dialectical vision of human beings, between stability and evolution.

43. For Commons, the relation that economics studies is not the so-called exchange of goods, but a transfer of property rights: 'Transactions, as thus defined, are not the exchange of commodities, in the physical sense of delivery, they are the alienation and acquisition, between individuals, of the rights of future ownership of physical things, as determined by the collective working rules of society. The transfer of these rights must therefore be negotiated between the parties concerned, according to the working rules of the society, before labour can produce, or consumers can consume, or commodities be physically delivered to other persons' (1934, p. 58). This conception justifies that legal and economic perspectives cannot be analytically separated.

44. For a very detailed exposition see Ramstad (1990).

45. Lachmann embraces the 'public choice' idea that laws are made by judges in a political process in accordance with a pure methodological individualism (Lachmann, 1979).

46. According to Commons, a transaction always involves a minimum of five protagonists: a seller and a buyer, an alternative seller and an alternative buyer, and the legal authorities that embody the process of arbitrating conflicts with rules. 'Consequently, if transactions are to go on peaceably without resort to violence between the parties there must always have been a fifth party to the transaction, namely, a judge, priest, chieftain, paterfamilias, arbitrator, foreman, superintendent, general manager, who would be able to decide and settle the dispute, with the aid of the combined power of the group to which the five parties belonged' (Commons, 1924, p. 67).

REFERENCES

Bazzoli, L. and V. Dutraive (1996), 'Theory of human agency and dynamics of social interactions: some legacy of J.R.Commons' Institutionalism', working paper, University of Lyon 2.

Boettke, P. (1989), 'Evolutions and economics: Austrians as Institutionalists', in W.J. Samuels (ed.), *Research in the History of Economic Thought and Methodology*, London: JAI Press Inc.

Boettke, P. and D. Prychitko (1994), 'The future of Austrian Economics', in P. Boettke and D. Prychitko (eds), *The Market Process: Essays in Contemporary Austrian Economics*, Aldershot, UK and Brookfield, US: Edward Elgar.

Boettke, P. and D. Prychitko (eds) (1994), *The Market Process: Essays in Contemporary Austrian Economics*, Aldershot, UK and Brookfield, US: Edward Elgar.

Boettke, P., S. Horwitz and D. Prychitko (1994), 'Beyond equilibrium economics: reflections on the uniqueness of the Austrian tradition', in P. Boettke and D. Prychitko (eds), *The Market Process: Essays in Contemporary Austrian Economics*, Aldershot, UK and Brookfield, US: Edward Elgar.

Carlsson, B. (1989), *Industrial Dynamics*, London: Kluwer Academic Publishers.

Commons, J.R. (1924), *The Legal Foundation of Capitalism*, London: Macmillan.

Commons, J.R. (1934), *Institutional Economics, its place in Political Economy*, Madison: University of Wisconsin Press. Macmillan.

Commons, J.R. (1950), *The Economics of Collective Action*, The University of Wisconsin, 1970.

Currie, M. and I. Steedman (1990), *Wrestling with Time*, Ann Arbor: University of Michigan Press.

David, P. (1988), 'Path-dependence: putting the past into the future of economics', *Institute for Mathematical Studies in the Social Sciences Technical Report 533*, Stanford University, November.

Dolan, E.G. (ed.) (1976), *The Foundations of Modern Austrian Economics*, Kansas City: Sheed & Ward, Inc.

Eldredge, N. and S.J. Gould (1977), 'Punctuated equilibria: the tempo and mode of evolution reconsidered', *Paleobiology*, **3**.

Fink, R. and T. Cowen (1985), 'Is the evenly rotating economy a useful economic construct?', *American Economic Review*, **75**.

Garrison, R. (1986), 'From Lachmann to Lucas: on institutions, expectations, and equilibrating tendencies', in I. Kirzner (ed.), *Subjectivism, Intelligibility and Economic Understanding*, New York: New York University Press.

Garrouste, P. (1994), 'Carl Menger et Friedrich A. Hayek à propos des institutions: continuité et ruptures', *Revue d'Economie Politique*, **104** (6), Nov.–Dec.

Garrouste, P. (1995), 'L'origine et l'évolution des institutions, pour un dialogue entre C. Menger et T. Veblen', in M. Basle, D. Dufourt, J.A. Heraud and J. Perrin (eds), *Changements institutionnels et changements techniques – évaluation, droits de propriété intellectuels et système national d'innovation*, Editions du C.N.R.S.

Garrouste, P. (1998), 'Does the Austrian Conception(s) of Institutions hold Water?', Paper presented at the Second Annual Conference of the ESHET at Bologna, 27 February–1 March.

Gloria, S. (1996), 'Discovery versus creation: implications on the Austrian view of the market process', Contribution to the EAEPE Conference in Antwerp, Belgium, 8–9 November.

Gordon, W. (1989), 'Comparing of the Austrian and Institutionalist Economics', in W.J. Samuels (ed.), *Research in the History of Economic Thought and Methodology*, London: JAI Press Inc.

Gunning, J.P. (1986), 'The methodology of Austrian economics and its relevance to Institutionalism', *American Journal of Economics and Sociology*, **45**.

Hamilton, W. (1973), *Evolutionary Economics: A Study of Change in Economic Theory*, Albuquerque: University of New Mexico Press.

Hicks, J.R. (1979), *Causality in Economics*, Oxford: Basil Blackwell.

High, J. (1994), 'The market process: an Austrian view', in P. Boettke and D. Prychitko (eds): *The Market Process: Essays in Contemporary Austrian Economics*, Aldershot, UK and Brookfield, US: Edward Elgar.

Hodgson, G.M. (1985), 'The rationalist conception of action', *Journal of Economic Issues*, December, reprinted in M. Tool and W.J. Samuels (eds), *The Methodology of Economic Thought*, Transaction Publishers, 1989.

Hodgson, G.M. (1988), *Economics and Institutions: A Manifesto for a Modern Institutional Economics*, Cambridge: Polity Press.

Hodgson, G.M. (1989), 'Institutional economic theory: the old versus the new', *Review of Political Economy*, **1**.

Hodgson, G.M. (1994), 'The return of Institutional economics', in Smelser and Swedberg (eds), *The Handbook of Economic Sociology*, Princeton University Press.

Hodgson, G.M. (1996), 'The viability of Institutional economics', mimeo.

Ioannides, S. (1992), *The Market, Competition and Democracy*, Aldershot, UK and Brookfield, US: Edward Elgar.

Jaffé, W. (1976), 'Menger, Jevons and Walras de-homogenized', *Economic Inquiry*, 14.

Kirzner, I. (1973), *Competition and Entrepreneurship*, Chicago: University of Chicago Press.

Kirzner, I. (1979), *Perception, Opportunity, and Profit*, Chicago: University of Chicago Press.

Kirzner, I. (1985), *Discovery and the Capitalist Process*, Chicago: University of Chicago Press.

Kirzner, I. (1992), *The Meaning of Market Process*, London: Routledge.

Lachmann, L. (1970), *The Legacy of Max Weber*, London: Heinemann.

Lachmann, L. (1976), 'On the central concept of Austrian Economics: market process', in E.G. Dolan (ed.), *The Foundations of Modern Austrian Economics*, Kansas City: Sheed & Ward, Inc.

Lachmann, L. (1978), *Capital and its Structure*, Kansas City: Sheed Andrews and McNeel, Inc., 2nd edition.

Lachmann, L. (1979), 'The flow of legislation and the permanence of the legal order', in Don Lavoie (ed.) (1994), *Expectations and the Meaning of Institutions, Essays in Economics by Ludwig Lachmann*, London: Routledge.

Lachmann, L. (1986), *The Market as an Economic Process*, New York: Basil Blackwell.

Lachmann, L. (1994), 'On the economics of time and ignorance', in P. Boettke and D. Prychitko (eds), *The Market Process: Essays in Contemporary Austrian Economics*, Aldershot, UK and Brookfield, US: Edward Elgar.

Langlois, R.N. (1986), 'The New Institutional Economics: an introductory essay', in R.N. Langlois (ed.): *Economics as a Process*, Cambridge: Cambridge University Press.

Langlois, R.N. (1989), 'What was wrong with the Old Institutional Economics (and what is still wrong with the New)?', *Review of Political Economy*, **1**.

Langlois, R.N. (1993), 'Orders and organizations: toward an Austrian theory of social institutions', in B.J. Caldwell and St. Boehm (eds), *Austrian Economics: Tensions and New Directions*, Dordrecht: Kluwer Academic Publishers.

Leathers, C.G. (1989), 'New and Old Institutionalists on legal rules: Hayek and Commons', *Review of Political Economy*, **1**.

Leathers, C.G. (1990), 'Veblen and Hayek on instincts and evolution', *Journal of History of Economic Thought*, **12**, Autumn.

Loasby, B. (1991), *Equilibrium and Evolution, an Exploration of Connecting Principles in Economics*, Manchester: Manchester University Press.

Menger, C. (1963), *Problems of Economics and Sociology*, Urbana: University of Illinois Press.

Miller, E. (1989), 'Comment on Boettke and Samuels: Austrian and Institutional economics', in W.J. Samuels (ed.), *Research in the History of Economic Thought and Methodology*, London: JAI Press Inc.

Mises, von L. (1949), *Human Action*, London: William Hodge.

Mitchell, W.C. (1935), 'Commons on Institutional economics', *American Economic Review*, **25** (4), 635–52.

Nelson, R. and S. Winter (1982), *An Evolutionary Theory of Economic Change*, Cambridge, MA and London: Belknap Press of Harvard University Press.

O'Driscoll, J. and M. Rizzo (1996), *The Economics of Time and Ignorance*, London: Basil Blackwell.

Perlman, M. (1986), 'Subjectivism and American institutionalism', in I. Kirzner (ed.), *Subjectivism, Intelligibility and Economic Understanding*, New York: New York University Press.

Polanyi, K. (1994), *The Great Transformation*, Boston: Beacon Press.

Ramstad, Y. (1990), 'The institutionalism of J.R. Commons: theoretical foundations of a volitional economics', *Research in the History of Economic Thought and Methodology*, **8**, 53–104.

Ramstad, Y. (1994), 'On the nature of economic evolution: John R. Commons and the metaphore of artificial selection', in Magnusson (ed.), *Evolutionary and Neo Schumpeterian Approaches to Economics*, Boston: Kluwer.

Robinson, J. (1962), *Essays in the Theory of Economic Growth*, New York: St. Martin's Press.

Rothbard, M.N. (1976), 'Praxeology: the methodology of Austrian economics', in E.G. Dolan (ed.), *The Foundations of Modern Austrian Economics*, Kansas City: Sheed & Ward, Inc.

Rutherford, M. (1989a), 'Some issues in the comparison of Austrian and Institutional Economics', in W.J. Samuels (ed.), *Research in the History of Economic Thought and Methodology*, London: JAI Press Inc.

Rutherford, M. (1989b), 'What is wrong with the New Institutional Economics (and what is still wrong with the old)? ', *Review of Political Economy*, **1**: 159–72.

Rutherford, M. (1994), *Institutions in Economics: Old and New*, Cambridge: Cambridge University Press.

Samuels, W.J. (1989), 'Austrian and Institutional economics: some common elements', in W.J. Samuels (ed.), *Research in the History of Economic Thought and Methodology*, London: JAI Press Inc.

Samuels, W.J. (1995), 'The present state of institutional economics', *Cambridge Journal of Economics*, **19**, 569–90.

Schotter, A. (1981), *The Economic Theory of Social Institutions*, New York: Cambridge University Press.

Schotter, A. (1994), 'Social institutions and game theory', in P.J. Boettke (ed.), *The Elgar Companion to Austrian Economics*, Aldershot, UK and Brookfield, US: Edward Elgar.

Setterfield, M. (1997), 'Should economists dispense with the notion of equilibrium?', *Journal of Post Keynesian Economics*, Autumn **20** (1).

Vanberg, V. (1989), 'Carl Menger's evolutionary and John R. Commons' collective action approach to institutions: a comparison', *Review of Political Economy*, no. 1, 334–60.

Veblen, T. (1898), 'Why is economics not an evolutionary science?', *Quarterly Journal of Economics*, **12**: 373–97.

Veblen, T. (1891–2), 'Böhm Bawerk's definition of capital and the source of wages', *Quarterly Journal of Economics*, **6**: 247–50.

Veblen, T. (1899–1900), 'The preconceptions of economic science', in W.C. Mitchell (ed.) (1964), *The Writings of T.Veblen*, New York: Augustus M. Kelley.

Veblen, T. (1904), 'The theory of business enterprise', in T. Veblen (1975), *The Writings of T. Veblen*, Clifton: Augustus M. Kellay.

Veblen, T. (1906), 'The place of science in modern civilization', in T. Veblen (1919) *The Place of Science in Modern Civilisation and Other Essays*, New York: Viking Press.

Veblen, T. (1919), 'The limitation of marginal utility', in W.C. Mitchell (ed.) (1964), *The Writings of T. Veblen*, New York: Augustus M. Kelley.

von Hayek, F. (1937), 'Economics and knowledge', in F. Hayek (1949), *Individualism and Economic Order*, London: Routledge & Kegan Paul.

von Hayek, F. (1945), 'The use of knowledge in society', in F. Hayek (1949), *Individualism and Economic Order*, London: Routledge & Kegan Paul.

von Hayek, F. (1978),*New Studies in Philosophy, Polirics, Economics and the History of Ideas*, London: Routledge & Kegan Paul, 2nd edition.

Waller, W.T. (1988), 'The concept of habit in economic analysis', *Journal of Economic Issues*, **XXII** (1).

Williamson, O.E. (1985), 'Reflections on the New Institutional Economics', *Journal of Institutional and Theoretical Economics*, March, **141** (1), 187–95.

Wynarczyk, P. (1992), 'Comparing alleged incommensurables: Institutional and Austrian economics as rivals and possible complements?', *Review of Political Economy*, **4** (1), 18–36.

4. Schumpeter and the pendulum: how evolution was whipped out in the construction of canonical economics

Francisco Louçã

1 INTRODUCTION

Joseph Schumpeter's work inspires a large part of the evolutionary programme in economics and particularly economics of technological change, in spite of his own contradictory relation to the mainstream, and inability to develop a fully alternative programme. This chapter addresses one of the major instances of his perplexities: Schumpeter's relation to the conceptualization of evolutionary dynamics in models of innovation. In particular, it discusses the debate on the limitations of the mechanical methods in the early econometric programme, which Schumpeter considered to be unable to represent his own model of change under capitalism.

In 1933, Ragnar Frisch, the founder of econometrics and a dominant figure in the construction of the institutions which would dominate the discipline for a long time (*Econometrica* and the Econometric Society), and a close friend of Schumpeter, published a paper with a seminal model of cycles. The paper, which was responsible later on for the attribution to Frisch of the first Nobel Prize in economics (*ex aequo* with Tinbergen), explained the cycle as the juxtaposition of a dampening propagation mechanism and a la Slutsky random impulses. One of the extensions of the model, incorporated in the paper but never elaborated, was the consideration of Schumpeterian innovations as one of the sources of impulses. Furthermore, Frisch emphatically stated that the model was prepared after consultation with Schumpeter.

Nevertheless, this model was deeply contradictory with Schumpeter's theory. This chapter discusses the correspondence between Frisch and Schumpeter on the issue, and how Frisch reached his conclusion in the preparation of the 1933 paper. The unpublished correspondence between both authors is examined,[1] emphasizing how the metaphor of the pendulum changed their way of thinking about models and cycles, and how influential it was in the development of early econometric confirmation. Finally, this chapter discusses Schumpeter's contraditions in the assessment of the evolutionary characteristics of economics and economic reality.

2   DEBATE AND MISUNDERSTANDINGS

Joseph Schumpeter was a most paradoxical theoretician. Divided between a late adhesion to historicism and a long-life faithful allegiance to general equilibrium, between evolutionary and organic thought and the adoration of the power of the physical metaphors in economics, Schumpeter was apparently unaffected by his own ambiguity. In spite of all contradictions, his main contribution to economics was a passionate defence of the historical approach to cycles and to the dynamics of capitalism. Indeed, although a stubborn supporter of the use of mathematics, a founder of the Econometric Society in 1930 and the writer of a programmatic paper in the first issue of *Econometrica* presenting its antecedents and project, Schumpeter distinguished himself mostly as an intensely dedicated researcher of concrete historical processes. Thanks to that, he eventually became the most quoted economist of the first decades of the 20th century, until the glamorous triumph of Keynes' *General Theory*.

Schumpeter's main publications are historical in the sense of applied historical and conceptual work (*Business Cycles*, 1939 – hereafter BC), of a polemic interpretation of the historical trends (*Capitalism, Socialism and Democracy*, 1942 – hereafter CSD) and of a historical account of the science itself (*History of Economic Analysis*, posthumously published in 1954 – hereafter HEA). His single most important contribution, and indeed the major reason for contemporary attention in relation to his work and inspiration, was the analysis of innovation, of creative destruction and of disequilibrium processes in modern economies.

This section presents an important and ignored discussion which challenged Schumpeter's concept of innovation, from the viewpoint of the requirements for an econometric approach to cycles and to economic structural change, as presented by Ragnar Frisch. It also highlights the crucial importance of metaphors – the rocking horse, the pendulum, the violin, and the Magellanic Oceans – both for persuasion and for concrete representation and abductive creation of new hypotheses in economics.

2.1   Frisch's Formal Model

Frisch's crucial paper on cycles, published in 1933 in the volume honouring Cassel, 'Propagation problems and impulse problems in dynamic economics' (hereafter PPIP), represented a crucial departure for the econometric approach of time series and of cycles. It was quite an achievement at that time:

1. $y = mx + \mu \, dx/dt$, which represents the depreciation of capital
2. $z_t = \int D \, y_{t-1} d\tau$, which represents the production activity τ, from instant 0 until ∞.
3. $d^2x/dt^2 = -\lambda \, (r \, dx/dt + s \, dz/dt)$, the consumption equation.

The model established a sophisticated deterministic system of differential and difference equations representing capital accumulation, Walrasian *encaisse désirée*, and consumption, and simulated quite well the business cycle, as a dampening process (see Figure 4.1).

Yet this was not a realistic picture of the cycles, since their recurrence is one of the impressive stylized facts about growth and fluctuations. Consequently, in order to account for the sustained movement, random shocks *à la* Slutsky were added to this mechanism. The system represented therefore a combined form of a deterministic and a probabilistic view. But, at the very end of the paper, Frisch still added another type of disturbances, larger and regular shocks accounting for the Schumpeterian innovative impulses.

On 25 October 1933 Frisch wrote to Schumpeter, announcing the conclusion of the paper, and the inclusion of the two types of impulses, random shocks and Schumpeterian innovations. These were contrasted as alternative views:

> You will probably remember our long correspondence back and forth about the pendulum analogy in business cycles. (...) In a rather big paper to be published in the volume in honour of Cassel I have insisted upon these two ways of looking upon the maintenance problem: on the one hand the idea of erratic shocks (starting with Wicksell, being developed by Slutsky and perhaps having being carried to a sort of relative completion by my theory of linear operators and erratic shocks soon to be published in *Econometrica*) and on the other hand your idea of the stream of energy coming in through the 'innovations'. (...) In the paper in the Cassel volume I was not able to devote more than a brief section to your theory (...), but I hope that I have succeeded in exhibiting the gist of your viewpoint as contrasted with the viewpoint of erratic shocks. (Oslo Archive, Institute of Economics)

The first type of disturbances, the Slutsky shocks, were represented with the help of the metaphor of the rocking horse, while the second, Schumpeterian shocks, was represented with the recourse to the metaphor of the pendulum. The pendulum analogy is presented as a second 'source of energy' maintaining the oscillations, but acting in a 'more continuous fashion' that the random shocks. The importance of the mechanical representation was emphasized again and again, since it permitted the understanding of Schumpeter's basic idea. Frisch went as far as mentioning that 'After long conversations and correspondence with Professor Schumpeter I believe the analogy may be taken as a fair representation of his point of view' (Frisch, 1933, p. 203).

Frisch argued for this solution for all his life, and indeed considered it to be one of his major contributions to economics – in spite of his doubts about the

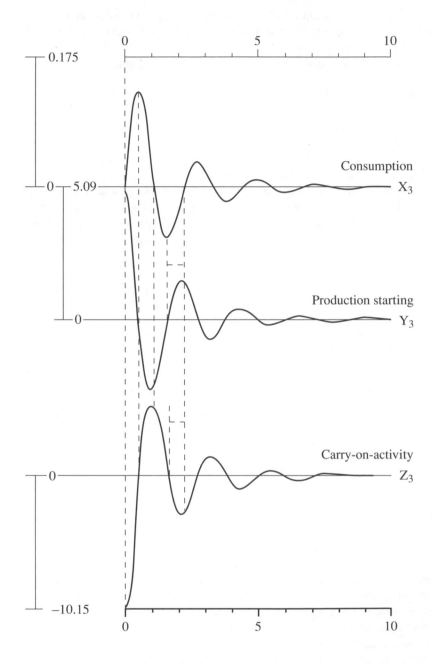

Figure 4.1   Frisch's rocking horse

incorporation of the probabilistic approach in economics and of his own arguments with his disciple Haavelmo about the issue. Indeed, this model established the dominance of the linear stochastic differential or difference equations as the adequate representation of the cycle, and buried for a long time the alternative non-linear auto-relaxation models.

At the end of the 1933 paper, Frisch considered very briefly some of Schumpeter's reservations to this interpretation, although not referring to the inspiration of the argument. Recognizing that the analogy with the pendulum gave a picture of an oscillatory system but 'not of the ['irreversible'] secular or perhaps supersecular tendency of evolutions', Frisch suggested that a simple solution would be to elevate the suspension point as a consequence of the movement itself. In that case, the trend would be generated by the cycle: 'Thus there will be an intimate connection between the oscillations and the irreversible evolution' (Frisch, 1933, pp. 205). Nevertheless, although insinuating that it would be a simple task, Frisch decided not to formulate that mathematical model.

Schumpeter did not immediately answer the October letter, since he was travelling at that time. His comment, on 28 December 1933, is part of a larger digression on the baroque and medieval cathedrals of France, just adding a few lines kindly expressing his remaining distance in relation to the solution suggested by Frisch:

> I am (...) looking forward to both your papers, the one on the erratic shocks (if these are only small, many, independent!) and the other in the Cassel volume (...), from which I hope to devise usual help in my perplexities. (Oslo, Institute of Economics)

Curiosity, but some reservation, recognition of the 'usual help' but lasting 'perplexities' – that was Schumpeter's attitude. The narrative of the debate preceding this epilogue highlights how Frisch and Schumpeter elaborated this metaphor, indicates their differences and their parallel evolution on the topic. That is the task for the remaining sections of this chapter.

2.2   Inner or Outer?

Schumpeter referred again and again and always with approval to this paper in his next books,[2] in spite of the obvious difference between his own explanation and that simplification, which amounted to a reduction of the cyclical mechanism to simple exogenous impulses impinging on the propagation and equilibrating system. Indeed, Frisch's view followed Wicksell and Ackerman's metaphor of the rocking horse – which became the long-standing paradigm for the analysis of cycles – but Schumpeter suspected the ability of these mechanical descriptions to describe an organic phenomenon. In the mechanical framework, innovations were just considered to be one of the sources of strictly exogenous impulses, and therefore the theory could not account for internally generated mechanisms of historical change.

This contradiction remained unnoticed for most authors working on the subject, since Schumpeter's relation to Frisch's work is still to be studied, and since the relevant documents, some private letters, were neither published nor even circulated or subject to academic research until now. But evidence shows that both authors discussed these topics at length, that their concepts were not equivalent and that decisive misunderstandings remained, that Schumpeter never fully adhered to the powerful explanation and method his colleague was using and, consequently, that he could never follow the econometricians in their own territory.

This is quite obvious from the inspection of Schumpeter's theories. His own concept of innovation is well known since his first influential book, *The Theory of Economic Development* (1911). Innovation was systematically presented as the encapsulation of a drive for change, emerging from the contradictions of the industrial capitalist development and pioneered by social deviant entrepreneurs, a process akin to that of biological mutation. That concept was influenced both by the tragic tradition in German thought and by the early impact of J.B. Clark's 1899 book, *The Distribution of Wealth*, but was developed by Schumpeter in an original framework which accounts for his fame (on the influence of the German cultural environment and of Clark, see Louçã, 1997a, pp. 237 f.).

It is well known that Schumpeter's life project was to create a general theory including that of Walras, an economist he admired among all others, but whose theory was considered to be wrong if taken in isolation, since it just accounted for static processes. 'I felt very strongly that this [the presentation of economics as the exclusive explanation of static processes] was *wrong* and that there was a source of energy within the economic system which would of itself disrupt any equilibrium that might be attained' (Schumpeter, 1937, p. 160, original emphasis), wrote Schumpeter about his conversation with the ageing Walras in 1909. Therefore, a truly general theory ought to include equilibrium and statics as well as disequilibrium and dynamics, that is, economic abstractions as well as economic processes describing the reality of capitalism. This was emphasized by Schumpeter again and again in his most important works and constituted a crucial contribution to the study of innovation:

> industrial mutation – if I may use the biological term – that incessantly revolutionises the economic structure from within, incessantly destroying the old one, incessantly creating a new one. This process of Creative Destruction is the essential fact about capitalism. (CSD, 1942, p. 83)

Or as he put categorically in his last text:

> Social phenomena constitute a unique process in historic time, and incessant and irreversible change is their most obvious characteristic. If by Evolutionism we mean not

more than recognition of this fact, then all reasoning about social phenomena must be either evolutionary in itself or else bear upon evolution. (HEA, 1954, p. 435)

This evolutionary approach comprised several important features not discussed in this chapter, such as the consideration of distinct modes of change and time dimensions, determining the analysis of fluctuations. But the decisive point, distinguishing Schumpeter among his colleagues, was the claim that innovation and destructive change emerged as a central characteristic of self-organization under capitalism. Therefore, the dominant evolutionary process was that of an internal change in the structure of the economy. An undated manuscript found at Harvard, *Statistical Evidence as to the Causes of Business Fluctuations*, presents the argument in a nutshell:

Summing up, it may be stated that statistical evidence suggests and in a sense even proves that business fluctuations are produced:

a. By the impact of factors external to the business organization;
b. By an evolutionary process within the business organism which is what is popularly meant by economic progress;
c. By the reactive response to the business organism to both. (Harvard Archive)

This represents quite faithfully Schumpeter's life adhesion to the distinction between external and secondary factors in the developmental process, and internal changes which represented the strength and the essence of entrepreneurial capitalism (in the same sense, BC, 1939, p. 68). Yet, a contradiction is obvious when Schumpeter acknowledged and accepted a quite different representation of his own theory by Frisch, who modelled points (a) and (c) as the exclusive factors responsible for fluctuations and the dynamics of the economic system. In that case, we have exogenous causality plus an endogenous filtering mechanism determining the shape of the movement, that is, a closed epistemic distinction between causality and intelligibility.[3]

2.3 Magellan's Dreams

Schumpeter and Frisch first met in 1927 at Harvard, when Frisch was giving a series of seminars on time series at Yale at the invitation of Irving Fisher, and Schumpeter was also travelling in the country. The difference between the two men was striking: Frisch was a 12-years-younger, mathematically inclined economist with left wing ideas, whereas Schumpeter was a respected and widely quoted theoretician, who had already published some influential books, had occupied a position as Minister of Finance in Austria and later directed a bank, and who was politically a conservative, to say the least. Yet, they became close

friends and enthusiastically shared some projects, such as the creation of the
econometric movement and the publication of *Econometrica.*

They corresponded intensely for many years until Schumpeter's death (1950),
and whenever they could meetings were arranged: in the period now under consideration, they met in September 1931 at Bonn, where Schumpeter was
teaching before his departure to Harvard, and direct discussions eventually went
on. The evidence considered in this section just precedes that meeting.[4]

It must be added that by the end of the 1920s and in the early 1930s,
Schumpeter and Frisch shared not only the passion for the creation of the
econometric movement: they were both engaged in time series analysis,
although using different methods and concepts. Frisch had just circulated his
paper on time series (1927), with the precious help of Mitchell, and Schumpeter
was already engaged in the preparations of his *magnum opus*, the seminal
Business Cycles (1939). There was an obvious common ground they were glad
to recognize: they intended to explain how change occurred, both accepted the
existence of different modes of cycles (Juglar and Kondratiev cycles) and
wished some formal model could be created in order to represent in an analytical
and rigorous framework, the cyclical processes. It is therefore quite natural that
their first meetings were largely devoted to this topic. Evidence shows
furthermore, that their respective points of view were quite different and that
it was not easy to create a common conceptual language in order to understand
and to compare their respective models.

The first piece of evidence is the letter Frisch wrote to Schumpeter on 28
May 1931. It indicates that Frisch was already close to the definition of his
analytical framework, and that a previous debate was engaged:

> I think I understand now your point about dynamics. Those things you mention: the
> more or less unpredictable innovations are those things that in my terminology would
> form the substance of the impulse problem, as distinguished from the propagation
> problem. Some other time I want to write you more fully about this. (Box 761, Oslo
> Library collection)

This letter proves that, by 1931, the metaphor of the rocking horse was
already clearly drawn and that its implications were well understood by Frisch,
who tried to reduce Schumpeter's theory to his own conceptual model. The
metaphor was originally suggested in a discrete footnote by Wicksell, and then
referred to by Ackerman in his doctoral thesis. Both references would have
been condemned to obscurity, if Frisch had not considered Wicksell the greatest
economist and if he was not part of Ackerman's jury in 1928: he quickly
embodied the metaphor in his own research and formulated a seminal model of
cycle inspired by this insight.[5] But, curiously enough, this metaphor of the
rocking horse, in spite of its influence in the dissemination of the piece in the

Cassel *Festschrift*, did not play any important role in the correspondence with Schumpeter, since both immediately felt that it could not account for the specificity of innovations. Instead, another metaphor came to dominate the construction of the argument – that of a pendulum hit by shocks and driven by some innovative process.

It is well known that the pendulum was already at that time an important reference for the analysis of cycles, and that it dominated the rhetoric of cycle analysis before the rocking horse: Yule and Fisher (the pendulum hit by peas), among others, used the metaphor earlier. Frisch used it in 1931, when he developed the first efforts to model cycles as an economy submitted to frictions. Strictly speaking, there was no analytical difference between the dissipative pendulum and the horse, if both were conceived of as mechanisms filtering and damping free oscillations.

Frisch wanted precisely to stress the antinomy between the role of Slutsky's random shocks in order to generate change, and the stability properties of the body of the system in order to reduce those impacts to the precise form of the cycle. As a consequence, the movement of a propagation damping mechanism was represented by the wooden horse, which was supposed to be under the impact of frequent kicks, making it rock. On the other hand, Frisch saw the concept of the pendulum as a much more elaborate mechanism which attempted to respond to Schumpeter's innovations, quite different from small, random and insignificant shocks. The striking extension of the metaphor was in fact related to the impulse system, which then came into the discussion. Yet, the forced pendulum under Schumpeterian shocks was a distinctive mathematical entity, and Frisch apparently did not understand the implications of the extension (Louçã, 1998).

This discussion highlights some of the reasons for the simultaneous use of both metaphors and their distinctions, and how Schumpeter and Frisch tried to reach an agreement that finally collapsed, although neither explicitly recognized the failure and the abyss between their conceptions. Indeed, there were quite obvious differences between the two approaches. On 10 June 1931,[6] Schumpeter stated his reservations and differences in relation to the pendulum, and suggested instead the biological analogy (mutation):

> This [the discussion of the nature of statics, 'a problem *à la* pendulum'] would be all, if data did not vary except by influences which we could call influences 'from without' or by 'growth'. But there is an agent, within the economic world (=system of quantities) which alters data and with these the economic process: entrepreneurial activity, which I have elsewhere given the reasons for considering as something sui generis (and the sociology of it). This is the agency which accounts for what may be termed in a special sense 'specifically economic evolution'. It not only destroys existing equilibrium, but also that circuit-like process of economic life, it makes economic things *change* instead of making them *recur*. And its effects are not

recurring – Ford can never be repeated – but 'historic' and definitely located in historical time. They are also irreversible. This distinction acquires importance owing to the importance of the phenomena incident to the mechanism by which 'innovations' come into existence. I do not like the analogy with 'growth', else I could express that distinction by comparing it to the distinction between the circulation of blood in a child and the growth of that child. Biological mutations would be a better analogy.

Schumpeter added a postscript to the same letter:

> On rereading this letter I do not know I have exceeded in clearing things up. But always think of the pendulum which, given mass force and so on, and no resistance of medium, would eventually swing in the same way, perfectly [.], and displaying no relevant historical dates. Now let its mass swell from within or a new force act upon it with a sudden push, shifting and deforming it *for good*, and you have a case of 'Dyn. S.' or 'Evolution'. (in Box 14, Frisch Rommet, Institute of Economics, Oslo)

This letter defines the terms of the discussion, as far as Schumpeter was concerned. First, it indicates that the relevant movements were the irreversible changes in the economies ('Ford can never be repeated'), historical changes instead of simple and mechanical recurrence. Second, it points out the nature of the changes emerging from internal forces (entrepreneurial activity), which determine economic evolution. Third, it is not a process of simple physical growth, and the analogy with biological mutation is thus more appropriate – and that was the precise distinction between Schumpeter and neoclassical economists.

Consequently, Schumpeter added the outstanding postscript: if the model is to be represented by the pendulum, then the mechanism must be subject to deformations and changeable by the impacts of innovations, so that it can 'display relevant historical dates'. In that sense and just two weeks later, on 24 June, Schumpeter insisted in his critique of the pendulum analogy:

> I am not *quite* satisfied by your classification of the 'innovations' as part of the impulse problem (...), because this seems to coordinate them with events, which come from outside the economic system such as chance gold-discoveries. The problem with these is simply to discover the reaction of the economic system on them. (...) Now as I look at it, any innovations are something different to impulses in this sense. They come from inside, they [are] economic phenomena sui generis (...). The reason why I so much insist on this and why I should like to convince you, is not pedantry: it is of some importance for a number of problems, and especially for the problem of the cycle, which affords a good example for the reason of my insisting: If you class innovation simply among impulses you arrive at some [.] position as Pigou, and miss what seems to me the heart of the matter: you only catch the 'vibrations' [.] to the impact of the 'impulse' and not the phenomena attaching to the impulse itself. (in Box 14, Frisch Rommet)

The critique is now very clear: innovations should not be considered as part of the impulses, since this implies ignoring both their causes and their real qualitative structural impacts. For Schumpeter, and that was indeed his unique contribution, innovations were part of the economic system itself, since 'coming from inside'. Otherwise, the 'heart of the matter' would be missed, since the effect of the phenomenon would be studied without any attempt to inquire into its causes – as implied by the mechanics of the pendulum.

The long and detailed answer by Frisch is a magnificent example of a rhetorical effort of persuasion, and a quite effective one, as we shall see. The letter was dated 5 July 1931[7] and recognizes the persistence of differences between the two authors. In spite of that, it argues that a mechanical analogy is indispensable to develop the argument and to define the problem, and insistently tries to convince Schumpeter:

> You say that you are not satisfied with my classifications of the innovations as disturbances (part of the impulse problem), and I think I understand now why you are not satisfied, but I believe you will be so when you have read this letter.
> (...) Let me tell you right away that I am glad you did not smooth out our differences in a more or less formalistic adoption of my pendulum analogy, but took the trouble to attempt to convince me that there is something fundamental which is not represented in the picture of the pendula as I gave it originally. (...) The reason why I did never under our conversations in Harvard or Cleveland seize your meaning exactly has been I suppose that I never was able to translate it into a mechanical analogy. I think I am able to do so now.

This is a very important statement, since Frisch acknowledges that they had different languages and that different problems were to be addressed by the respective models. Consequently, some rules of correspondence should be established, and that was the precise role of the metaphor. This is how Frisch proceeded to demonstrate his mechanical analogy:

> Your San Francisco letter [10 June 1931] must have been working in my subconscience even after I sent you my all too simple answer classifying your innovations under the impulse heading. In fact, about two weeks ago (...) my thought got started along the following mechanical analogy:
> Suppose you have a pendulum exposed to friction so that its motion would die down if it were left to itself. Now build a container for water on the top of the pendulum (...). Further build a pipe down through the length of the pendulum and arrange an outlet for the water at the very lowest point of the pendulum. This outlet shall be of the following peculiar sort: Its opening points to the left and equipped with a valve that is regulated by the *velocity* of the pendulum (...). The regulation of the valve is such that the opening is largest when the pendulum moves towards the right, and in particular the opening is largest when the speed of the pendulum (towards the right) is at its maximum. We can imagine that the opening is some simple function of the speed. When the pendulum moves towards the left the opening is nearly (but not completely) closed, the opening being at the smallest when the speed towards

the left is the largest. (...) Now let the container be alimented with water from some source which we may consider as datum in the problem. In other words the stream flowing into the container we consider as a known function of time (for instance a constant). (Oslo Archive)

This interpretation became part of Frisch's writings on cycle and economic evolution, as well as part of his teaching. In 1933–4, he represented his pendulum metaphor by the drawing in Figure 4.2, included in his mimeographed lessons at the Institute of Economics, *Makrodynamikk*.

Finally, Frisch applied this analogy in order to explain the two different sources of impulses, Schumpeterian innovations and random shocks:

If you now let the system loose it will evolve in cycles whose length will be determined partly by the length of the pendulum, partly by the friction and partly by the law that regulates the opening of the valve. Of course you understand already the whole analogy: The water represents the new ideas, inventions, etc. They are not utilized when they come, but are stored until the next period of prosperity (or even longer, some of the molecules in the container may rest there indefinitely). And when they are finally utilized they form the additional surplus of energy which is necessary to maintain the swings, to prevent them from dying out. The amount of energy which will thus be released depends on whether there is a large amount of *potential* innovations stored, and also on the velocity of the upswing (...).

I hope you are more satisfied with this interpretation of the innovations. And you understand of course how much I owe you for being led into this avenue of approach, which I hope will be a fruitful one. As I see it now there are two aspects to the impulse

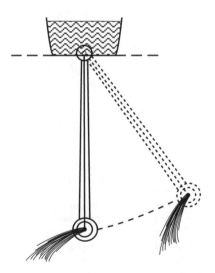

Figure 4.2   Schumpeter's pendulum, according to Frisch (adapted).

(or 'energy') problem: On the one hand the more or less random irregularity of inventions and progress in the arts. (...) On the other hand the periodic release in the actual utilization of stored inventions, which is your idea.

Which one of the two that is actually the most important in the sense of representing the largest source of 'energy' for the maintenance of the economic swings I think nobody can say today. This can only be found out by painstaking studies that are *econometric* in the best sense of the word. I should be very much mistaken if such studies would not lead us to new Magellanic Oceans in cycle theory. (Harvard Archive)

Again, this represented a peculiar vision of Schumpeter's idea, but also a major departure from Frisch's previous models, since it required the abandonment of the universe of free oscillations, replaced by a parametrically forced oscillation.

Schumpeter reacted to the letter less than two weeks afterwards, 17 July 1931. In spite of the ingenious mechanism, he was not at all convinced. The distinctive role of creative destruction, of the systemic change imposed by innovations, was not encapsulated in the model. *Et pour cause*: it could only deal with Slutsky shocks, not with complex objects as these, 'partly elastic and partly subject to deformation', non-computable and poorly defined changes. And the latter were required by Schumpeter to form his model of cycles *cum* trend. After dealing with the preparations for the Lausanne meeting of the Econometric Society[8] (22–24 September 1931), he insisted again that one should consider irregularities, deformation and shifts in the body of economic relations along the cycle:

Now the *pleasure* (after the *duty* [the preparation of the Econometric Society meeting]): I have to thank you for the papers you were good enough to send me, all of which interest me very much, but I want to hurry on to our discussion on 'impulses'. I have been fascinated by your analogy, which I think is much superior to one I had formed myself: I tried to think of the process I have in mind (and which claims precedence as against irregularities which are the consequence of influences acting from without the economic sphere, but being part and parcel of that sphere itself and sure to display themselves even if we abstract from outside or chance disturbances as we must in a theoretical approach) as of a force acting intermittently on a body (or system) which is partly elastic and partly subject to deformation.

This force pushes the body or system up, deforming it in the process, after which we observe a sagging back with further deformations, and besides vibrations, elastic reactions, etc. A new system (or form and position of the body) establishes itself, after which the force starts acting again. Now your analogy grips one element of the whole thing so elegantly that it will be possible to proceed with it while very little progress seems (...) to me to be possible with that clumsy and complicated model of mine. I think highly of the importance (...) of such analogies for one type of theory, which will grow in importance – that type of which I think a *Jasturnsgleischung* [approximating reality] (I don't know the English term) of economic life would be at the centre.

Schumpeter praised the illustrative role of the metaphor: it facilitated the discussion and imaginary representation of each other's arguments. But still, a crucial disagreement remained, and Schumpeter stressed the limits of the pendulum models, which ignore structural change or the consequences of the cycle itself:

> They [the analogies] are, however, of less service for another type [of theory], which in constructing its models (...) primarily thinks of the inner life and structure of the economic process – primarily asks, e.g., *what* interest is the price of and so on. In judging my *Entwichlung* [Theory of Economic Development] you must not forget that it was problems such as this I was aiming at. In this connection I by leave to touch upon two things. First, being truly glad to see that my *manière de voir* may possibly, in your hands, [.] of being gripped by the tools of the other type, I am anxious to point out where I am not yet quite satisfied with your brilliant construction: On the other hand, something within me rebels at our pendulum keeping its suspension point. I do think it a great improvement, provided it be feasible, to shift the suspension point in the process.

Indeed, the equivocation lies in the fact that both authors shared the metaphor but meant two types of theories: Frisch's mode of theorizing was the translation of the assumptions and the hypotheses into the language of formal logic and mathematical deduction, while Schumpeter suspected the limitations of such an endeavour. This was why Schumpeter listed the three main inconveniences of the formal model his colleague was arguing for: (i) it assumed constant mass, i.e. a constant structure, (ii) it was not possible to represent the trend as the result of the cycle, and (iii) the inner process of generation of change was not explainable in this framework. In one word, the dynamics of the system was unsatisfactory:

> Other considerations quite apart, this cannot be done because the shift is *no phenomenon* sui generis, around which the cycle moves, as another phenomenon sui generis, but the *net result* of the cyclical movement, *which is the essential point of evolution*, of the sort that our model, to express the theory, would have to be constructed such that the water must arrive *at the same time* which it creates the pendulum movement, who displaces the suspension point *and does so only by and through* the pendulum movement (...) and of disturbances (among which I think once *again* current random inventions and progress in arts[)].
>
> On the other hand, I do not quite like the mass of the pendulum remaining constant. I should like our water mechanism to *increase* it in the process. Finally, if the pendulum is to represent not only the social product in the sense of the consumer goods, but the whole of the economic system with all the higher values of goods and commercial activity, an *inner vibratory system* would be extremely useful if it could be [.]. (Box 14, Oslo Institute of Economics)

Frisch replied with a polite letter on 24 July, briefly acknowledging Schumpeter's comments but adding no further argument and dealing with the preparations for the Lausanne meeting. It is quite obvious that he considered the matter to be closed and his pendulum metaphor to be enough, although the differences remained as far as Schumpeter was concerned.

The differences were related to at least two major points. The first was the formal and analogical representation of those specific disturbances, 'inventions' as designed by Frisch or 'innovations' as Schumpeter preferred since they emerged from the inner system itself.[9] As Frisch's reasoning was dominated by the necessity of the mechanic encapsulation of the theory and of the formal mathematical representation, he could only consider the two alternative positions: either the variable was endogenously determined by the system of equations describing the process, and therefore was explained by it, or it was exogenous to that system, and therefore was explanatory of the changes in the process. The representation of two types of exogenous variables – *à la* Slutsky and *à la* Schumpeter – assesses the difficulty, since there are obvious analytical differences between them, one being an aggregation of unknown irrelevant exogenous impacts, and the other a description of the cause of crucial changes in the economies.

But this was rather artificial, since the narrative introduction of Schumpeterian shocks had no analytical counterpart in the model. Indeed, Frisch's model asserts that the variables accounting for innovation do not change the structure of the process, and merely generate self-similar cycles – a *perpetuum mobile*. Yet, Schumpeter's reasoning was dominated by a completely different requirement, since he took a literary approach of the innovative process, under the influence of a non-defined biological metaphor, mutation. And mutation was designed to understand concrete historical change and essentially the drive for change in capitalism, and not the mechanical contrivance of the formal model Frisch had in mind. Indeed, one of the relevant contradictions in this polemic is the epistemic distinction between the concepts of 'exogenous' and 'endogenous' variables used by Frisch, as defined by the formal models, and the non-equivalent concepts of 'external' and 'internal' forces, defined by Schumpeter in relation to the scope of the theory itself, as the limits of what was reachable by the theoretical effort of explanation at a given moment. Innovation was for Schumpeter part of the explainable economic system, although not determined by it, since it referred to social deviance and abnormal behaviour, the charac-teristics of entrepreneurship. In summary, the difference was that for Schumpeter causality is not equivalent to mechanical determinism, which is the only form of determination Frisch could accept in the framework of his model.

Indeed, Frisch worked in the area of formal mathematical models, whereas Schumpeter worked in the area of narrative and appreciative theories, and con-sequently their discussion is largely a case of mistaken identities. Nevertheless and paradoxically, the rhetoric used by the authors provided the only possible medium for communicating as previously indicated, although it could not by itself prevent wrong interpretations. This case is in fact a good example high-lighting the importance of the use of metaphors in order to create a shared conceptual platform and to understand each other's arguments, for two economists departing from rather opposite points of view. In this framework, the metaphors related both arguments to commonly understood mechanical models – the rocking horse, the pendulum – that allowed for the identification of the representation of their main points. The debate did not depend on the handling of sophisticated formal representations that Schumpeter could not fully understand, but rather on the image of the model. This is why, in spite of the different approaches to the problem of innovation, and moreover of the incomparability of their arguments, Schumpeter and Frisch could elaborate their arguments and evolve in the discussion, trying to solve this puzzle.

Yet the solution was particularly difficult, since there was a second decisive difference in their positions: Schumpeter was in fact requiring a very complex system in order to represent the innovative process. If the pendulum was modelled in order to change its suspension point – as a result of the cycle itself, it should be noted, so that the trend be indeed indistinguishable from the oscil-lations – and if its mass should also increase or if its shape should be deformed as part of the effects of the 'inner vibratory system', this obviously implied a nonlinear representation. Schumpeter argued for this solution while ignoring the method of proceeding along those lines, since he did not and could not even attempt to represent that model formally. It required and still requires some adventurous travel in the unknown, with unpredictable results if any, just as Magellan dared to do. Schumpeter wanted to advance in that direction, but did not know how to do so. Conversely, Frisch knew what it meant but did not want to follow that path, since it would move him away from formal modelling and to *mare incognita*. And that Frisch knew better than anyone at the time.

3   THE LAST EPISODES

Although the topic was never more the subject of discussion after 1931, both Frisch and Schumpeter maintained and elaborated their positions. In the preparation and writing of *Business Cycles*, Schumpeter came back again and again to the same perplexity, implicitly indicating quite a different solution as an alternative to the mechanical device of Frisch. The *leitmotiv* was obvious: 'It [innovation] is an internal factor because the turning of the existing factors of production to new users is a purely economic process and, in capitalist society, purely a matter of business behaviour' (BC, p. 86). As a consequence, the innovative process of change and destruction should be modelled as an internal feature of capitalism, and that would be the proper explanation in economics (ibid., p. 7). Furthermore, the relevant external events could not be appropriately represented as random shocks on a pendulum, and Schumpeter stated that rather bluntly: 'But the influence of external factors is never absent. And never are they of such a nature that we could dispose of them according to a scheme of, say, a pendulum continually exposed to numerous small and independent shocks' (ibid., p. 12).

However, Schumpeter took pains to explain at the very same time that Frisch's model of impulse and propagation was really distinct from the available alternatives, namely the allegedly *perpetuum mobile* systems such as that of Kalecki, or those of Wicksell and Slutsky which were the inspiration of the rocking horse (BC, pp. 181 n., 189, 560 n.). Yet, he could not answer the obvious fact that Frisch's pendulum was indeed also a *perpetuum mobile* device, close to Kalecki's – since both shared the framework and the analytical solution they imposed as the standard model of cycles.

Later on, in the *History of Economic Analysis*, Schumpeter expressed his suspicion in relation to the mechanical analogies in an inspiring text against reductionism. He went as far as suggesting a new and alternative metaphor, that of the violin being played by a gifted musician:

> It has been said above that macrodynamics helps us to understand mechanisms of propagation. It will perhaps assist the reader if he will look upon the economic system as a sort of resonator, which reacts to the impact of disturbing or 'irritating' events in a manner that is partly determined by its physical structure. Think for instance of a violin which 'reacts' in a determined manner when 'irritated' as the player applies the bow. Understanding the laws of this reaction contributes to a complete 'explanation' of the phenomenon that we call a violin concert. But evidently this contribution, even if reinforced by the contribution of the neurophysiologist, does not explain the whole of it: aesthetic evaluation and the like apart, there is a range of purely scientific ground that acoustics and physiology are constitutionally unable to cover. (HEA, pp. 1167–8)

And here Schumpeter introduced a sharp critique of the claim of unlimited explanatory power of formal models:

> Similarly macrodynamics, while quite essential to an explanation of cyclical phenomena, suffers from definite limitations:[10] its cyclical models are what acoustic models of resonators are for the violin concert. But its votaries will not see this. They construct macrodynamic models that are to explain all there is to explain, for economists, in the cyclical phenomena. The very attempt to do so involves several definite errors of fact.[11] And flimsy structures based upon arbitrary assumptions are immediately 'applied' and presented as guides to policy, a practice that of course completes the list of reasons for irritation in the opposite camp. One sometimes has the impression that there are only two groups of economists: those who do not understand a difference equation; and those who understand nothing else. It is therefore a hope, rather than a prognosis to be presently fulfilled, which I am expressing if I venture to say that this entirely unnecessary barrier – but one which

is no novelty in our science – to fertilizing interaction will vanish by virtue of the logic of things.' (HEA, pp. 1167–8)

The intrinsic limitations of the previous metaphors were indeed, according to Schumpeter, those of formal macroeconomics as such: resonance, from the aesthetic pleasure or from social interaction, was outside the scope of modelling. But this is finally how evolution was whipped out in the construction of the canon: the legitimate mode of theorizing being established as formal modelling, the Schumpeterian reservations were ignored as a romantic protestation from the pre-scientific past of economics.

Now, the reader must accept that this is the convenient epilogue for the story of an intense, useful and quite misunderstood discussion on the foundations of the econometric programme for the analysis of cycles. The debate highlights the crucial role of metaphors as a way to direct the construction of the argument, of its formal representations and of alternatives. Schumpeter was eventually under the impression that the mathematical capacities of his friend and colleague restricted his thought to a narrow domain and prevented the consideration of the decisive qualitative features of innovation under capitalism; moreover, he was conditioned by the public claim, made in the influential 1933 paper by Frisch, that the pendulum accurately represented his own point of view. He chose not to challenge that claim; yet, he stressed again and again that the mechanical representation was finally of no use in understanding change, evolution and irreversibility of real cycles or even the aesthetic pleasure of a violin concert. Quite rightly, Schumpeter intuited that the explanation and this generation of alternative complex models were still submerged somewhere in the Oceans of Magellan's fantasies or dreams.

ACKNOWLEDGEMENTS

Arjo Klamer and Christopher Freeman commented on earlier versions of this paper. I thank them for their contribution, with the usual disclaimer. I thank Mrs Ragna Frisch for permission to quote from her father's archives.

NOTES

1. The correspondence is to be found at Oslo University (Institute of Economics and University Library) and Harvard University. A complete transcription of this correspondence is in Louçã, 1997b, and a mathematical analysis of some of its implications is in Louçã, 1998. Frisch's letters were clearly typewritten, whereas Schumpeter's were hand-written and are in a very poor condition (some of the words are quite difficult to decipher, and whenever it was not possible they are marked as [.]). Emphasis is by the authors.

2. References to Frisch's 1933 paper can be found in *Business Cycles* (pp. 171 n., 181 n., 189) and in *History of Economic Analysis* (p. 1162 n.). Schumpeter never mentioned any direct criticism of the paper.
3. In 1931, Frisch clearly explained why the cycles should be conceived of as free oscillations: 'Here it cannot, as far as I understand, any longer be a question of a forced oscillation. The bundle of phenomena we call business cycles is, I believe, a complex we have to attack as composed of free oscillations if we as economists are ever to be able to understand it. The explanation of the cyclical character of the oscillation must be sought in the inner structure of the system' (quoted in Andvig, 1981 pp. 708). Intelligibility requires endogenous explanation, in the context of these standard models.
4. The fact that they met in September after an intense correspondence in the summer of 1931 was damaging for the future interpretative work on their points of view, since there is no more written trace of the developments of their discussion. Furthermore, some of the letters of this period are apparently lost, since they could not be found either in Harvard or in the Oslo Collection.
5. The Cassel paper is careful enough to refer to this origin of the metaphor, although with a wrong date. It constituted the single most important departure for the econometric analysis of the cycle, and the metaphor explicitly or implicitly dominated the research programme until very recently (Louçã, 1997a, pp. 117 f.). Wicksell's metaphor appeared in 1918 in a review of a paper by Karl Petander, 'Karl Petander: Goda och darliga tider', in *Ekonomisk Tidskrift*, **19**: 66–73, in a footnote to page 71: 'if you hit a rocking horse with a stick, the movement of the horse will be very different from that of the stick. The hits are the cause of the movement, but the system's own equilibrium laws condition the form of the movement' (quoted in Thalberg, 1992, p. 115 n.).
6. This is the first letter dispensing with the formal treatment between Schumpeter and Frisch. It was sent from San Francisco.
7. This is the only letter here quoted that was already partly reproduced elsewhere (Stolper, 1994, p. 70 f.).
8. In that meeting, Tinbergen presented several models of endogenous and regular cycles. Frisch was of course much closer to the subsequent solution that would come to be accepted as the pattern of cycle models, as represented by the rocking horse or the pendulum in PPIP. But it is relevant to note that both shared the same fascination for Aftalion's explanation of the cycle created by lags in the production of capital goods.
9. This difference of conceptualization is already highly revealing of the alternative approaches: invention can be considered as exogenous and emerging from the external scientific system, whereas innovation was precisely described as the result of the market selection process of invention, that is, of the specific economic system. Innovation should never be described as a purely exogenous variable in the Schumpeterian framework.
10. A note by Schumpeter emphasized the evolutionary character of economic data and therefore strengthened the critique: 'The simile limps, of course, like all similes. Cycles run their course in the *historical* evolution of the capitalist economy. Even neglecting all the economic sociology that must therefore inevitably enter into their explanation, we cannot help recognizing that their theory or, to avoid this word, their analysis must be largely bound up with the theory or analysis of evolution rather than with dynamics, which is the theory or analysis of sequences that do not carry any *historical* dates. No doubt there are certain mechanisms that played as great a part in 1857 as in 1929, and these must be taken account of in any observed cycle by more or less generally applicable macrodynamic schemata, just as, on a lower level of technique, the ordinary theory of supply and demand. But they are only tools and do not in themselves suffice, even if supplied with all conceivable time series, to reconstruct the phenomenon as a whole and, of course, still less its long-run outcomes' (HEA, p. 1167 n.).
11. Again, Schumpeter's footnote is very telling: 'Three of these may serve as illustration. They will at the same time show why the respective objections do not tell against the models themselves but only against the claim alluded to. (1) Macrodynamic models, presented with that claim, involve the proposition that the 'causes' of the business cycles must be found in

the interaction between the social aggregates themselves, whereas it can be proved that business cycles arise from sectional disturbances. (2) With the same proviso, macrodynamic models carry the implication that the structural changes that transform economics historically have nothing to do with business cycles, whereas it can be proved that cycles are the form that structural changes take. (3) Constructors of macrodynamic models, almost always, aim at explaining all the phases of the cycle (and the turning points) by a single 'final' equation. This is indeed not impossible. But it spells error to assume that it must be possible and to bend analysis to that requirement' (HEA, p. 1168 n.)

REFERENCES

Andvig, C. (1981), 'Ragnar Frisch and business cycle research during the interwar years', *History of Political Economy*, **13** (4), 695–725.

Frisch, Ragnar (1927), *The Analysis of Statistical Time Series*, New York, April, mimeo.

Frisch, Ragnar (1933), 'Propagation problems and impulse problems in dynamic economics', in K. Koch (ed.), *Economic Essays in Honour of Gustav Cassel*, London: Frank Cass, pp. 171–205.

Louçã, Francisco (1997a), *Turbulence in Economics – An Evolutionary Appraisal of Cycles and Complexity in Historical Processes*, Cheltenham, UK and Lyme, US: Edward Elgar.

Louçã, Francisco (1997b), *The Intriguing Pendulum*, Working Paper 4/97, Departamento de Economia, ISEG.

Louçã, Francisco (1998), *Chaos in the Early Metaphors and Models of Business Cycles*, Working Paper, Departamento de Economia, ISEG.

Schumpeter, Joseph [1911] (1982), 'Teoria do Desenvolvimento Económico – Uma Investigação sobre Lucros', Capital Crédito, *Juro e o Ciclo Económico*, São Paulo: April.

Schumpeter, Joseph (1937), 'Preface to the Japanese Edition of Theorie der Wirtschaftlichen Entwicklung', in J. Schumpeter, (1951, ed. by R. Clemence), *Essays of Joseph Schumpeter*, Cambridge, MA: Addison-Wesley, pp. 158–63.

Schumpeter, Joseph (1939), *Business Cycles*, (BC) New York: McGraw-Hill.

Schumpeter, Joseph (1942), *Capitalism, Socialism and Democracy*, (CSD) London: Routledge.

Schumpeter, Joseph (1954), *History of Economic Analysis*, (HEA) London: Routledge.

Stolper, W. (1994), 'Joseph Allois Schumpeter – The public life of a private man', Princeton: Princeton University Press.

Thalberg, Bjorn (1992), 'A reconsideration of Frisch's original cycle model', in K. Velupillai (ed.), *Nonlinear and Multisectoral Macrodynamics – Essays in Honour of Richard Goodwin*, New York: New York University Press, pp. 96–117.

5. Veblen and Commons on private property: an institutionalist discussion around a capitalist foundation

Philippe Broda

1 INTRODUCTION

The area where the differences between Veblen and Commons are the strongest is certainly centred around their respective opinions in the debates on economic policy. Veblen is known as a radical, desperately hostile to capitalism. He praises a kind of revolution led by the engineers. As for Commons, his declared ambition is to save capitalism by making it 'reasonable'. He is simply a reformer.[1] Yet, one thing is certain: both institutionalists are very sceptical about any economic system based on *laissez-faire*.

This chapter is an attempt to account for this disagreement between Veblen and Commons through their analyses on one crucial theoretical point, which is property. This is because, in the capitalist system, the market is where individuals express and achieve their personal interests: thus it presupposes the institution of ownership as one of its cornerstones. Therefore, the investigation of how Veblen and Commons tackle property finally boils down to their analysis of the foundations of capitalism, and this allows better understanding of their positions on the questions of economic policy.

Since they do not subscribe to the ideal of *laissez-faire*, Veblen and Commons also oppose, each one in his own way, the analysis of the economic orthodoxy that firmly advocates the capitalist regulation. What unites them, comparatively to the orthodox conception of property, is striking: they focus on the conflictual aspects inherent in ownership and they grant them great importance (section 2). The following section then examines the divergences between them. Commons ascribes a positive function to property: after all, it limits the conflicts between the social actors. It plays a coordinating role. This is not the case with Veblen since, according to him, both ownership and all the predatory institutions, are responsible for these conflicts (section 3).

So, through these analyses on property, it is finally the connection between law and economics that is investigated. It is then possible to observe that

Veblen's and Commons' positions are prospectively critical of the more recent positions on that matter. Their point of view is relevant compared with these conceptions that affirm that the legal rules must be appraised on the basis of their efficiency.[2] Veblen, Commons and, more generally, old institutionalists, present an alternative to this nowadays dominant conception.

2   A COMMON CRITIQUE OF THE ORTHODOXY

Veblen and Commons may not conceive the economic orthodoxy in a similar manner. But, both of them regard Locke as being a founding father of the modern theory of ownership.[3] It is true that we can find in Locke elements that initiate this joint hostility. In the Lockean view, man is owner of himself and then of the product of his labour. Thus, the institution of ownership crowns a specific relationship between men and nature. The classics and labour value do not really question the nature of this link.

Besides, Marx reproached that in a system where property is taken as a given, the focus on commodities is a substitute for an authentic taking social relations into account. We know that Smith, Ricardo and the others were aware that there were conflicts between economic groups. But, for them, these antagonisms were not at the heart of the matter. Their resolution was supposed to result from considerations regarding the laws of production and the problem of rent, namely without real reflection about ownership itself.[4]

In standard neoclassical thought, property, like other institutions, remains too exogenous. The individual makes his choices while his resources and constraints are given. The interference of another person in his plan is called an 'externality'. In such a logic, the initial endowments of individuals and their social meaning are not to be questioned.

Veblen and Commons both propose a new kind of approach. Their views on ownership are crucial to their analysis of the economic system. Their specificity is expressed in two points. First, ownership is interpreted as an interdependence between men, not as a link between men and nature (2.1). Secondly, this interdependence introduces social conflicts directly into economics through the idea of 'vested interests' (2.2).

2.1   A Social Dimension

According to Veblen, the role of the institution of ownership is fundamental in the modern era – the 'machine era' if we keep his terminology. It is an indication of personal success. In fact, in the present context of competition, rivalry between individuals, the collected properties measure the place of each one in the social scale. Therefore, men direct their activities in order to accumulate goods.

In *The Theory of the Leisure Class* ([1899] 1978), the book that made him famous, Veblen describes the mechanisms ensuring the functioning and even the stability of such an institutional framework. His starting point is 'self-esteem'. He argues that social actors are driven by self-esteem, that is 'the usual basis of self-respect is the respect accorded by one's neighbours', and he adds that 'only individuals with an aberrant temperament can, in the long run, retain their self-esteem in the face of the disesteem of their fellows' (Veblen, [1899] 1978, p. 22).[5]

The transition from self-esteem to disposition for 'emulation' is barely perceptible and this emulative tendency is the principal factor inherent in human nature for the advent of competition. An additional condition required is peculiar to the material environment. People are supposed to live in a state of relative abundance. In other words, there must be something to waste.

All these considerations are connected. The rise of a 'leisure class' came together with the appearance of the institution of ownership (Veblen, [1899] 1978, p. 17). Before, there was a kind of solidarity within the community whereas, from then on, the members of this leisure class acquired an honorific status that exempted them from industrial and common tasks. The reasons for their domination over the 'underlying population' are not to be explored here but, since these 'barbarian' times, the display of their high position takes the same form: 'conspicuous' consumption and leisure. Then, their inclination towards emulation expresses itself fully. By means of their trophies, properties or futile activities, their intention is to demonstrate how far they keep their hands from any efficient or industrial occupation.

With the passing of time, the nature of the objects that men appropriate has changed. It depends on the cultural circumstances. Thus, the ownership of captive wives is specific to the beginning of the institution during the barbarian epoch, whereas modern capitalism requires the appropriation of pecuniary wealth. Nevertheless, ownership is always characterized by two features. Firstly, it conveys the idea of competition among individuals. Secondly, a connotation of waste, of futility, is associated with the canons of taste.

The desire for 'invidious distinctions' incites the lower classes to take an example from the leisure class and to try to imitate its members, thereby involving a process of self-enforcement. Veblen insists on the obstacle that the existence of a leisure class – that is, the institution of private property – constitutes to cultural evolution (Veblen [1899] 1978, p. 135).[6] Besides this social stability, the analysis of ownership provides another interesting element directly related to the tendency towards emulation: the quest for ownership is endless.

As far back as 1892, in answer to Spencer, Veblen explained that

> the existing system has not made, and does not tend to make, the industrious poor poorer as measured absolutely in means of livelihood; but it does tend to make them relatively poorer, in their own eyes, as measured in terms of comparative economic importance, and, curious as it may seem at first sight, that is what seems to count. (Veblen [1919] 1990, p. 392)

His judgment was definitive: capitalism could not promote general welfare because each person appraises his own situation only in relativistic terms, compared with the other people who belong to the community.

We can find in Commons' reflection the main points that have been developed in Veblen's argumentation set out up till now: he considers ownership as a mark of interdependence between individuals, he is aware that its forms changed through history, and he links it to a logic of social stability. However, whether about external or human factors, his theoretical foundations are different from those of Veblen. Commons does not correlate property with a context of abundance, but with a world of scarcity. As for man, what makes him so specific here is not any emulative bent, but consciousness.

It is interesting to observe how Commons' scheme leads to conclusions close to Veblen's results:

> wherever there is a permanent scarcity of particular objects [...], the self-conscious person recognizes his dependence upon them, and these objects then come to have a conscious value to him. (Commons [1899–1900] 1967, p. 11)

The need for appropriation obviously stems from the constraints imposed on men by the environment. Put another way, property is the human answer to a scarcity problem. But it is not conceived in the first place as a relation between individuals and an object. It is principally a relation between individuals. Commons points out that ownership means at least as much to withhold an object from the others as to hold it (Commons [1924] 1959, pp. 52–3). The idea of relations of power between men is then connected to this institution. Therefore, the social dimension of property appears clearly.

Commons surmises that, historically, one of the most significant forms of ownership is indisputably the capture of women. In this regard, we can easily see why ownership is assimilated to a relation of coercion, that is 'a means of commanding and securing for consumption the services of others' (Commons, [1899–1900] 1965, p. 20). Nowadays, things are much more complicated. The capitalist system is not a simple expression of individual liberties. Coercion remains, but is less visible: 'this basic fact of private property is veiled by the wage system and the practice of purchasing commodities on a world market' (Commons, [1899–1900] 1965, p. 19).

The outlines of ownership are in ongoing evolution. Like Veblen, Commons interprets its transformations in the direction of a lesser brutality. While conscience stops being 'empirical' and becomes 'reflective', persuasion replaces coercion progressively but not entirely.

Since the emergence of the state which assumes the monopoly of legitimate violence, ownership does not grant the possibility of using physical sanctions. Nonetheless, whatever historical era it belongs to, it allows regulation of society. And if ownership fulfils a social function – it brings order – it is not only content to secure the expectations of the community members, but it also protects their position in the economic competition. On that aspect, we can find another agreement between both institutionalists.

2.2 Some 'Vested Interests'

Veblen's approach is cultural. He defines culture as a 'complex of the habits of life and of thought prevalent among the members of the community' (Veblen, [1919] 1990, p. 39). According to his historical reading, cultural evolution underwent four stages in the Western world.

During the first, the 'savage' era, individuals lived in small communities. Their activities were mainly agricultural. It stemmed from the important relationship between men and the earth that the biological rates steered their habits of thought. The ideas of birth, growth and death were essential to their interpretation of events. The second period was the 'barbarian' and its origin went back to the appearance of a surplus of resources. Its distribution provoked conflicts between communities and even within these groups. Life was no longer peaceful. So, 'the relation in which the deity, or deities, are conceived to stand to facts (was) no longer the relationship of progenitor, so much as that of suzerainty' (Veblen, [1919] 1990, p. 11). The understanding of reality then respected new canons of validity in view of the fact that the activities of men had changed. The 'handicraft' era came after barbarity; it lasted from about the 13th century until 1760 in Great Britain and a little later in the rest of Europe. Here again, life was relatively pleasant: people earned their livelihood with less violence. Small industry developed and the line of production was rather short. The skill of the craftsman left a mark on the human mind which was much more significant than his tools. In seeking to explain events, individuals transpose these habits of life in their imputation of conduct to the observed facts. Workmanship was now the guiding principle of the rules of interpretation. The realm of natural law settled down. The 'machine' era, in which our author lives, is the fourth and last one. The line of production becomes longer and the task of the worker seems to be unimportant. The habits of thought are again transformed. The productive activities have taught men to step aside when confronted by the size of the machine. The traces of animism and teleology disappear and the preconceptions of the speculative systems become 'matter-of-fact'.

Veblen argues that the problems of his day come from the lag in the adaptation of some spheres of the cultural system to the new habits of life. He thinks especially about the law and the juridical principles which include the rights of free contract and the security of property. The new state of the industrial arts declares them obsolete. In other words, the cultural framework is in some respects schizophrenic. Two types of institutional forces are confronting each other. The logic of technological process, of industrial efficiency, is in opposition to the logic of conservatism towards pecuniary interests.[7]

Thus, the requirements of modern technology cannot tolerate self-help and ownership which act as pure hindrances to the industrial process. From Veblen's point of view, pecuniary gains only disrupt production lines. He has in mind mainly corporate property, 'absentee ownership'. Yet, his analysis applies to any kind of property.[8] In this perspective, 'sabotage' that boils down to 'secure or defend, or to defeat or diminish ; some preferential right or special advantage in respect of income or privilege' (Veblen, [1921] 1965, p. 4), property and 'vested interest', which is a 'marketable right to get something from nothing' (Veblen, [1919] 1946, p. 100), are almost interchangeable terms because they embody the same obstruction.

The 'kept classes' are those classes which try to secure for themselves advantages to the detriment of the community. According to Veblen, it is evidently true for the capitalists but it can also concern the workers. For instance, he qualifies the trade union AFL as 'vested interest' because its policy endeavours to get an increase in wages, an improvement in the conditions of work. This means that, finally, AFL helps to support the existing system and its lack of efficiency. In contrast, Veblen's judgement about IWW, another trade union which is revolutionary, is more positive. In short, the single role of ownership is to express the individual tendencies for emulation and, in the present economic situation, its pecuniary value is a function of the disturbance it can cause to the industry.

Commons summarizes some of Veblen's arguments about 'vested interests'. Property vests interests. In his view, when individuals share the same position regarding ownership of goods, class consciousness emerges. The social classes then appear.[9] The defence or the appropriation of 'vested interests' is the main source of conflict in the community. In spite of that, Commons refuses any clear-cut division. There is no rift between an industrial and a leisure class. For the same reason, although he admits the danger of abuse inherent in the coercive dimension of property, he rejects the radicalism of the theory of exploitation. First, social conflicts need not necessarily lead to an uprising. Furthermore, they do not oppose above all capitalists and workers. According to Commons, Marx has overlooked the conflict between white-collar and blue-collar workers, and the importance of the small property owners, especially the farmers (Commons, [1934] 1990, p. 878).

Concerning property, Veblen and Commons indeed agree to consider that the social tensions it generates are an essential part of economic understanding. However, this does not prevent us from already discerning traces of divergence in their perception of the institutions, and particularly of ownership.

3   TWO WAYS OF INTEGRATING PROPERTY

When Veblen and Commons insist on the social problems that the coercive aspects of ownership are able to generate, their paths diverge. The reason why we can observe such a result comes from the function they ascribe to this coercion. While Veblen considers it as unnecessary, Commons argues it is crucial and positive.

The understanding of this opposition requires a flashback to the origins of human societies (section 3.1). There we can see that, according to Veblen, the relations between men are marked with a kind of harmony when the institution of property is missing. For Commons – the difference is obvious – ownership appears at the same time as humanity, in an atmosphere of conflict. So, it exerts a useful role: it limits the extent of the competition between the members of the community.

Institutions perform a coordination task in Veblen's and Commons' perspectives. But, from the initial distinction that has just been made, it is possible to check that each one tackles the connection between property – and, more generally, the institutions – with coordination in a very specific way (section 3.2). For Commons, coordination is an essential problem because it is never entirely ensured. In the case of excessive coercion, the economic order could even be called into question. Consequently, his investigation focuses on this point.

On the other hand, Veblen assumes the realization of this coordination. The danger is not that coercion can be equivalent to exploitation and then evoke a revolution. It is that the coercion inherent in the existence of ownership leads inevitably to tremendous waste in the economy, to such an extent that there is a genuine threat to cultural survival.

3.1   Back to the Origins

During his career, Veblen's positions evolved. He developed new concepts – 'idle curiosity' for example. It seems that his theory took its final form in *The Instinct of Workmanship* ([1914] 1990).[10] Yet, a constancy is traced as well, underlining the permanence of his views on a subject like property.

It is recurrent, in Veblen's works, that ownership is not an institution present in every social organization. Its rise is related to the barbarian epoch. This means that the preceding era did not know it. In this respect, the 'savagery' may be considered as a 'Golden Age'. In this way and in contrast with the other periods, the historical data about the savage stage are not numerous in Veblen's writings. Such fuzziness lends credence to the belief that, like a myth, the savage culture plays the role of a value standard.

The border between the savage and barbarian epochs is not easy to identify. Veblen tells us of more or less 'naïve' savagery, of 'lower' and 'upper' barbarian periods. The transition seems indeed to have happened progressively between the former, when social cohesion was strong, and the latter, when predatory attitudes spread. What is certain is that, at the beginning of the savage era, the conditions of life were rather hard. That contributed to the reinforcement of solidarity within the community. The primitive instincts of man, especially the 'parental bent' and the 'instinct of workmanship', are on favourable ground.

In those circumstances, an improvement in the conditions of production is observed in the long run. The advancement in the state of the industrial arts explains that men finished by overcoming the harshness of life. The problem is that the appearance of a surplus corrupted the primitive instincts. Predation followed solidarity and 'the instinct of sportsmanship' took the place of the 'instinct of workmanship'.

There is then a kind of paradox: the savage culture contains the forces that will lead to its destruction. In fact, close to the habits of thought that ensure the stability of the cultural framework through a process of self-enforcement, there are forces that threaten these ceremonial practices.[11]

'The beginnings of ownership' (Veblen, [1898] 1934) is only a sketch of the Veblenian definitive system. But, it contributes to our understanding of Veblen's view of human life during the mythical savage era. It allows us to grasp how he dissasociated possession from property. Moreover, this article is interesting because Commons, refers to it in order to explain his position on ownership (Commons [1899–1900] 1965, p. 13 n. 1).[12]

In Veblen's mind, the savage man is 'unsophisticated'. Even if there is strong collective solidarity, he personally uses weapons, clothes and so on.... It is not specific to this historical period, it happens in any human group. What makes him so primitive is that he does not perceive these objects as his property. According to Veblen, ownership requires an external perception of the item (Hegel [1821] 1995, pp. 88–98). This is obviously not the case then: the savage's 'individuality is conceived to cover, somewhat vaguely and uncertainly, a pretty wide fringe of facts and objects that pertain to him more or less immediately' (Veblen, 1934, p. 36). For a man like him, his weapons have the same status as his shadow. This relation is described as 'organic' rather than 'economic'. So, the conversion to individual use implies possession but not property.

Veblen points out that, for a savage, the things which are part of his 'quasi-personal fringe' of facts and the things owned by him do not necessarily coincide. An object may belong to the personality of a man by way of pervasion and may be used by another one. This is true especially for the objects located in the periphery of the personal 'zones of influence'. There is additional evidence that possession during the savage period must not be confused with the institution of ownership.

However, it could be attractive to consider that the modern conception of property derived from savage possession. The idea is that it emerged from its presumed precedent through a progressive development of consciousness. For example, at the end, man would have stopped believing that his weapons belonged to the 'quasi-personal fringe' of facts peculiar to him. He would have slowly understood that these objects were external to him – this being essential for the rise of ownership. Nevertheless, by contrast, the Veblenian theory does not admit any kind of continuity between possession and property.

Veblen argues, indeed, that, even if it has been introduced very gradually into human groups, the institution of ownership shows a real break with the previous institution of 'possession'. To allow such a radical change, ownership had to apply first to an object that could not be easily included in the individual sphere of influence. The captives fulfilled the condition because they were 'distinct from their captor in point of individuality, and so (...) not readily brought in under the quasi-personal fringe' (Veblen, 1934, pp. 46–7). This is why, with the rise of predatory life, the seizure of persons preceded the seizure of goods.

Accordingly, Veblen maintains that the original human communities did not know the institution of property. Savage people were supposed to live in a state of simplicity and kindness. It is only in a second phase called barbarian that ownership appeared. His conclusion is that property is not indispensable to the institutional framework of a peaceful collectivity. Commons, by contrast, denies that there are 'human' characteristics in societies where ownership is missing. In this regard, his analysis of the family is illuminating, given his emphasis on the capture of women. Until the appropriation of women is institutionalized, it is just possible to compare any human group to an animal society.

Of course, questions about the nature of a community where life is simple and naïve – human or animal – do not strictly speaking constitute an economic problem.[13] However, they have entered into the core of the disagreement between Veblen and Commons, for the latter refutes the existence of a human society with no institution of property. He cannot conceive of a 'state of innocence' for human beings because, in his view, humanity appears concomitantly with consciousness.

Commons writes that 'self-consciousness implies not merely feeling, but, especially, knowledge of self. Such knowledge is, however, at the same time knowledge of others and of the world about' (Commons, [1899–1900] 1965, p. 11).

As it has already been said, thanks to their consciousness, men have an external perception of the objects present in their environment. Although the seizure of persons is meaningful in Commons' reflection, it is not a mandatory passage for the beginnings of ownership. The institution of ownership appears everywhere there is scarcity. It concerns the land where there is a scarcity of land, the animals where there is a scarcity of animals, the men where there is a scarcity of men, and so on. It is interesting to note that, while Veblen relates the beginnings of ownership to an evolution in the state of the industrial arts, Commons invokes a human dimension, an increase of the population which is the cause of scarcity (Commons, [1899–1900] 1965, p. 13).

The divergence between Veblen and Commons about the rise of property tells us finally that the former does not see any inevitability of human conflicts in societies, whereas the latter takes the individual antagonisms as his starting point. The opposition between both institutionalists in their analysis of ownership stems from here. And, behind this evidence, it is their conception of the social coordination that is questioned.

3.2   Institutions and Coordination

Commons' point of view about the regulating function of the institutions is summarized in this short passage:

> Individuals begin as babies. They learn the custom of language, of cooperation with other individuals, of working towards common ends, of negotiations to eliminate conflicts of interest, of subordination to the working rules of the many concerns of which they are members. (Commons, [1934] 1990, pp. 73–4)

In fact, he defines them as 'Collective action in control of individual action' (Commons, [1934] 1990, p. 69). He is aware that they embrace a range of phenomena as wide as the language, the family, the business firm and the State. But he is mainly interested in their active dimension, hence his emphasis on the concept of 'going concern'.[14] People are 'Institutionalized minds' but they always keep a space of freedom: their behaviour is not considered as determined.

Through their 'working rules', institutions actually play a coordinating role.[15] They tend to make individual conducts compatible. Nevertheless, they cannot succeed in eradicating social conflicts. They are only able to mitigate them, for there is a serious risk. In the case of bad coordination, the existence of the 'going concern' is even endangered if their members do not feel that they have 'joint expectations'[16] any more. Commons is afraid of the vacuum. Therefore, it is not surprising that the last chapter of his *Institutional Economics* (1934) is principally devoted to fascism and communism, what could happen if the capitalist system did not generate a correct institutional coordination (Commons, [1934] 1990, pp. 876–903).

The active dimension of the institutions and the place of coordination are, in Commons' system, linked to his understanding of the specificity of the social sciences. Unlike the physical or the natural sciences, the data in the social sciences are characterized by 'willingness'.[17] The social stability is fragile and must be constructed at any moment. The question of the compatibility between the individual and the collective interests, as expressed in the definition of the institution itself, includes economic, legal and ethical aspects.[18] To put it very simply, the material constraints (the economy) are not forgotten when men try to find a 'reasonable' social compromise (the law) so that the members of the community will accept it (ethics).

So, Commons does not deny that institutions are also related to external factors, to the environment. All the same, he focuses on their volitional dimension. His perception of property illustrates this logic. Thus, in the *Legal Foundations of Capitalism* (1924), he devotes a great part of his attention to the evolution of its meaning in the work of the courts. It is in no way argued that the decisions of the judges are disconnected from the structure of economic relations. On the contrary, the development of jurisprudence depends on and goes with it.[19] From the interpretation of the fourteenth amendment of the Constitution of the United States by the judicial authorities, Commons writes that the sense given to ownership has progressively changed. The idea of 'exchange-value' has replaced the one of 'use-value' (Commons, [1924] 1959, pp. 11–19). The widening of the scope of the concept of property is even clearer in the conceptual framework he depicts: from 'corporeal property', ownership of goods, to 'incorporeal property', ownership of debts, and to 'intangible property', ownership of 'expected opportunities to make a profit by withholding supply' (Commons, [1934] 1990, p. 5).

Despite the elements peculiar to the economic infrastructure over which the judges have no control,[20] their action is considered as essential. They have to guarantee that the coercion associated with ownership will not be excessive. Their task is not passive. Otherwise, they would have admitted without turning a hair the trend to economic concentration. Now, we know that Commons was reluctant to attribute too much power to the same hands. He thought that monopolies should be regulated.[21] Then, the institution of ownership must be seen in an outlook where there is no inevitability of social order. In this perspective, it plays a role of coordination, but provided that men are careful, it remains within limits.

In the Veblenian analysis, there is neither a problem of orientation of the social process, nor of coordination, because there are self-enforcing mechanisms ensuring social stability. In other words, men are conditioned so that no conflict jeopardizes the organization of the economy. The compatibility between individual conducts is already stated by the cultural complex. This feeling of human passivity is a result of Veblen's definition of institutions as habits of thought and of life. They embody all the inertia that human behaviour can integrate. Their coordinating function is then performed *a priori*. Moreover, the social process is supposed to be 'blind'. For all these reasons, we can understand why Veblen despises the juridical discipline: it is only an external and rigid stratum.[22]

According to Veblen, there are two kinds of cultural model. The relationship between the members of the community may be either peaceful, as during the savage era, or conflictual, as in the modern capitalist epoch. Property is a central institution belonging to the second model. But, in any case, even in the antagonistic configuration, a coordination between the individuals' actions is presumed. People are subject to habituation. They are accustomed to follow some rules of behaviour in such a way that their conducts, although resulting from opposing interests, will not bring about social confusion.

The drawback specific to the conflictual model, the risk of cultural collapse, is not then relative to a lack of coordination (Veblen, [1914] 1990, p. 24–5). Its problem arises from the waste it encourages. In the capitalist economy, the 'instinct of workmanship' and the 'parental bent' are likewise neutralized. Industrial efficiency is diminished. Veblen identifies numerous reasons for the 'sabotage' of production.[23] Yet, we have to remember here that, in his thinking, the institution of property crystallizes the responsibility of these wastes. Thus, if its existence is not inevitable – the model with strong solidarity and without ownership is an alternative – its disappearance is a condition for the recovery of productive efficiency.

Veblen's position on the fate of capitalist regulation is marked by some doubts.[24] Meanwhile, one point poses no problems. Its hypothetical aim in the direction of abandonment of the spirit of competition was not really supposed to spring from the action of men frustrated by their poverty. The change was to be derived from a technological revolution. In the vanguard of the movement were to be found the industrial experts, that is the engineers.[25] After all, the exit from capitalist logic was to arise from the discipline of the machine. Under its sway, in the modern era, the mentality of the working population, especially the engineers among them, was to be transformed. Their habits of thought were to become impersonal, 'matter-of-fact'. Hence, a consciousness of the industrial wastes.[26] So, in Veblen's mind, the main shortcoming associated with property and coercion is not exploitation, but inefficiency in the process of production.[27]

4   CONCLUSION

Veblen rejects the spontaneous character of the compatibility between individual and collective interests. He thinks that individualist inclinations cause awful disturbances at a social level. In other words, the 'invisible hand' turns out to be rather 'bloodstained'. In order to prevent an economic collapse, the technologists must replace the businessmen at the head of the economy.

Commons defends a more moderate opinion. He says that private corporations 'have made possible the present marvellous development of industry' (Commons, [1894] 1967, p. 126). In this case, the argument is that collective control is only necessary in order to avoid individual rationales generating harmful effects on society, as if a kind of 'visible hand' was required to help the famous 'invisible hand'.

Moreover, Veblen's and Commons' analyses on the institution of private property finally shed new light on the intensity of their respective reserves concerning an economy based on *laissez-faire*. Commons insists on the coordinating function of ownership. Like Veblen, he thinks that property has a coercive dimension. But, unlike him, he admits its inevitability. And if he suspects the danger of a drift towards exploitation, he also considers that it is possible to set up mechanisms to control this coercion. So, capitalism remains, despite all its imperfections, a valuable system when its abuses are corrected. Veblen's so-called radicalism may be connected to his absolute rejection of ownership. In his theory, this institution is associated with industrial waste, not with exploitation. If we can imagine, as Commons does, a system of a balance of power where the central problem is expressed in terms of domination, there is no such counterweight in his case of 'sabotage'. To make a parallel with Commons, nothing like a 'balance of waste' is conceivable.

Through the debate on the harmony between collective and individual interests with its implications for economic policy, it is finally the connection between law and economics that is questioned. Here again, Commons and Veblen do not agree perfectly. In Commons' view, since it is neither necessary nor impossible that social and personal interests are compatible, the fundamental issue is to succeed in coordinating them. Law must oppose the centrifugal individualistic tendencies of economic behaviour. Commons' key word is not 'efficiency' but 'reasonableness'.

It is true that Veblen concentrates on efficiency. But it is not the same concept as is generally used by economists. More than this, his industrial efficiency is contradictory to economic efficiency. As a matter of fact, a system without industrial waste requires the disappearance of individualist inclinations. Law and economics that are supposed to deal with them are only interesting in a cultural scheme that is much more global.

Therefore, it is clear that, according to Veblen's and Commons' positions, connection does not mean annexation of law by economics, or more precisely by economic efficiency. The result of their multidisciplinary approach is not a transformation and an adaptation of what is law to the economic logic but an original analysis that calls into question traditional economics itself.

NOTES

1. Hence, Kennedy's accusation against Commons relating to his 'conservatism' (Kennedy, 1962, pp. 29–42). See Harter's reply (Harter 1963, pp. 226–32).
2. Kirat studies this point thoroughly (Kirat 1998, pp. 1057–1087).
3. See Veblen, [1904] 1978, pp. 71–2 and Commons, [1934] 1990, pp. 30–40.
4. It has been said that Marx was 'the last of the classics'. In a sense, the institutionalists – especially Veblen – share this opinion. Veblen accuses Marx of being under the sway of the idea of natural rights. That is, even though his theory of exploitation is critical of 'sanitized' aspects of the classical views concerning ownership, and he locates this institution directly in a social perspective, yet he admits this natural relation between men and the product of their labour when he argues that they are illegitimately deprived of it (Veblen, [1919] 1990, pp. 411–13).
5. Dowd emphasizes how basic this point is in Veblen's construction (Dowd, 1964, pp. 6–7, 12–13).
6. About phenomena like 'self-enforcement' and 'lock-in', see Hodgson 1992, pp. 292–3. In his treatment of institutional dynamics, Corei also quotes this excellent paper (Corei, 1995, pp. 22–3).
7. Ayres and his followers have developed their theory around this dichotomy between what they called 'instrumental' and 'ceremonial' institutions. For a good synthesis of their stream of thought, see Bush 1987, pp. 1075–116.
8. It must just be added that Veblen is more indulgent towards the institution of ownership in the handicraft era. It is also associated then to a stimulation of the industrial bent that had disappeared during the barbarian epoch. The appropriation of the means of production does not penalize the community too much compared to the machine era.
9. See Commons, [1899–1900] 1965, pp. 46–7 and [1924] 1959, p. 248. Gonce has already noticed this point (Gonce, 1971, p. 84).
10. Of all his books, this was the one he preferred (Dorfman, [1934] 1972, p. 324).
11. Veblen resorts to this type of argumentation to study a way out of the capitalist system (see, for instance, Veblen, [1921] 1965).
12. Rather strangely, because of his deep disagreement with Veblen, he writes that this work is 'original and discerning'.
13. Moreover, Veblen and Commons did not inaugurate the debate. Strauss reminds us that the Greek classics had already confronted each other about the virtual humanity of the 'state of innocence' (Strauss, [1989] 1993, p. 232).
14. See his definition of the 'going concern'. Commons mentions the idea of 'joint expectation' (Commons, [1934] 1990, p. 58).
15. For further developments on this coordinating function, see my PhD dissertation (Broda, 1996).
16. 'A going concern exists only as long there are expectations' (Commons, [1934] 1990, p. 620).
17. Gruchy's comments about that point are very explicit (Gruchy, 1940, pp. 825–33).
18. Commons' unit of analysis, the 'transaction', proves it (see, for instance, Commons 1935, p. 124–44).
19. Through the experimental methods of reasoning of 'exclusion and inclusion' (Commons, [1934] 1990, pp. 715–17).

20. According to Commons, capitalism has undergone three stages: a 'merchant' one, an 'employer' one and a 'banker' one.
21. Harter gives a very good account of Commons' cautiousness towards monopolies (Harter, 1962, pp. 213–18).
22. See, for example, Veblen, [1919] 1946, pp. 17–34.
23. Mainly in Veblen, [1921] 1965, chapter V.
24. For a summary, see Rutherford, 1984, pp. 341–3.
25. Veblen even proposed the foundation of a 'Soviet of Technicians' (Veblen, [1921] 1965, chapter VI).
26. The last chapter of *The Theory of Business Enterprise* (1904), headed 'The Cultural Incidence of the Machine Process', is striking in this regard (Veblen, [1904] 1978, pp. 302–400).
27. Tilman defends the opposite view since he asserts that Veblen's writings about the central function played by the engineers do not reflect the real nature of his views. He thinks they express a 'despair' and a 'satirical intent' (Tilman 1989, p. 15), as if Veblen was finally exposing in a curious manner a theory of exploitation. My objection is that Tilman's attitude does not seem to be very 'matter-of-fact'. Am I right Mr. Veblen?

REFERENCES

Broda, Philippe (1996), 'Marché et institutions chez les institutionnalistes américains', University of Paris I: PhD Dissertation.

Bush, Paul D. (1987), 'Theory of institutional change', *Journal of Economic Issues*, September: 1075–116.

Commons, John R. (1894), *Social Reform and the Church*, New York: Kelley, 1967.

Commons, John R. (1899–1900), *A Sociological View of the Sovereignty*, New York: Kelley, 1965.

Commons, John R. (1924), *Legal Foundations of Capitalism*, Madison: University of Wisconsin Press, 1959.

Commons, John R. (1934), *Institutional Economics, its Place in Political Economy*, New Brunswick and London: Transaction, 1990.

Commons, John. R. (1935), 'The problem of correlating law, economics and ethics', in *Mélanges Geny*, Paris: Sirey, pp. 124–44.

Corei, Thorstein (1995), *L'Economie institutionnaliste. Les fondateurs*, Paris: Economica.

Dorfman, Joseph (1934), *Thorstein Veblen and his America*, Clifton: Kelley, 1972.

Dowd Douglas F. (1964), *Thorstein Veblen*, New York: Washington Square Press.

Gonce, Richard A. (1971), 'John R. Commons's legal economic theory', *Journal of Economic Issues*, September: 80–95.

Gruchy, Allan G. (1940), 'John R. Commons' concept of twentieth-century economics', *Journal of Political Economy*, **48**: 823–49.

Harter Jr. and G. Lafayette (1962), *John R. Commons: his assault on laissez-faire*, Oregon State: Corvallis.

Harter (Jr.) and G. Lafayette (1963), 'John R. Commons, conservative or liberal', *Western Economic Journal*, Summer: 226–32.

Hegel, Friedrich G.W. (1821), *Principes de la philosophie du droit*, Paris: Tel Gallimard, 1995.

Hodgson, Geoffrey M. (1992), 'Thorstein Veblen and the post-Darwinian Economics', *Cambridge Journal of Economics*, September: 285–301.

Kennedy, William F. (1962), 'John R. Commons, conservative reformer', *Western Economic Journal*, Autumn: 29–42.

Kirat, Thierry (1998), 'De l'analyse économique du droit à de nouvelles alliances', *Revue Economique*, **49** (4): 1057–87.

Rutherford, Malcolm (1984), 'Thorstein Veblen and the processes of institutional change', *History of Political Economy*, **16** (3): 331–48.

Samuels, Warren J. (1989), 'Austrian and Institutional economics: some common elements', *Research in the History of Economic Thought and Methodology*, **6**: 53–71.

Strauss, Leo (1989), *La Renaissance du rationalisme politique classique [The rebirth of classical political rationalism]*, Paris: NRF Gallimard, 1993.

Tilman, Rick (1989), 'John R. Commons as a critic of Thorstein Veblen', communication presented at the *Western Social Conference*, Albuquerque, 27–30 April: 1–26.

Veblen, Thorstein (1899), *Théorie de la classe de loisir [The Theory of the Leisure Class]*, Paris: Gallimard, 1978.

Veblen, Thorstein (1904), *The Theory of Business Enterprise*, New Brunswick: Transaction, 1978.

Veblen, Thorstein (1914), *The Instinct of Workmanship and the State of the Industrial Arts*, New Brunswick and London: Transaction, 1990.

Veblen, Thorstein (1919), *The Place of Science in Modern Civilization and Other Essays*, New Brunswick and London: Transaction, 1990.

Veblen, Thorstein (1919), *The Vested Interests and the Common Man*, New York: Viking Press, 1946.

Veblen, Thorstein (1921), *The Engineers and the Price System*, New York: Kelley, 1965.

Veblen, Thorstein (1934), 'The Beginnings of Ownership' in L. Ardzrooni (ed.), *Essays in our Changing Order*, New York: Viking Press.

6. Competition, competitive selection and economic evolution

John Foster

1 INTRODUCTION

We live in an era in which there has been rising support for policies that increase the exposure of both individuals and organizations to an ill-defined notion called 'competition'. It is now routine to hear, in a range of settings, how more exposure to this intangible force leads to increased efficiency, favourable adaptations of products and processes, and enhanced economic welfare for all. Should there be, along the way, some transitional suffering, committed believers are inclined to argue, in Panglossian terms, that it is justified. Correspondingly, egalitarian concerns for equity are increasingly downplayed and the twin evils of working poverty and unemployment are tolerated to an extent unthinkable thirty years ago.

Proponents of 'competition' argue that the pursuit of individual self-interest must be promoted and there is an associated acceptance that a 'healthy', evolving society must involve the competitive selection of 'winners' and 'losers'. Although such a view is often expressed in the context of economic policy, it becomes apparent that its supporters are upholding something much wider – a 'world view' based upon a 'survival of the fittest' analogy drawn from evolutionary biology. In parallel, there has been an upsurge in interest in evolutionary approaches to economics that, in the main, are built upon competitive selection mechanisms. Some evolutionary economists deny any connection between their work and policies based upon competitive selection thinking, preferring to associate these only with well-known economic liberals: 'In contrast to the theories of Spencer in the nineteenth century, and Friedman, Hayek and Williamson in the twentieth, an evolutionary paradigm is not the basis for the policy outlook of Dr Pangloss' (Hodgson, 1993 p. 259).

In this chapter, it is contended that such a stance is too simplistic, born of a lack of clarity as to what is meant by 'competition' and from the inappropriate use of biological analogies to understand evolutionary economic processes. In section 2, the concept of competition applied by economic policymakers will be

107

discussed. The shifting perception of competition in economics will be examined in section 3. Section 4 looks at the development of evolutionary thinking in economics, with particular reference to biological analogies concerning competitive selection. In section 5, suggestions are made as to how competitive selection and economic self-organization might be integrated into a unified treatment of economic evolution. Section 6 contains some concluding comments.

2   COMPETITION AND ECONOMIC POLICY

> Competition policy is not about the pursuit of competition *per se*. Rather it seeks to facilitate effective competition to promote efficiency and economic growth, while accommodating situations where competition does not achieve efficiency or conflicts with other social objectives. (Commonwealth of Australia 1993, p. xvi)

This statement, contained in a highly influential Australian report concerning competition policy, is typical of those we see in the formulation of competition policy. Nowhere is 'competition' adequately defined nor is any theory of the competitive process offered or referred to. Thus, an undefined term concerning an unexplained process has played a central role in policy formulation in Australia, and similar examples can be found in other OECD countries. The reduction of protection, privatization, deregulation and the removal of various subsidies have all been common in resultant policy packages and, in Eastern Europe, a massive withdrawal of government from the economic system has also been enacted rapidly in the name of 'competition'.

When pushed for an explanation as to what 'competition' is, both economists and non-economists alike tend to resort to analogy: something about the 'survival of the fittest' – a biological analogy concerning competitive selection. However, amongst economists, this was not always so. Back in the 1950s most economists would, in all probability, have offered, not a biological analogy, but actual industrial examples, explaining why it was difficult to apply simplistic analogies to complex processes that involve interactions between both individuals and organizations, such as firms. Often, it would be concluded that it was necessary for government to intervene in some way to ensure that beneficial economic coordination would be the end result.[1]

By the mid-1980s, the New Right, with a neo-Spencerian political philosophy, had ensured that the biological analogy of competitive selection became central to the economic policy of the Thatcher government in the UK. However, even in countries with socialist governments, such as Australia and New Zealand, it was no longer very controversial to assert that more 'survival of the fittest' competition was necessary in ailing industries. Many socialists, long nurtured upon a Keynesian view of the economy and, therefore, one that is almost exclusively preoccupied by demand-side considerations, had little idea of how supply-side processes operated. It was something to do with the degree of 'competition' that prevailed: economists had ensured that the notion of 'perfect competition' had become well-established in socialist thinking concerning market failure, and 'imperfect competition' became widely accepted as a better characterization of the supply-sides of real economies in the 1980s. The work of Michael Kalecki, which became increasingly influential on the political left in the 1980s as a distributionally based macroeconomic model with an explicit supply-side, also stressed that the degree of 'competition' was crucial.

However, these conceptualizations are static and equilibrium in character and, as such, could not deal with the process of competition but, rather, alternative market structures that might or might not be the outcome of some unspecified competitive process. This theoretical vacuum was filled increasingly, not with new 'theories of process' or careful discussion of case studies, but with biological analogies concerning competitive selection. Disaffected socialists were particularly vulnerable to a fundamental change of heart concerning the cooperative possibilities of human beings after the failures of collectivism. After all, if your view of the world centres upon conflict between classes and you then decide that solidarity does not exist, what is left but a Hobbesian competitive struggle between individuals?

Despite the fact that those on both the right and the left of politics became free and easy in the application of competitive biological analogy, mainstream economists, to their credit, tended to be much more careful in their use of the term 'competition' in the context of policy advice. Because of their moderating influence, many of the new policies implemented simply involved the removal of unwarranted economic rents accruing to groups, which were able to exercise power, either through the political process or the market. More 'competition' was just less 'exploitation'. However, economists did not always get their way and, particularly in the UK, policies were enacted that did not accord with the principles of neoclassical economics. For example, privatization was sometimes implemented in such a way that monopoly power was bestowed on economic organizations and tax reform did not always act upon marginal economic incentives, yielding large windfall gains to the already rich at the expense of the poor. The British case is instructive because it offers a reminder that traditional political agendas, serving established interest groups, can often be more important than economics in economic policymaking. This danger had been anticipated as far back as 1947 by Friedrich von Hayek:

> There is some justification in the taunt that many of the pretending defenders of 'free enterprise' are in fact defenders of privileges and advocates of government activity in their favour rather than opponents of all privilege. There is no hope of a return to a freer system until the leaders of the movement against state control are prepared to

impose upon themselves that discipline of a competitive market which they ask the masses to accept. (Hayek quoted in Cockett, 1995 pp. 111–12)

Of course, those implementing the new economic policies used the writings of economic liberals, such as Friedrich von Hayek and Milton Friedman, to justify their actions. However, close scrutiny of the writings of both soon reveals inconsistencies and contradictions. For example, Hayek did not see competition primarily as a competitive struggle:[2]

Competition is essentially a process of the formation of opinion: by spreading information, it creates that unity and coherence of the economic system, which we presuppose when we think of it as one market. It creates the views people have about what is best and cheapest, and it is because of it that people know at least as much about possibilities and opportunities as they in fact do. (von Hayek, 1948 p. 106)

Also, Friedman did not concur with neo-Spencerians that trade unions had the power to cause wage inflation and, as a monetarist, he continued to see a role for government to intervene in the economy to stabilize nominal income growth using monetary means. However, he did resort to the use of biological analogy in order to argue that the neoclassical general equilibrium model with profit maximization can be viewed as a valid 'as if' construct. It could be viewed as the logical outcome of a competitive selection process that weeds out non-profit maximizers.

These difficulties and confusions arise, first, because of a lack of clarity as to what is meant by competition and, second, because biological analogies are employed without careful consideration as to their role and validity in economic settings. Thus, it is comparatively easy for politicians to establish superficial connections between political philosophy and economic liberalism and then to use the ideas of economists to provide intellectual support for a political agenda to which the latter only subscribe in a limited sense.

3   PERCEPTIONS OF COMPETITION IN ECONOMICS

The rise of the view that economies should be more 'competitive' gained most strength in the 1980s, as the decline and fall of many communist regimes stemmed the flow of propaganda promoting collectivism. There was a parallel loss of trust in the competences and motivations of politicians and government officials in many social democracies. Of course, to the mainstream economist, the idea that 'competition' should be encouraged was not new – for decades, economists had used the 'competitive' general equilibrium model to promote the idea that 'perfect competition' yields maximum economic well-being. The problem was that such an abstract representation of the economic system says nothing at all about the process of competition but, instead, represents an idealized equilibrium state of perfect coordination at an appropriate set of prices.

Those interested in inquiring into the actual workings of the competitive process, such as Kirzner (1973) and Loasby (1991), have pointed out that the 'competitive' general equilibrium model was, in fact, used as a model to aid government intervention in the economy. Fifty years ago, it was regarded as a guide for planners in communist countries or as an inspiration for government intervention in mixed economies to correct for 'market failures'. The absence of any identifiable competitive process in the 'competitive' general equilibrium model was stressed by Friedrich von Hayek as long ago as 1948 to a seemingly uninterested community of economists and policymakers:

> ...it seems as if economists by this peculiar use of language were deceiving themselves into a belief that, in discussing 'competition' they are saying something about the nature and significance of the process, by which the state of affairs is brought about, that they merely assume to exist. In fact, this moving force of economic life is almost altogether undiscussed. (von Hayek, 1948, p. 93)

By 1968, nothing seemed to have changed: 'There is probably no concept in all of economics that is at once more fundamental or pervasive, yet less satisfactorily developed, than the concept of competition' (McNulty, 1968, p. 639).

Use of the 'competitive' general equilibrium model to motivate intervention in the economy enabled economists to avoid the difficulties involved in confronting the meaning of competition in actual historical processes. Important processes, such as the rise and fall of productive organizations, technological and organizational change and the emergence of institutions could be set to one side. The price system in the 'competitive' general equilibrium model, far from being represented in evolutionary terms, expresses the idea that the economic system is fundamentally different from biological systems. It is the outcome of rational human behaviour within a fixed structure of rules that operates in a manner analogous to a Newtonian system in physics. Thus, we see little use of 'survival of the fittest' imagery by influential economists or policymakers in the early postwar period. Economic development was viewed as centring on government intervention to prevent instability, through discretionary fiscal policy, and to promote growth, through the provision of infrastructure, education and subsidies to stimulate private investment. Thus was forged a benign compromise between the Smithian ideal of an economy full of interacting individuals willing to pursue their self-interest in producing, exchanging and contracting and the Keynesian ideal of an 'ethically-correct' government, intervening to undertake those aspects of economic coordination that are deemed to be outside the scope of market forces. A formal, timeless, theoretical system was offered which had enormous analytical versatility but no connection whatsoever to the historical processes taking place in real economies. Through the 1950s and the 1960s, competition began to be widely discussed in these terms and inquiries into the detailed workings of competitive processes were increasingly regarded as a secondary consideration. Even governmental bodies, such as the Monopolies Commission in the UK, vested with the task of protecting society from the ravages of organizations exploiting a monopoly position or engaging in restrictive practices, shifted away from a 'case by case' approach towards general principles concerning the distance of the case from the ideal state of perfect competition.

Many economists in the 1950s who had set about building up an analytical understanding of the organization and evolution of industry from Marshallian principles, such as Penrose (1952) and Richardson (1960), found, to their dismay, that they were accused of using 'bad' theory (i.e. 'partial' rather than 'general' equilibrium theory) and inadequate representations of competition and markets. Significantly, both rejected biological analogy as a useful basis for understanding such processes. By the early 1970s, Richardson (1972) would publish an intemperate article, which signalled the beginning of his eventual withdrawal from academic life. In it, he stressed that vertical cooperation in industry led to most innovative developments and, thus, diminished the relevance of horizontal competition between firms. The exception was very homogenous products where there existed numerous firms with vertical market linkages but little profit or stability to allow them to innovate. The accumulated wisdom of George Richardson and many other economists concerning such processes was increasingly ignored in the 1960s. The outcome was predictable: policy mistakes and policies that favoured interest groups. When the target was held to be a state of perfect competition, which could never exist in the historical dimension, a *carte blanche* was provided for virtually any kind of policy.

Through this period, accumulated knowledge concerning the processes of competition and cooperation in industry was eroded in favour of a theory of 'competitive' outcomes that could never eventuate. As real economies evolved, continual analytical revision had to be undertaken to obtain an approximate match between the chosen formal model and new circumstances. This was not too difficult because the model was timeless and, thus, capable of infinite variation. From the early 1970s onwards, OECD economies ran into economic difficulties in the form of simultaneous rises in inflation and unemployment. Political philosophies of both the right and left of politics began to take a stronger hold upon economic policymaking. Economists responded appropriately, first of all designing ill-fated prices and incomes policies then, later, offering advice as to how the supply-side of the economy could be liberalized. Economic liberalism was, of course, very appealing to economists. What economist would object to the proposition that markets should be more extensive? Keynesianism had already been cast by the mainstream in terms of market failure, and government had not succeeded in compensating for such failure, so why not simply get the market to work better?

As had been the case in the past, neoclassical economists could revise their infinitely adaptable 'competitive' general equilibrium model to suit the times. It became a vehicle for arguing that governments should not intervene to stabilize the economy or to lead economic development, but should only intervene in ways that could facilitate the improved competitive functioning of the market, through the removal of subsidies, deregulation and privatization. The general equilibrium model mutated from a planning model to one that could characterize the outcomes in real economies where the forces of competitive selection were released. This was an idea that was wholly inappropriate in the days of planning and the Smith–Keynes consensus, but it is now a convenient fiction to argue that government intervention got in the way of economic evolution. Thus, neoclassical economists did not, in the main, resist the takeover of political philosophy in the field of economic policy but, rather, attempted to tailor their core theoretical model to be consistent with it.

Despite the adaptation of the 'competitive' general equilibrium model to the new political climate, it remained an inadequate expression of the competitive process. At base, the model is an expression of the Smithian ideal concerning the benefits to be had from a system where self-interested people are willing to engage in trade and contract with each other within an over-arching system of collectively upheld ethics. As ubiquitous as ever, economists thinking in terms of 'competitive' general equilibrium began to imagine that such an equilibrium could be seen as the outcome of a continual process of competitive selection, following the old suggestion of Friedman (1953), raised in a quite different methodological context. Decades of familiarity with their model had led neo-classical economists to forget its fundamental Smithian construction. It is an ideal representation of a trading and contracting system which, in reality, has never been approximated. More importantly, improvements in the functioning of markets, which could, in some sense, be seen as a move towards the ideal, have been hard won over decades of institutional change. In the Smithian model, market activity evolves, not through the operation of 'competition' but through a process of self-organization that involves the emergent cooperation of parties involved and ratification, through regulation and the rule of law, by governing authorities. In classical political economy, this emergent process was regarded by many as the key aspect of capitalist progress.

In modern times, this classical tradition has been kept alive by the Austrian School, whose members have always tended to be unimpressed by biological analogies concerning competitive selection:

> What elevates man above all other animals is the cognition that peaceful cooperation under the principle of the division of labour is a better method to preserve life and to

remove felt uneasiness than indulging in pitiless biological competition for a share
in the scarce means of subsistence provided by nature. (Mises, 1978, p. 97)

The Austrian view of competition can be viewed as a development of Adam
Smith's thinking. Morgan (1993) has pointed out that he used the term 'free
competition' to refer to a condition where people have rights to trade and
contract with each other, denied to them in the mercantilist era. He also used
the term 'competition' to cover a condition where there exists a state of excess
demand or supply in a market that has to be resolved by buyers and sellers.[3] So
there appears to be a dilemma: on the one hand, neoclassical economists are
good Smithians with regard to statics but, on the other, they envisage the
existence of a process of competitive selection that cannot be inferred from
their theorizing and that is alien to Smith's view of economic development. In
contrast, Austrians uphold the Smithian tradition, yet Hayek is the favourite
economist of the New Right, a movement which believes that competitive
selection is a vital feature of both societies and their constituent economies.
This really raises two issues: first, what is the political economy of the
interaction between economics and political philosophy and, second, what
constitutes economic evolution?

4   EVOLUTIONARY THINKING IN ECONOMICS

Up until the middle of the 19th century, the evolution of the economic system
was mainly thought of as a development process involving synergies between
individuals and between organizations of individuals. By the late 19th century
the view that economic evolution was driven by competitive struggle began to
spread. There is little doubt that it was the publication of Darwin's *The Origin
of the Species* that stimulated this shift, although it was through Herbert Spencer
and Karl Marx, with their very different depictions of competitive struggle in
the social sphere, that made the greatest impact upon political economists.

Despite the static depictions of the Smithian system in modern neoclassical
economics, there is little doubt that Smith offered a depiction of a process that
was evolutionary in character.[4] However, it was a process that was seen as pre-
dominantly concerned with synergies. He emphasized the inherent tendency
for people to 'truck and barter' and to enter into commercial contracts, provided
that appropriate institutions existed and were cultivated to facilitate such
economic cooperation. This was a revolutionary idea in its time and one which,
through the introduction of laws to protect from exploitation those who engaged
in trade and contracting, provided a fundamental force for the development and
refinement of capitalism in the 19th and 20th centuries.

Adam Smith's famous example of the pin factory and the division of labour provided a lasting and vivid depiction of how synergies occur in the economic system, yielding increased complexity, increased organization and increased productivity. This was not a description of the 'market' working; neither was it simply 'economies of scale' at work. It involved the interaction of organizational and technological innovations catalysed by the existence of an entrepreneur. The self-organization of the economy depended upon the anchor of a structure of ethics yielded by the socio-cultural system; otherwise it would be very difficult for self-interested producers to engage in any trade or contracting at all. Much of capitalist development in the 19th century centred upon the translation of prevailing ethics into a system of contractual law which could enable the system of trading and contracting to become more complex. Such law was not introduced as an initiative of governments, which tended to represent established interests, but through pressure from those engaged in commerce. By the end of the 19th century, the stress on the synergies available through the promotion of economic liberty, in an appropriate ethical and legal climate, remained strong in the classical tradition.

Alfred Marshall, one of the acknowledged founders of neoclassical economics, maintained Smith's view and consequently confined use of his 'mechanical analogy' to short periods when 'statical' assumptions could only hold approximately. By Marshall's time, the institutions of capitalism had developed to such an extent, along with improvements in the storage and transmission of information, that the operation of markets had become much more important in eliminating gluts and shortages in systematic ways. Capitalism had developed markets in certain commodities that acted as homoeostatic mechanisms and provided valuable information to suppliers and demanders. It was necessary to provide an analytical framework within which these could be understood. However, Marshall steadfastly rejected the notion that the Newtonian mechanical analogy that he applied in the short period could be used to understand economic development in the long period – he continued to see the development of capitalism, as Smith had, as an evolutionary process, centred upon synergies, made possible by the existence of a compatible ethical system. Marshall considered the use of biological analogy, but was never comfortable enough with Darwinian (or more, accurately, Spencerian) depictions of competitive selection. In Foster (1993), it is argued that his intuitions were strongly self-organizational in character, keeping him solidly in the Smithian synergies tradition.[5]

Marshall's speculations concerning biological analogy reflected a rise in interest in them by political economists in the late 19th century, particularly in the United States. The interest of Veblen (1898) in such analogies is well known. What is less well understood is that Thorstein Veblen was one example in a group at that time who sought to understand the nature of 'competition' in the economic system in the late 19th century, when rivalry between firms in the United States reached unprecedented levels, along with a parallel rise of cooperation in the form of the rapid concentration of firms into monopolies. Morgan (1993) examines the definitions of competition of five economists – Veblen, Hadley, Ely, Clark (J.B.) and Sumner. She discovers a bewildering array of definitions but concludes that this is due to the fact that the process of change going on was quite different from the past. She notes that all of the economists examined felt compelled to use, in some sense, the Darwinian biological analogy to deal with the rapid transition which took place.

Thus, thinking of economic evolution as a Darwinian struggle became firmly fixed in the American psyche and was perpetuated in economics in the American institutionalist tradition that remained a powerful force until the Second World War. Neoclassical economics was firmly rejected by institutionalists in preference for an emphasis on power relations. However, as the 20th century unfolded, organized market activity continued to increase as the institutions created to encourage and protect it were strengthened. Gradually neoclassical economics came to prosper and institutionalist approaches went into decline. Neoclassical economics was either Marshallian and concerned with the operation of the price mechanism in practical, short period settings or, following Leon Walras, preoccupied with the elegant, welfare maximizing properties of an ideal theoretical system of general equilibrium. In both, competitive struggle of the Marxist or Veblenian type was downplayed.

However, after Marshall's death, neoclassical economists began to equate general equilibrium theory, not with utopia, but with the actual state that market systems tended towards in the long period if they were competitive. The corollary was that such a tendency was only held back by the presence of 'imperfect competition'. Ideological considerations demanded that the myth of the perfect price system had to be linked, explicitly, with actual capitalist economies in the West. By the 1940s, neoclassical economists were coming under increasing pressure to present a general equilibrium model which, as Oskar Lange pointed out, looked more like a device to guide 'shadow price' central planning than a description of a competitive economy. Being entirely static, the model was unconvincing as a depiction of the capitalist system – it dealt with the theoretical outcomes of competition but said nothing about the process of competition.

After the Second World War, neo-Darwinism swept through the biological sciences and, in the form of analogy, began to enter the social sciences and the humanities. Alchian (1950) was one of the first to see how neo-Darwinian analogy could help to justify the use of neoclassical general equilibrium economics to determine the outcome of unobservable economic processes. He argued that a high level of Darwinian style competitive selection amongst firms would lead to the most efficient surviving. The latter did not optimize but competitive selection ensured that the best of all possible worlds would prevail in an efficiency sense. However, Alchian stressed that the outcome of such a process would not necessarily match the general equilibrium solution:

> What really counts is the various actions actually tried, for it is from these that 'success' is selected, not from some set of perfect actions. The economist may be pushing his luck too far in arguing that actions in response to changes in environment and changes in satisfaction with the existing state of affairs will converge as a result of adaptation or adoption toward the optimum action that should have been selected, if foresight had been perfect. (Alchian, 1950, p. 220)

However, if the most efficient *was* a profit maximizer in the traditional neo-classical sense and the level of knowledge was high enough for imitation to spread rapidly, then a close correspondence with GE theory could be made. Alchian knew that this raised empirical questions and that there was little evidence to support the notion that such a conjunction between competitive selection and general equilibrium theorizing could be made. Nonetheless, over four decades later he was bolder: 'Competitive trial and error will evolve toward the fittest – whom economists characterise as profit maximisers' (Alchian, 1996, p. 520).

Alchian's approach ultimately proved to be significant because it constituted the first use of an analogy drawn from the R.A. Fisher-inspired neo-Darwinism that was sweeping biology at the time: 'in college, I had a course in biology which was all Darwin and evolution. Finally, at the graduate level, I was fortunate to have worked with Professor Wallis, who introduced me to R.A. Fisher's *Statistical Methods for Biological Research*' (Alchian, 1996, p. 522). In drawing such an analogy, Alchian provided a new perspective on static general equilibrium: the possibility now arose that such an equilibrium could be the outcome of an unobserved historical process of competitive selection.

In a world of now highly developed contractual law and sophisticated markets, the synergies that Smith fought to promote were gradually taken for granted and the stress was increasingly on selective competition. This emerging perspective had little impact in the 1950s, when social democracy was spreading and state welfare and stabilization programmes were being set up. However, the creative, developmental dimension of the classical tradition was gradually de-emphasized. Economic expansion came to be seen, not as due to synergies, but rather exogenous factors, such as technical change which, significantly, was likened to 'manna from Heaven'. This approach was manifested in the neo-classical growth model that was devised in the 1950s and the 1960s. In the microeconomics, which underlay neoclassical growth theory, there arose a 'supply side' concern to encourage competition at all costs. Ethical concerns were dismissed as 'normative' and firms, eliminated because of deregulation and microeconomic reform, deserved their fate.

By the 1980s, many economic theorists accepted the notion that perfect competition was an unacceptable component of their idealization: in a long run characterized by economies of scale, imperfect competition must prevail. Paradoxically, the preoccupation with imperfect competition led to a greater concern with the actual mechanics of competition than was ever evident in the 'competitive' general equilibrium theory. Game theory became the vehicle for analysis, resulting in a body of theory which was no longer centred around a simple static idealization but upon a complex tangle of situation-specific deductions linked, increasingly, to the parallel game theoretical developments of, for example, Maynard Smith (1983), in evolutionary biology.[6] Gradually, evolutionary game theory in economics began to take on a strong resemblance to neo-Darwinian evolutionary biology.

Selection mechanism analogies, drawn from evolutionary biology, contain presumptions concerning the survival of atomistic units, usually genomes, through competition at a phenotypical level. Thus, the evolution of a species can be reduced to the replicative success of genomes. Through the competition of phenotypes, genomes maximize fitness and minimize the generation of adverse mutations. One of the most extreme, but well-known, modern presentations of this type of genetic theory is to be found in Richard Dawkins' *The Selfish Gene* (1976). Dawkins conceives of competitive selection as operative further down than the genome, at the level of the gene. Thus, Dawkins takes neo-Darwinist reductionism down to a level where Lamarkian and other types of evolutionary theories cannot be sustained. Unlike Dawkins, most modern neo-Darwinian biologists stay at the level of the genome in their reductionist accounts of competitive selection. However, in principle, they share the same individualist ontology as Dawkins. For an economist, the striking feature of neo-Darwinist reductionism is its remarkable similarity with neoclassical economics. The Dawkins version stresses the anthropomorphism involved, given that selfishness is a concept that relates to behaviour of individual human beings, not bits of genetic material, and one which became the foundation of *laissez-faire* economics. Thus, the notion that microscopic units, such as genes, are 'selfish' involves the use of a social science analogy. How did such an analogy come to be imported into biology?

We can begin to answer such a question by examining the writings of Charles Darwin, which constitute the 'scriptures', as far as evolutionary biologists, such as Dawkins, are concerned. We find that, in constructing his theory of natural selection, Darwin was influenced by, among others, Thomas Malthus, the economist. As Hodgson (1993) points out, although we cannot discover the precise use of an economic analogy, the economic metaphors that Darwin imports are critically important in his theorizing.[7] In the words of Karl Marx: 'It is remarkable how Darwin recognises amongst beasts and plants his English society, with its division of labour, competition, opening up of new markets, "inventions" and the Malthusian struggle for existence. It is Hobbes' *bellum omnium contra omnes* [war against all]' (Marx to Engels, 1862, in Marx and Engels, 1937).

There is no strong evidence that the writings of Adam Smith influenced Darwin. However, they both shared the idea that the Newtonian system of equilibrating interactions could be used as an analogy in their respective ecological and economic contexts. All self-respecting scientists in the late 18th and early 19th centuries placed their ideas concerning the mechanism in systems in the Newtonian tradition. However, it was the Malthusian inspiration that was crucial. He offered the idea that population will always grow faster than resources, resulting in a permanent scarcity and a competitive selection environment reaching down to the level of the individual organism. Permanent scarcity is, of course, a central idea in economics and, after Darwin, it was this economic analogy which was stressed in the 'scientific' refinement of neo-Darwinian evolutionary biology. In parallel, economics also underwent a similar process of refinement, whereby informal propositions, set in the context of political economy, concerning the selfish materialism of individuals in the face of scarcity, combined with the effects of competition through markets, became formalized into a neoclassical economic mainstream.

On close examination, there is a close resemblance between the selfish gene and *homo economicus*, despite their separate development from common roots in 18th and 19th century political economy. Both involve abstract selfishness constructs relating to microscopic units of analysis. In the former, fitness is maximized and adverse mutations are minimized. In the latter, utility (or profit) is maximized and inefficiencies are minimized. Both are highly reductionist and involve heroic aggregation propositions. Competition is the maximizer, removing the unfit genetic mutant in biology and the inefficient producer in economics. Maximum 'fitness' and 'utility' are non-teleological outcomes. The common Newtonian heritage allows both to use equilibrium theories to capture the outcome of selection processes.

Friedman (1953) took the step that Alchian (1950) had hesitated to make and argued that we could regard the general equilibrium optimizing outcome *as if* it was the outcome of a process of competitive selection. However, this was cast, not within an explanatory, but rather an instrumentalist, methodology of science. The existence of the market price mechanism allows the possibility of a general equilibrium, in terms of prices and quantities, to exist. Firms, products, tastes can all come and go as economic evolution proceeds. At each instant, competition ensures utility maximization, cost minimization and equilibrium. The focus is not on the underlying evolutionary process but rather on the continual efficiency and welfare outcomes yielded by material selfishness and competition. It is an *as if* assumption to aid economic model construction, not a depiction of the Hobbesian society of Thomas Malthus and Dr Pangloss.

In both neoclassical economics and neo-Darwinian evolutionary biology, external shocks push the system out of equilibrium, which is re-established through the force of competition. Both systems are fundamentally Newtonian – they are timeless and do not depict a process unfolding in history. In the biological case, this is less obvious because the goal is to understand structural change in biological organisms in a historical setting. However, the neo-Darwinian gradual process of evolutionary change is also Newtonian. A random distribution of mutations at the microscopic level yields a dominant gene through competitive selection. These gives rise to increases in efficiency and a moving macroscopic equilibrium that is stable and not subject to nonlinear discontinuities. As Maynard Smith (1970) pointed out, neo-Darwinian natural selection is a time reversible process and, as such, ahistorical. Ruse (1982) also argued convincingly that Darwin attempted to make his theory of natural selection consistent with Newtonian dynamics. Thus, even though the inherently static and idealistic nature of modern neoclassical economics precluded its proponents from understanding the *process* of structural change in the economic system, an analogy could be struck with neo-Darwinian evolutionary biology in terms of *outcomes*. Thus, much discourse in neoclassical economics came to be conducted through the medium of evolutionary game theory and was compatible with modern variants of Spencerian political philosophy and sociobiology. In contrast, both Milton Friedman and Friedrich von Hayek stuck to more traditional Smithian versions of economic liberalism.

It has been argued that the common ancestry and resultant compatibility of neoclassical economics and neo-Darwinian evolutionary biology made it inevitable that neoclassical economists would espouse a particular view of economic evolution. However, an alternative tradition followed on from Veblen (1898). After the demise of the Keynesian/Smithian consensus in the late 1970s, there arose a chorus of objections to the narrowly defined nature of neoclassical competitive selection as a theory of economic evolution. The seminal book by Nelson and Winter (1982) is representative of the rise of a new group of evolutionary economists who rejected static, neoclassical general equilibrium depictions of the economy and used biological analogies concerning competition in a different way. Many stressed that competition must be understood as a process, not as a set of outcomes, and that competition in the economic domain is different in character from that dealt with in evolutionary biology. Many of these evolutionary economists did not choose the neo-Darwinian theory of natural selection as their biological analogy. Instead, they tended to favour a Lamarkian analogy. The latter allows for the inheritance of behavioural characteristics acquired from experience in particular environments. Thus, 'routines' (Nelson and Winter, 1982) or 'techniques' (Mokyr, 1990), are viewed as counterparts to genes which can be modified through experience in particular circumstances. The economic system does not need to rely entirely upon natural selection to adapt firms. Techniques can be devised through creative endeavour and can spread to other organizations through learning and imitation. However, the Lamarkian approach continues to use the gene as a biological analogy. The gene has simply become 'more clever' in adapting to experience and spreading itself.

As in the 'selfish gene' approach of Dawkins (1976), firms are mere vehicles in which routines and techniques replicate. Indeed, there is a close correspondence with Dawkins' notion of the 'meme'. As Kelm (1997) points out, the evolutionary economists have tended to provide an integration of Darwinian biological analogy and Joseph Schumpeter's ideas on innovation and development. However, Ruth (1996, p. 128) has heavily criticized the preoccupation of Nelson and Winter (1982) and others with related approaches with competition between firms as a source of evolutionary economic change. He argues that there is a 'failure to properly treat fundamental dissimilarities in the acquisition and maintenance of knowledge of the firm and the organism.' He points out that this criticism was made by Penrose (1952), following Alchian (1950), and Businario (1983), following Nelson and Winter (1982).

The pivotal nature of competitive selection in these modern developments in evolutionary economics tends to place them close to the evolutionary game theory tradition in neoclassical economics. The theoretical context is much looser and there is a greater preoccupation with non-linear dynamical mathematics and, correspondingly, more model simulation and less deduction. It is striking that in this so-called neo-Schumpeterian tradition, evolutionary economists use biological analogy and dynamical mathematics, both eschewed by Joseph Schumpeter in his representations of economic development. So, is it really very helpful to base economic evolutionary arguments on biological analogies concerning techniques or routines as genes and firms as competing phenotypes? Would it not be much better, as Joseph Schumpeter argued, to forget about such reductionist biological analogies altogether and examine economic evolution in its own unique social, political and psychological context?

Those in the Veblenian evolutionary economic tradition argue that this is exactly what they attempt to do. However, economic evolution is depicted as a more open struggle between organizational groups, from which evolutionary change emerges. Since the role of the market is delimited, power struggles play a much greater role. Power struggle is a political process, so the door is opened for the intervention of interest groups in the process of economic evolution and for the imposition of preferred value systems. If the New Right can be viewed as neo-Spencerian, then modern Veblenians are reminiscent of neo-Marxians. Competitive selection is the dominant mechanism for change, but at the group level and socio-economic in nature. Thus, many Veblenians depart, fundamentally, from the Smithian tradition of self-organization in the economic system. They may well not advocate the policies of Dr Pangloss but they share with him, Thomas Malthus and Herbert Spencer a vision of society as driven by competitive struggle, but between groups rather than individuals.

In the 19th century, the Darwinian revolution in biology spawned the opposing competitive selection visions of Spencer and Marx, ultimately pushing the Smithian tradition into a static, equilibrium model which came to define, to a large extent, the modern discipline of economics. The New Right and the Veblenians represent the old positions concerning societal evolution as driven by individual versus group selection while the Smithian tradition has weakened dramatically, as its static representation of the more narrowly construed economic system has also come to be interpreted as an outcome of competitive selection, using neo-Darwinian biological analogy. In contrast, although neo-Schumpeterians have espoused biological analogy in their discussions of competition, the influence of Schumpeter has remained strong, ensuring that competition has been studied as a unique economic phenomenon. Furthermore, due regard has been taken of the creative and cooperative organizational inter-actions that are so important in economic evolution. Appropriately, it is in the neo-Schumpeterian tradition that we discover some of the most innovative thinking concerning economic evolution.

5   COMPETITIVE SELECTION AND SELF-ORGANIZATION

Metcalfe (1994), following in the neo-Schumpeterian tradition of Nelson and Winter (1982), has argued that competitive selection is not to be viewed as a biological analogy but, rather, a universal principle which operates in the presence of variety. Generalizing in this particular way allowed him to consider competitive selection specifically in an economic context. Like Alchian (1950), Metcalfe builds his model of competitive selection from that of Fisher (1930), but that is where the biological similarity ends – there is no Malthusian 'struggle for survival' analogy, but rather a process of differential economic growth emanating from variety in creativity, innovation and imitation. The resolution of variety generates growth towards a stationary state that is not a Newtonian equilibrium state, but rather a state of uniformity that is likely to have unstable characteristics. Crucially, in the case of competition between firms, the outcome is monopoly: competition destroys itself. Thus, the notion that neoclassical general equilibrium is the outcome of competitive selection is decisively rejected.

Selection comes from variety, but where does variety come from? The Metcalfe model holds variety constant and shows how one technique or routine will become dominant. To prevent a state of homogeneity from happening, new variety must be generated. Thus, Metcalfe's model locates the origins of economic evolution in the domain of the Austrian School, namely, the generation of novelty, knowledge and uncertainty. Thus, in explaining how competitive selection can be envisaged in terms of growth processes, Metcalfe demonstrates the limitations of a competitive explanation of economic evolution and the need for a Smithian story as to how variety emerges from novelty and becomes 'fixed' in something upon which competitive selection can act. Metcalfe's careful attempts to understand what competitive selection actually means, provides a clear understanding of the limits of biological analogy and stresses that we cannot understand economic evolution only from a competitive viewpoint. In Foster (1997) and Witt (1997) it is argued that it is necessary to introduce the notion of economic self-organization to fill this analytical gap. Economic self-organization is different from physio-chemical and biological self-organization and from the Austrian conception of 'spontaneous order' but, at the same time, shares common features with all of them.

Remarkably, despite the fact that the Smithian tradition in economics is fundamentally about what we might regard as a form of self-organization in the economic system, most economists continue to select analogies which involve competitive selection to envisage processes between outcome states which are depicted in terms of Newtonian physical analogy. Perhaps the modern emphasis upon competitive selection is due to the fact that scarcity gradually became the defining characteristic of modern economics and, thus, echoing Thomas Malthus, economics must be about competition. The dictum of Mill (1848) that 'only through the principle of competition has political economy any pretension to the character of a science' had, a century later, become entrenched. On the other hand, perhaps modern economics has assumed a degree of path dependence because of a commitment to reductionism, and a focus upon individuals.

However, none of this explains why evolutionary economists, critical of neoclassical economics, continue to emphasize competition over self-organization.[8] Many are well read in evolutionary biology, yet do not seem to have grasped the self-organizational revolution that has been going on.[9] For example, Hodgson (1993) makes only passing references to self-organization, recognizing only some relation between the term and the Austrian notion of 'spontaneous order'. This imbalance in treatment is manifest in his treatment of Joseph Schumpeter who is seen as dealing, in the main, with economic development, not evolution. In contrast, Thorstein Veblen is viewed as more of an evolutionary economist because he provided a competitive selection analogy that is more accurately Darwinian and, thus, a biological analogy (Hodgson, 1997).

As we have noted, the evolutionary models of Metcalfe (1994) offer the most formal representation of competitive selection. However, he stresses that the generation of variety is crucial, but difficult to represent formally. Instead, he follows the time-honoured Marshallian tradition of engaging in *ceteris paribus* and confronts the same problem as Marshall: he has stated a mechanism which yields a stationary state conditioned by history, while holding the non-deterministic aspects of reality fixed. In Metcalfe's case, variety is held constant, yet the 'true' evolutionary process is that which causes variety to change. Markets do not generate variety; they process it to obtain outcomes. Variety can be generated in response to market outcomes but it is also the outcomes of hierarchical arrangements which extend far beyond the economic, into the political, social and cultural realms. These gain dimension in institutions that can both promote and restrain the generation of variety. Hayek stressed the former and Veblen the latter. The problem with Fisher models of competitive selection is that, if variety is always changing, often because firms access new niches as they innovate, and the unit of selection changes as more organization parallels increasing complexity, how can they be applied in real world settings? Typically, the fear of competition is itself a stimulus to innovation, thus the tendency towards a stationary state affects the stationary state itself and we have a non-equilibrium process.

What we have to accept is that, in economic systems, variety at the individual level leads to further variety through the formation of organizations. Thus, we have a process of economic self-organization and the cumulative formation of organized complexity. For Schumpeter, a subset of individuals, namely entrepreneurs, were instrumental in generating such variety by bringing together new techniques and/or new organizational arrangements. They, in turn, draw upon the mass of variety in knowledge and skills that exists. The Metcalfe model comes into its own when variety generation slows down and best practice production comes to dominate. Through imitation, this practice spreads and becomes dominant across firms. Inasmuch as this spread is restricted, then firms that cannot adapt will decline in importance.

It is easy to overstate the importance of this kind of competitive selection for the failure of firms. Firms fail for many reasons relating to many dimensions of human decision-making. Irreversibility and chance will be important. If firms can take advantage of economies of scale and/or erect barriers to the flow of imitation, this will be much more important as a source of firm failure than competitive selection of techniques. We must resist using the biological analogy of the gene because, ultimately, it is the behaviour of people in organizations that is decisive. Organisms do not engage in internal selection processes to come up with modified genes in order to develop and avoid phenotype competition. We should think of routines, techniques and institutions as the outgrowth of the creative and cooperative capabilities of particular people, in the presence of stocks and flows of free energy.

Competitive selection is not the cause of economic evolution, but an outcome of a myriad of endogenous and exogenous influences. When are we likely to see it at work in the economic system? Before we can apply a selection model to, for example, firms, we need to be able to establish that conditions exist where variety is relatively constant and that other factors influencing the expansion and survival of techniques and the firms in which they are used are relatively unimportant. First of all, it is unlikely that competitive selection will occur when the elements of the population dealt with are entering a niche that is still open. When the niche is open, individuals will cooperate to their mutual advantage and, in so doing, may develop organizational links and, thus, continually alter the unit of selection. Secondly, when a niche limit is approached, variety is most likely to tend towards the static variety requirement of the competitive selection model. However, even in these conditions, a process of selective competition and attendant homogenization need not occur, simply because awareness of the possibility of some form of competition, is in itself, a spur towards the generation of new variety and structural adaptation.

Even if we do have the required conditions of creative and cooperative impoverishment and severe lock-in, there can be no presumption that the outcome of competitive selection will be more efficient firms. It is in such circumstances that political considerations of power, rather than efficiency, can become decisive. The formation of political alliances and the deliberate elimination of competitors may well be much more important than cost differences in production. As variety dilutes to homogeneity, we can expect firms to engage in defensive strategies, erecting entry barriers and engaging in cosmetic research and development.[10] Furthermore, since all such activities are recorded as value added in the economy, economic growth can continue even though there is little fundamental development going on. However, we should also observe rising inequality and structural unemployment as the powerful engage in expropriation, rather than innovation. Sorting will also occur because of chance – simply being in the wrong place at the wrong time.

Thus, we must take great care in using the term 'competition'. Competition, which yields beneficial outcomes, is associated with some sort of overarching cooperation. All participatory games are defined by the collective acceptance of rules. Thus, rivalry can mean different things at different times. Early in an innovative diffusion process, rivalry exists, but cooperation tends to dominate. There is no defined game; the rules and the creative participants are both evolving through cooperative interactions. Early in this process, the situation appears to be chaotic – both opportunities and mistakes are plentiful. On the 'frontier economy' emergence of rules and organizations to reduce uncertainty are the key to development.

A *ceteris paribus* sequence of prominent stages that self-organizing systems go through could be delineated as follows:

Dominant Organisational State
DISORDER →CO-OPERATION →RIVALRY →CONFLICT → DISORDER

Dynamics of Complexity
DISCOVERY → INNOVATION → ECONOMIZING → EXPLOITATION →
COLLAPSE

In no sense is such a characterization intended to be deterministic. The essence of self-organization is the presence of openness. Thus, the phase of cooperation/innovation may not lead to the next stage but a discontinuous switch may occur on to a new cooperation/innovation phase. The rivalry/economizing phase may, as Schumpeter suggested, lead to unenvisaged opportunities to deviate on to new innovation paths. The last disorder stage may result in the demise of the system, its componentization into a greater system or a new phase of cooperation/innovation.

Development is a parallel process of increasing organization and complexity. The key distinction between the biological and the economic is that the latter involves the formation of organizational arrangements between individuals, which results in *new variety*. Furthermore, the hard distinction between the organism, which has strong informational connections between components, and the notion of ecology, which involves some kind of selection environment, is not present in the economy. In the words of biologists Depew and Weber (1995): 'What makes an organism different from an ecological system is...the ability that it has to internalise the relevant information for processing energy and matter. That is precisely what the ecosystem lacks' (p. 475). Economic organizations are highly adaptable in this regard. Even the whole economy is subject to internalized informational connections between components. Institutions exist at all levels of the economy and these allow informational connections to function. As Dobzhansky (1951) pointed out, biological organisms accumulate a store of variety. Similarly, economic organizations accumulate a store of knowledge and the formation of more complex organizations yields new variety in knowledge. Because economic agents actually seek novel knowledge, rather than simply acquiring it from environmental interactions, the self-organizational character of economic systems is much more pronounced than in biological systems. It is for this reason that economic evolution has been so rapid – reliance upon only competitive selection may well have slowed, or even stopped, this process.

Thus, the competitive selection model of Metcalfe approximates conditions in stage 3 in which, for example, firms sell comparable products and attempt to raise productivity by introducing labour saving technologies to cut overall costs. Because goods-producing industries are usually subject to strong economies of scale, this can be done with a smaller increment of labour than that which is released by this process. The market winners are those which can adapt their organizations to cope with such change. Thus, the emergent variety that is really important as an organization grows is organizational adaptability that tends to vary dramatically across firms. The process of translating discoveries into innovations is attributable to the creative organizational skills of entrepreneurs. These innovations are spread by imitation. However, the process of capital/labour substitution to raise productivity is due to the adaptive organizational skills of managers. The conflictual process of collusion, merger and takeover in order to obtain economic rents is attributable to the political skills of directors (Veblen's 'captains of industry'), under pressure from shareholders to maintain an acceptable rate of return. Any organization that can draw upon all three of these skills, should be adaptable and long-lived.

Recognition of hierarchy is crucial. All economic organizations do not inevitably decline and fall because some are selected, not by competition, but by the emergent hierarchical needs of the greater system, to play a 'core' role. 'Embedded' organizations become integral to the success of peripheral organizations and, as such, are permitted to receive economic rents under strict rules. Thus, the legal system is integral to the social and economic systems and has to operate under rules that regulate rent flows; otherwise the burden involved would interfere with the development of the system. Lawyers must be incorruptible and not be allowed to charge on the margin in line with the expected future lifetime earnings of someone facing a possible conviction for a crime.

Thus, the Schumpeterian process of innovation diffusion, followed by creative destruction, contains: organizations which adapt to new processes or products, organizations which are removed by conflict, or simply by chance, and organizations which stay the same but are selected to be in the core of the evolving greater system. The limited relevance of the analogy of biological competitive selection in this process is clear. There is rivalry, which is a state of economizing, and conflict, which is a state of emergent collusion, domination and submission. The homogeneity that exists in such a state is not indicative of efficiency and it must be broken before a process of self-organizational development can recommence, as varied knowledge concerning technology and organization becomes effective again.

6   CONCLUSIONS

The distinctive feature of the economic system is the manner in which it has transcended the functioning of the biological system. Thus, to attempt to understand economic evolution using biological analogies or metaphors, beyond the initial stages of conceptualization, can be very misleading. Pursuit of such a research strategy has led many evolutionary economists to take theoretical positions based upon outdated and inappropriate biological analogies. The result has been over-emphasis upon the biological variant of competitive selection in economic evolution. An unintended consequence has been to provide the New

Right with a menu of selectionist arguments to bolster their crude Spencerian views of society and to provide justification, however unwarranted, for the application of what could be described as 'economic eugenics' in a range of contexts, ostensibly to enhance economic efficiency.

In stating this we do not mean that it is not important to understand the connections between the economic and the biological domains or the common systemic features that each shares. Indeed, any conceptualization of economic behaviour must be consistent, in some sense, with the biological dimensions of human behaviour. What we learn from modern biology is that the self-organization approach is redefining its systemic and ontological character, as has been the case in both physics and chemistry. However, we can also see that the energetic and informational character of biological self-organization differs from its physical and chemical counterparts. Equally, self-organization is distinctively different in the economic domain (see Foster, 1997). As such, we are not using analogy or metaphor in applying self-organization – it is a process that must, necessarily, be present in the economic system.

It has been argued that Metcalfe's (1994) highly perceptive analysis of the nature of competitive selection in the economic domain opens up evolutionary economics for the incorporation of economic self-organization. The focus upon 'variety' is specifically because he wishes to provide a better theoretical representation of a competitive process. However, he makes it clear that the flow of new variety is crucial and that it is not likely to be random in the economic case, following the lead of Joseph Schumpeter. He also accepts that non-deterministic and historical factors will be important. Competition does not lead to economic evolution, but to a tendency towards homogeneity and, if successful firms can set up barriers on information flow, monopolistic exploitation is the outcome. Thus, competition can be self-destructive. Schumpeter's evocative 'creative destruction' involves something more important: the liberation of new novelty into the creative and cooperative process of technological and organizational innovation. It is a small step to see that economic self-organization might be made compatible with the Metcalfe model in order to render it more fully Schumpeterian. Economic self-organization involves the quest for novel information, so that variety emanates, endogenously, from organizational formation. Variety is not fixed but is the outcome of tractable developmental processes.

The distinction with self-organization in the natural world is simple: internalized information in the natural world is imposed from experience, and this may well involve natural selection, at some appropriate level, in biological settings. In contrast, internalized information in the economic world is knowledge that is actively acquired. There is no equivalent of biological natural selection, even though we observe competition acting decisively in appropriate economic contexts. Again, in the words of Depew and Weber (1995):

The use of brains and symbolic communication to store and transmit culturally acquired information, and to keep finding more of it, is a remarkable adaptation that confers on species that have sophisticated means of enhancing autocatalysis and making other species pay their entropic debts. It signals another level of natural selection, for it results in, and relies on, an autonomous form of *cultural* selection that cannot be reduced to natural selection, just as natural selection cannot be reduced to chemical selection, or chemical selection to physical selection. (pp. 470–71)

'Cultural selection' is no more than the rise and fall of particular ideas in the process of economic self-organization. As such, it diminishes greatly the role for natural, chemical and physical selection. Despite this, we shall still see firms failing and rising, only to decline again, and there will be episodes when such processes will look strikingly like natural selection at work. However, closer inspection is likely to show that the exercise of acquired power is involved. Firms do not always compete in fixed resource niches but prosper or fail depending on their ability to persuade consumers to buy their products, suppliers to accept their contracts and employees to act in creative and cooperative ways. Competitive selection of the biological type is not the main engine of economic evolution, but a boundary phenomenon.

ACKNOWLEDGEMENTS

I have received many helpful comments on earlier drafts of this article. I would like to offer particular thanks to: Guido Bunstorf, Burkhard Fleith, Antonio Calafati, Karen Knottenbauer, Jan Kregel, Brian Loasby, Paulo Ramazzotti, Christian Sartorius and Ulrich Witt. The usual caveat applies.

NOTES

1. Buchanan (1996) notes, in assessing the contributions of Armen Alchian that 'evolutionary thinking permeates economics and is now becoming a very natural way of thinking, but nobody thought about evolutionary processes in the 1950s'.
2. See also Hayek (1978).
3. Endres (1995) reviews the origins of conceptions of competition in Austrian economics and he notes the close connection with Smith. He also points out that, in the 20th century, Austrians did, increasingly, introduce the notion of 'conflict' into their analysis, but mainly in the context of bargaining over prices.
4. See Backhouse (1990) for an assessment of the classical view of competition and its transition into a static representation.
5. You and Wilkinson (1994) offer a modern example of the application of the Marshallian approach, with its implicit self-organizational perspective, to deal with both competition and cooperation in the context of industrial districts.
6. See Maynard Smith and Szathmary (1996) for a recent presentation of these ideas.
7. This powerful impact is stressed in Darwin's notebook on 28 September 1838. See Jones (1989) who examines the connections between Darwin and the writing of Malthus.

8. A few exceptions exist. In particular, see Silverberg, Dosi and Orsenigo (1988) for the presentation and simulation of models that attempt to integrate self-organization and competitive mechanisms. However, the conception of self-organization used is drawn from a natural science analogy, rather than one developed explicitly for use in the economic domain.
9. See Depew and Weber (1995) for a modern history of evolutionary thought in biology. They make clear that there has been a rise in self-organizational thinking in biology over the past decade and that it tends to be more integrative, rather than competitive with the neo-Darwinian competitive selection approach. See, for example, Kauffman (1993).
10. Even in the biological context, Eldredge (1985) speculates that it may have been the case that the powerful eliminate mutations that are both detrimental and beneficial. This leads to protracted periods of stasis and a gradual increase in structural instability, in the sense that the species becomes increasingly vulnerable to the impact of exogenous shocks.

REFERENCES

Alchian, A.A. (1950), 'Uncertainty, evolution and economic theory', *Journal of Political Economy*, **58**: 211–22.

Alchian, A.A. (1996), 'Principles of professional advancement', *Economic Inquiry*, **34**: 520–26.

Backhouse, R.E. (1990), 'Competition', in J. Creedy (ed.), *Foundations of Economic Thought*, Oxford: Basil Blackwell.

Buchanan, J.M. (1996), 'Principles of professional advancement', *Economic Inquiry*, **34**: 520–26.

Businario, U. (1983), 'Applying the biological metaphor to technological innovation', *Futures*, **15**: 464–77.

Cockett, R. (1995), *Thinking the Unthinkable; Think Tanks and the Economic Counter Revolution, 1931–1983*, London: Harper Collins.

Commonwealth of Australia (1993), *National Competition Policy*, Report by the Independent Committee of Inquiry (the Hilmer Report), Commonwealth Government Printer, Canberra.

Darwin, C. (1859), *The Origin of The Species by Means of Natural Selection*, London: Watts.

Dawkins, R. (1976), *The Selfish Gene*, Oxford: Oxford University Press.

Depew, D.J. and B.H. Weber (1995), *Darwinism Evolving: System Dynamics and the Geneology of Natural Selection*, Cambridge, MA.: MIT Press.

Dobzhansky, T. (1951), *Genetics and the Origin of the Species*, 3rd edn, New York: Columbia University Press.

Eldredge, N. (1985), *Time Frames*, New York: Simon and Schuster.

Endres, A.M. (1995), 'Conceptions of competition in Austrian economics before Hayek', *History of Economic Review*, **23**: 1–19.

Fisher, R.A. (1930), *The Genetical Theory of Natural Selection*, Oxford: Oxford University Press.

Foster, J. (1993), 'Economics and the self-organisation approach: Alfred Marshall revisited?', *Economic Journal*, **103**: 975–91.

Foster, J. (1997), 'The analytical foundations of evolutionary economics: from biological analogy to economic self-organisation', *Structural Change and Economic Dynamics*, **8**: 427–51.

Friedman, M. (1953), 'The methodology of positive economics', in M. Friedman, *Essays in Positive Economics*, Chicago: University of Chicago Press.

Hodgson, G. (1993), *Economics and Evolution: Bringing Life Back to Economics*, Cambridge: Polity Press.

Hodgson, G. (1997), 'The evolutionary and non-Darwinian economics of Joseph Schumpeter' *Journal of Evolutionary Economics*, **7**: 131–46.

Jones, L.B. (1989), 'Schumpeter versus Darwin: In re Malthus' *Southern Economic Journal*, **55**: 410–22.

Kauffman, S. (1993), *The Origins of Order: Self-Organisation and Selection in Evolution*, New York: Oxford University Press.

Kelm (1997), 'Schumpeter's theory of economic evolution; a Darwinian interpretation', *Journal of Evolutionary Economics*, **7**: 97–130.

Kirzner, I.M. (1973), *Competition and Entrepreneurship*, Chicago: University of Chicago Press.

Loasby, B. (1991), *Equilibrium and Evolution: an Exploration of Connecting Principles in Economics*, Manchester: Manchester University Press.

McNulty, P.J. (1968), 'Economic theory and the meaning of competition', *Quarterly Journal of Economics*, **82**: 639–56.

Marx, K. and Engels, F. (1937), *Selected Correspondence*, I. Lasker, trans. Moscow.

Maynard Smith, J. (1970) 'Time in the evolutionary process', *Studium Generale*, **23**: 266–72.

Maynard Smith, J. (1983), *Evolution and the Theory of Games*, Cambridge: Cambridge University Press.

Maynard Smith, J. and E. Szathmary (1996), *The Major Transitions in Evolution*, London: W.H. Freeman.

Metcalfe, J.S. (1994), 'Competition, Fisher's principle and increasing returns in the selection process', *Journal of Evolutionary Economics*, **4**, 327–46.

Mill, J.S. (1848), *Principles of Political Economy*, London: John W. Parker.

Mises, L. (1978), *The Ultimate Foundations of Economic Science*, Kansas City, Missouri: Sheed, Andrews and McMeel.

Mokyr, J. (1990), *The Lever of Riches*, New York: Oxford University Press.

Morgan, M.S. (1993), 'Competing notions of "competition" in late nineteenth-century American economics', *History of Political Economy*, **25**: 563–604.

Nelson, R. and S. Winter (1982), *An Evolutionary Theory of Economic Change*, Cambridge, MA: Belknap Press.

Penrose, E.T. (1952), 'Biological analogies and the theory of the firm', *American Economic Review*, **42**: 804–19.

Richardson, G.B. (1960), *Information and Investment; a Study in the Working of the Competitive Economy*, London: Oxford University Press.

Richardson, G.B. (1972), 'The organisation of industry', *Economic Journal*, **82**: 883–96.

Ruse, M. (1982), *Darwinism Defended: a Guide to Evolutionary Controversies*, Reading, MA.: Addison-Wesley.

Ruth, M. (1996), 'Evolutionary economics at the crossroads of biology and physics', *Journal of Social and Evolutionary Systems*, **19**: 125–44.

Silverberg G., G. Dosi and L. Orsenigo (1988), 'Innovation, diversity and diffusion; a self organisation model', *Economic Journal*, **98**: 1032–54.

Veblen, T. (1898), 'Why is economics not an evolutionary science?', *Quarterly Journal of Economics*, **12**: 373–97.

von Hayek, F. (1948), 'The meaning of competition', in F. von Hayek, *Individualism and Economic Order*. Reprinted in S. Littlechild (ed.) (1990), *Austrian Economics Vol 3*, Aldershot UK and Brookfield, US: Edward Elgar.

von Hayek, F. (1978), 'Competition as a discovery process', in F. von Hayek, *New Studies in Philosophy, Politics, Economics and the History of Ideas*. Reprinted in S. Littlechild (ed.) (1990), *Austrian Economics Vol 3*, Aldershot, UK and Brookfield, US: Edward Elgar.

Witt, U. (1997), 'Self-organisation and economics – what is new?', *Structural Change and Economic Dynamics*, **8**: 489–507.

You, J-B. and F. Wilkinson (1994), 'Competition and co-operation: toward understanding industrial districts', *Review of Political Economy*, **6**: 259–78.

7. Evolutionary themes in the Austrian tradition: Menger, Wieser and Schumpeter on institutions and rationality

Richard Arena and Sandye Gloria-Palermo

1 INTRODUCTION

During the last two decades, the rise of a 'new' microeconomics (Cahuc, 1993) and the revival of institutionalism strongly contribute to point out the problem of the nature of the economic reasons that explain the emergence of institutions or of forms of organization. The treatment of this problem is essential for institutionalist as well as for evolutionary economists. It indeed plays a central role in the building process of a more satisfactory economic dynamics. The importance of this problem for contemporary theorists does not mean, however, that it is entirely new. The Austrian tradition, for instance, devoted particular and permanent attention to it, even if this interest was frequently neglected by commentators.

Now, the purpose of this chapter is precisely to reconsider this attention and, therefore, to investigate what were the specificities of the tribute paid by Austrian economists to the analysis of the problem. Here, it is obviously impossible to take each of these authors into account. This is why we focus our approach on the works of only three of them: Carl Menger, Friedrich von Wieser and Joseph Schumpeter.

The contributions of these authors indeed offer two important common features.

Firstly, they are sometimes described as the fundamental steps of the Austrian version of the so-called marginalist revolution. Menger is the creator of the tradition and he is often presented as one of the founding fathers of neoclassicism. Wieser belongs to the second generation; the author is credited to have given a more pedagogic and systematic form to the original Austrian marginalist message. Finally, Schumpeter is considered as one of the first builders of a neoclassical synthesis able to welcome Austrian as well as Walrasian theoretical ingredients. Our contribution will necessarily contradict this type of interpretation since it will stress the elements of continuity of an evolutionary line of thought linking our three authors.

Secondly, these elements correspond to the way according to which Menger, Wieser and Schumpeter coped with the problems of the genesis and the emergence of social institutions. They all indeed faced the question of the characterization of a process in which different groups of agents associated with different types of economic rationality interact, create and, then, reinforce an institution.

The contributions of the three authors will be considered in turn and, according to our view, in spite of their differences, they exhibit common evolutionary and institutionalist features which characterize the Austrian tradition in economic analysis.

The first part of the chapter considers Menger's conception of the emergence of institutions and especially of money and markets. In this framework, Mengerian agents are supposed to introduce new economic rules or devices in a world characterized by radical uncertainty. These individual choices lead to specific social–institutional arrangements, interpreted as unintended consequences of individual behaviours. These arrangements become mere institutions if agents who did not participate in this process of emergence confirm its social utility through mimetic behaviours, which consist in following the rules, pointed out by the first group of agents.

Von Wieser reconsidered Menger's approach distinguishing *leaders* and *masses*. Wieserian leaders behave exactly as Mengerian creators of institutions. However, the result of their process of building new institutions can only work if it is followed and therefore accepted by the major part of agents, namely what Wieser calls the masses. If masses are not satisfied with the new institutional rules or devices, they might refuse them; in this case these rules and devices are discarded and new leaders must introduce new institutional proposals to be confirmed by masses. This conception of the distinction between leaders and masses is directly related to Wieser's definition of a social economy and to the role given to social stratification and power relations within the realm of individual interaction.

It is interesting to notice that in the first German edition of his *Theory of Economic Development*, Schumpeter distinguishes *hedonistic* and *energic* rationality. While the former is perfectly compatible with the usual economic conception of rationality, the latter clearly excludes it. It has nothing in common with maximization but rather refers to the realization of ideal rules or objectives. This opposition between hedonistic and energic rationality was discarded in its original form in the subsequent edition of the *Theory of Economic Development* and replaced by a dichotomy between innovative and mimetic entrepreneurial behaviours.

2 MENGER'S ANALYSIS OF THE EMERGENCE OF ORGANIC INSTITUTIONS

Various contradictory interpretations of Menger's contribution to economics have been proposed in the history of economic thought: Stigler (1941) considers our author as one of the main founders of the marginalist revolution, while Streissler (1972) disputes this interpretation, focusing on Menger's specific advances within the theory of production.

One of the explanations of this heterogeneity amongst commentators might be related to the exclusive stress they generally put on the main book written by Menger, the *Grundsätze der Volkwirtschaftslehre*. The analytical aim of the book is however hardly characterized and Menger's analytical objectives become clearer and more precise only if the reader also takes into account the *Untersuchungen*, that is, a book which is generally confined to a tribute to methodology. It is then easier to understand that, to Menger, economists have to solve a major problem, namely, the emergence and evolution of spontaneous complex economic phenomena (Gloria-Palermo, 1999). Now, the right way to do it is

> to reduce the complex phenomena of human economic activity to the simplest elements that can still be subjected to accurate observation, to apply to these elements the measure corresponding to their nature, and constantly adhering to this measure, to investigate the manner in which more complex phenomena evolve from their elements according to definite principles. (Menger, [1871] 1950, pp. 46–7)

With this methodological device, it is possible to understand the main problem related to the existence of 'organic institutions', that is spontaneous institutions. These institutions indeed come about as the unintended result of individual human efforts (pursuing *individual* interests) without a *common will* directed toward their establishment (Menger, [1883] 1963, p. 133). Now, a question necessarily arises: 'How can it be that institutions which serve the common welfare and are extremely significant for its development come into being without a common will directed toward establishing them?' (ibid., p. 146).

In his *Untersuchungen*, Menger deepens the analysis of the emergence of money that he has been elaborating since the *Grundsätze*. The theory of the appearance of the monetary institution perfectly illustrates his view on organic institutions. The emergence of money is a spontaneous process, as is the simultaneous disappearance of barter. Both processes do not result from an explicit or legislative agreement but are the outcome of individual interaction, economic agents following their personal plans of action and self-interest. Menger is then addressing the following challenge which consists in explaining the emergence of an institution – money as a generalized medium of exchange – starting only from individual behaviours and therefore, excluding a priori any role to a common will or a social encouragement to individuals.

> The problem which science has to solve here consists in the explanation of a social phenomenon, of a homogenous way of acting on the part of the members of a community, for which public motives are recognisable, but for which in the concrete case individual motives are hard to discern. (Menger, [1883] 1963, p. 152)

Menger starts his analysis from a barter economy, which is described as the 'natural' system of exchange, in contrast with the 'monetary' system. Menger emphasizes the difficulty in reaching trade agreements in the barter economy, due to the usual problem of finding the required double-coincidence between individual needs. The first solution put forward by individuals is to proceed to indirect exchanges; Menger underlines the negative consequences of such a solution on the development of the division of labour and on economic progress in general (Menger, [1871] 1950, p. 258):

> [this] difficulty would have been insurmountable and would have seriously impeded progress in the division of labour, and above all in the production of goods for future sale, if there had not been, in the very nature of things, a way out. But there were elements in their situation that everywhere led men inevitably, without the need for a special agreement or even government compulsion, to a state of affairs in which this difficulty was completely overcome. (Menger, [1871] 1950, pp. 258–9)

Individuals then found out another more efficient way of overcoming the difficulties attached to barter, thereby noticing that some goods are indeed more marketable than others. 'The causes of the different degrees of saleableness in commodities' are related, according to Menger (1892, p. 246), to different motives: to the organization of supply and demand (number of buyers, intensity of their needs, importance of their purchase power, volume of supply), to the organization of the market (degree of development of exchanges, importance of speculation, degree of free trade); to the inner characteristics of goods (divisibility for instance); to temporal limits (permanence of needs, durability and cost of preservation of goods, periodicity of market, development of speculation); some of the causes are also spatial (degree of distribution, transportation, communication on the market) (Menger, 1892, pp. 246–7).

The intensity of indirect exchanges is thus led to decrease: agents progressively learn to select more and more marketable commodities, to proceed to indirect exchange, even if they do not need them for their own consumption, till the moment when the number of commodities used as medium of exchange is reduced to one.

> The economic interest of the economic individuals, therefore, with increased knowledge of their *individual* interests, without any agreement, without legislation

compulsion, *even without any consideration of public interest*, leads them to turn over there wares for more marketable ones, even if they do not need the latter for their immediate consumer needs. (Menger, [1883] 1963, p. 154)

Menger here is clearly describing a self-organizing process. The selection of specific commodities as a medium of exchange is first due to the inner quality of saleableness of these goods but is also due to a large extent to chance. The diffusion of the use of these commodities is depicted as a process of imitation by agents who, in pursuing their self-interest, are progressively becoming aware that through the use of these specific goods, they can proceed 'to [their] end much more quickly, more economically and with a greatly enhanced probability of success' (Menger, [1871] 1950, p. 258).

Even if at first only a minority of agents perceives the advantage of exchanging goods against more marketable commodities, the recognition of the success attached to such a way of exchanging will progressively convince the other individuals to adopt the same behaviour. In that way, a good which was initially used as a medium of exchange partly by chance, and partly for its intrinsic qualities, ultimately imposes itself as a systematic means of trade. The phenomenon is self-enforcing because the more this commodity is used as an intermediary of exchange, the more it becomes an *efficient* medium of exchange, so that in the long run, holding this commodity represents a *certain* means for achieving individual ends. Money is thus not a sudden phenomenon but rather the result of an on-going process involving learning. This is why for Menger,

> [...] money is neither the product of an agreement on the part of economising men nor the product of legislative acts. No one invented it. As economising individuals in social situations became increasingly aware of their economic interest, they everywhere attained the simple knowledge that surrendering less saleable commodities for others of greater saleability brings them substantially closer to the attainment of their specific economic purposes. Thus, with the progressive development of social economy, money came to exist in numerous centres of civilisation independently. (Menger, [1871] 1976, p. 262)

Notice, however, that although money may be considered as universal if viewed as an institutional device, its concrete manifestation depends on 'particular peoples' and 'particular historical periods' (ibid., pp. 262–3). Different marketable commodities have indeed been selected by individuals at different times and in different places.

An analogous approach could have been implemented using Menger's conception of the emergence of markets as institutions (Arena, 1997). In his *Principles*, our author indeed describes how economies *evolve* from the 'isolated household' to the 'organised market economy' (Menger, [1871] 1963, pp. 236–9).

The first of these economies is a completely closed productive system in which no exchange occurs; goods are distributed by a central familial authority according to an a priori conception of division of labour (ibid., pp. 236–7).

The second type of economy incorporates both the institutions of money and 'middlemen', the latter constituting a special class of agents whose function is to improve the organization of markets. More precisely,

> [they correspond to] a special class of economizing individuals who take charge of the intellectual and mechanical parts of exchange operations for society and who are reimbursed for this with a part of the gains from trade. (Menger, [1883] 1963, p. 239)

It is interesting to notice that the path from the former to the latter economy goes through the systems of production 'on order' (ibid., p. 237) which is another example of production economy working without markets. In this type of economy, craftsmen offer their services to consumers who directly provide them with the necessary raw materials and products and collect back the final product. Now, these systems offer a precise example of an inefficient institution. Production on order has been abandoned because 'several serious disadvantages' convinced agents that neither their interests nor common will could be satisfied by this economic system (ibid., p. 238).

> The consumer must still wait sometimes for his product, and is never quite certain of its properties in advance. The producer is sometimes wholly engaged and at other times overburdened with orders, with the result that he is sometimes forced to be idle while at other times he cannot meet his demand.

The characterization of the processes of emergence of money and market clearly points out the existence of two groups of agents associated with two types of economic rationality.

On one side, we have innovators who have a greater knowledge of their personal interest, which leads them to improve the efficiency of exchanges. In Menger's 1892 article, they are described as 'the most effective' or 'the most intelligent bargainers' (Menger, 1892, p. 254). They are those who try to find new processes or new tools for improving the working of the market economy.

On the other side, we have imitators. Imitators progressively realize the potential impact of these new processes or new tools. They also understand that this impact might be profitable for them. Therefore, they decide to imitate innovators, transforming new devices into routines.

Institutions, therefore, emerge from the interaction between innovators and imitators. This interaction does not assume any reference to maximizing agents only looking for their self-interest. It rather relates to *Mengerian economizing men* whom Jaffé (1976) described in this way:

Man, as Menger saw him, far from being a 'lightning calculator', is a bumbling, erring, ill-informed creature, plagued with uncertainty, forever hovering between alluring hopes, haunting fears, and congenitally incapable of making finely calibrated decisions in pursuit of satisfaction. (Jaffé, 1976, p. 252)

3 WIESER'S ANALYSIS OF INSTITUTIONS AS THE RESULT OF THE INTERACTION BETWEEN LEADERS AND MASSES

Wieser's position on methodological individualism is carefully described in the following passage of his 1927 book, *Social Economics*:

> What valid substitute may we offer for the individualistic theory of society? In its naïve formulation it has become inadequate. But one cannot get away from its fundamental concept, that the individual is the subject of social intercourse. The individuals who comprise the society are the sole possessors of all consciousness and of all will. The 'organic' explanation, which seeks to make society as such, without reference to individuals, the subject of social activity, has patently proved a failure. One must hold himself aloof from the excesses of the individualistic exposition, but the explanation must still run in terms of the individual. It is in the individual that one must look for those tendencies that make the social structure that dove-tail (if we may use that expression) in such a manner as to give the firm cohesion of social unity and at the same time provide the foundation for the erection of social power. (Wieser, 1927, p. 154)

It is first clear that Wieser expresses strong doubts on what he calls 'naïve' individualism. Classical economists were not 'naïve' individualists but, in a way, they opened a road in this direction. Of course, they did not explain *all* economic phenomena by *mere* individual behaviours and found them on a *limitless* self-interest. Wieser notices that

> When they dealt with freedom of action they conceived of personal egoism as controlled by law and modality. Moreover, they clearly recognized that certain dangers inhered in personal egoism and that certain precautions must be taken against them. (Wieser, 1927, p. 153)

But Wieser considered that classical economists only took into account a part of the individual determinants of economic behaviours, that is, the 'forces of freedom' ('*Freiheitsmächte*'). They ignored the 'forces of compulsion' related to the existence of power in economics and this omission led them to cope with individuals as if they were perfectly autonomous, free and equal. On the other hand, Wieser considered that individuals were generally unequal and that 'compulsion' reduced their degree of freedom and autonomy. That is why the author attributed to classical economists the 'error' of giving individuals 'too much room for the play of personal freedom' (Wieser, 1927, p. 53). A different conception of individuals and individualism had therefore to be introduced:

> Man is too weak to assure his preservation and to develop his life if he stands as an isolated individual. The impulse to self-preservation and to further development – the egoistic interest that grows from an appreciation of weakness – leads to social organisation. In part, men are thus led by conscious deliberation. But fundamentally, a social impulse is operative; man is by nature a social being (...).
>
> They are two types of social force: natural controls [forces of freedom] and compulsion. Natural controls are recognized by the individual as aids to the assertion and development of his being. He feels them as increasing his individual power (...). When he is most completely dominated by them – when his innermost being assents to them – then for the first time does he believe himself to be quite free. Thus freedom does not consist in total lack of control. It consists rather in a relation of the individual to society.
>
> Compulsion, on the other hand, is recognized as a restriction on the individual life. Its powers are most keenly appreciated when they arise from the armed force which has subdued the vanquished to the will of the victor. But as we shall show later, these forces also develop within the ordinary intercourse of a society. (Wieser, 1927, p. 155)

In this prospect, Wieser does not deny that individuals seek their self-interest. In *Natural Value* as well as in the *Theory of the Simple Economy* (book 1 of *Social Economics*), individuals are indeed depicted as utility maximizers and they do not really differ from their Walrasian cousins. However, the economies represented in these two books refer to what Wieser calls 'the most abstract isolating and idealising assumptions' (Wieser, 1927, p. 6). Therefore, they differ from social economies which appear with a 'decreasing abstraction to conditions of reality' (Wieser, 1927, p. 9). Now, in contrast to the assumptions of *Natural Value*, individuals cease to have analogous natural abilities and identical endowments. They belong to social classes, they are constrained by institutions and they can exert (or undergo) power effects on (or from) other individuals. Therefore, individual decisions no longer reflect the 'forces of freedom'; they also depend on social inequalities and constraints. They contribute, however, to institutional changes, even if it is in an unintended way and if these changes will affect, in turn, subsequent economic behaviours.

One of the most significant examples of power relations is given by Wieser's relation between leaders and masses. Leaders are autonomous and their energy permits them to behave according to their individual aims. However, masses are not passive. They can accept or reject what leaders decided and their attitude is essential. If masses agree with leaders' actions, they are driven to copy them. Therefore,

> through the initiative of leaders and through initiative acceptance by the masses's, society develops certain institutions serving the common needs so well as to seem like

the creation of an organized social will. Money, markets, division of labour, the social economy itself are such creation. (Mitchell, 1917, p. 104)

In compliance with Menger's views, Wieser also introduces two different types of behaviour. One is *innovative*. It corresponds to leaders' decisions. The other one is *imitative*. It refers to the attitude of masses. The intervention of masses cannot be interpreted, however, as a pure act of recognition of the social utility of leaders' decisions. It generally transforms an individual invention into a real social device. Therefore, masses tend to create a final rule 'far beyond [leaders'] expectations' (Wieser, 1927, p. 165). This is the meaning Wieser attributes to Menger's idea according to which economic institutions are the 'unintended social results of individual teleological tendencies' (Wieser, 1927, p. 165). The distinction between leadership and masses is not, however, provisional or casual. It is first based on the existence of an inequality among the national community: 'Leadership is impossible without some inequality' (Wieser, 1927, p. 157).

But inequality is not sufficient. Permanence of inequality is also a determinant of the distinction between leadership and masses. It must be confirmed by the existence of social power:

> It is only when [the] superiority is so great as to give its possessor marked advantage that it gives him power (...). One speaks of social power, when the superiority places a large number of other people at a disadvantage and particularly when it is not individual possessors of power who are involved but social groups that are opposed. (Wieser, 1927, p. 157)

Social power can be reinforced by law but this is not a necessity. It gives birth to social classes and, within classes, to 'similar social groups' (Wieser, 1927, p. 158). These relations of 'social domination and subordination' (ibid., p. 158) generate what Wieser calls a 'social stratification' (ibid., p. 158), which influences substantially individual behaviours. From this standpoint, the example of the formation of prices in social economics is significant, since it shows how stratification modifies the natural effect of marginal utility on value.

We understand now why Wieser considers that his explanation of the working of the economic system 'involves a reduction of the individualistic stress' (ibid., p. 163).

Like Menger, Wieser clearly regards money as one of the founding institutions of social economy:

> For complicated social institutions the historical explanation requires further refinement. We shall show this by the classic illustration of money, whose unknown origin has provoked almost as much interest among men as the origin of the state or of speech. But we must also show that the more subtle explanation at which one finally arrives, necessarily involves a reduction of individualistic stress.

The long series of writers who sought to explain money as an individualistic institution, ends with Menger's penetrating investigation. He uses the phenomenon of money as a paradigm by which he assumes to show that all social institutions of the economy are nothing more than 'unintended social results of individual-teleological factors' (*Untersuchungen*, pp. 171–87). (Wieser, 1927, p. 163)

This quotation ought not to be interpreted, however, as a complete approbation of Menger's approach. Wieser indeed accepted it only partially. The author considers that money is something more than a social 'unintended result'. To put it briefly, for Wieser, Menger's story is substantially correct if we interpret what he calls 'individual efforts' as the efforts of the 'leaders'. In other words, Wieser implants his theory of the interaction between leadership and masses within Menger's approach. According to him, within the market process, the members of the society who had charge of the organization of exchanges very quickly realized the importance of the drawbacks implied by a barter economy. These drawbacks – which are familiar to economists – convinced the 'leaders' to introduce a simpler system which would have avoided the necessity of multiplying indirect and costly exchanges. Through a process of learning, little by little, they created several means of substitution according to their historical and cultural environment. Therefore these leaders, who only had their own interest in mind, indeed contributed to create a true unintended new monetary system. But, in Wieser's conception, these means only became a system when masses approved by imitating leaders, in other words, when everyone, in the least exchange processes, used the means introduced by the main participants to the market. Money is therefore an institution which is not understandable with the sole help of an individualistic approach.

4   ENTREPRENEURS AND MANAGERS IN SCHUMPETER'S ANALYSIS

We have checked how, in Menger's and Wieser's contributions, the existence of two different groups of agents, related to two difference types of economic rationality, contributed to the explanation of the emergence of specific institutions, as money or markets. All these ingredients are still present in Schumpeter's economic analysis. However, they no longer play the same role as in the contributions of the two other Austrian authors.

It is indeed clear that, in Schumpeter as well as in Menger or Wieser, two different types of economic rationality are present. This dichotomy specially appears in Schumpeter (1908) and (1912). The first corresponds to what Schumpeter calls 'hedonistic egoism' and is predominant in the framework of the circular flow. The second is related to 'energic egoism' and appears with economic development.

In Schumpeter (1908), hedonistic egoism is identified with Walrasian rational behaviour. Maximization of utility functions by equalization of relative prices to marginal utility ratios is the individual rule. In this theoretical framework, the use of the term 'hedonism' is the more disputable because Schumpeter supports Walras against the Austrian School in his attempt to expel psychology from economic theory:

> We have good reasons to be suspicious about sentences which we find everywhere in literature under the name of psychological assertions... Our examples show us clearly that the reference to psychology of crises does not mean anything but [banality]. (Schumpeter, 1908, p. 545)

Little by little, however, with the successive editions of *The Theory of Economic Development*, a different conception of 'hedonistic egoism' replaces Walrasian rational behaviour, in relation to the substitution of stationary circular flow by static equilibrium. This replacement had been rather slow. In the American edition of *The Theory of Economic Development,* Schumpeter still maintains the thesis of the compatibility between circular flow individual behaviours and consumers' and producers' micro-equilibria in the Walrasian sense (Schumpeter, 1934, p. 41). This does not yet imply that agents will actually behave as explicit and conscious maximizers:

> In this system of values a person's whole economy is expressed, all the relations of his life, his outlook, his method of production, his wants, all his economic combinations. The individual is never equally conscious of all parts of this value system; rather at any moment the greater part of it lies beneath the threshold of consciousness. Also, when he makes decisions concerning his economic conduct he does not pay attention to all the facts given expression to in this value system, but only to certain indices ready at hand. He acts in the ordinary daily round according to the general custom and experience. (ibid., p. 39)

This experience is the result of the past activity of individuals, which taught them 'sternly what [they had] to do' (ibid., p. 6). In other words, agents might have formed false expectations but, by trial and error, they were able to revise mistaken decisions. Individual behaviour, in circular flow, appears therefore to be *adaptive* rather than *optimal*. This adaptive behaviour is accurately described in the first pages of *Business Cycles* through the efforts of managers to perceive their environment and assign their own place with regard to a social norm, the 'normal business situation'. Here, hedonism is the equivalent of routine and adaptive rationality.

On the other hand, 'energic egoism' can be characterized as an active and 'voluntaristic' behaviour adopted by entrepreneurs. In this respect, the Schumpeterian approach contrasts strongly with the Walrasian one. In Walras's conception, entrepreneurs are pure intermediaries between services and product markets and do not earn any specific income.

Quite the reverse, Schumpeterian entrepreneurs play a central part in economic development. They do not adapt to their environment but adapt the environment to themselves. They shape technical methods of production, endowments as well as consumer preferences, being able to overcome the various resistances (psychological, social, and so on) that they meet in order to put their decisions into practice (ibid., pp. 119–24). Their rationality is not compatible with optimization because it excludes what Keynes called 'Benthamite calculation':

> Men who created modern industry were 'all of a piece men' and not cheap-jacks who were wondering continuously and with anguish whether every effort they expended promised them a sufficient increment of pleasure. These men were not very preoccupied by the hedonistic fruits of their actions... Such men create because they cannot help but do it. (Schumpeter, 1986, pp. 225–6)

It is therefore impossible to convert entrepreneurs' motives into measurable magnitudes. 'The will to found a private Kingdom', 'the will to conquer', or 'the joy of creating' cannot be evaluated or maximized (Schumpeter, 1934, p. 93). Consequently, Schumpeterian entrepreneurs differ drastically from neo-classical ones.

> For their success, keenness and rigor, but also a certain narrowness which concentrates on the immediate chances are essential. Schumpeter stresses that, in economic life, decisions must be taken 'without working out all the details' and he is by no means convinced that gathering and exploiting information is essential for the functioning of entrepreneurship. (Swoboda, in Seidl, 1984b, p. 18)

Schumpeterian entrepreneurs prefer intuitions to rational calculations (Schumpeter, 1934, p. 85). Innovations make precise calculations impossible. They reinforce uncertainty and oblige decision-makers to face it, sometimes being compelled to 'guess' the future rather than 'predict' it (Schumpeter, 1934, p. 85).

Finally, entrepreneurs are not permanent agents. They are submitted to a real process of selection, which eliminates 'losers' to the benefit of 'winners' or 'leaders' (Schumpeter, 1939, pp. 153–5). Moreover, entrepreneurs who cease innovating but survive become mere managers again.

This circumstance confirms the 'local' validity of hedonistic rationality: Schumpeter does not consider it as a universal type; it only appears as a static form of behaviour.

What we are doing amounts to this: we do not attack traditional theory, Walrasian or Marshallian, on its own ground. In particular, we do not take offence at its fundamental assumptions about business behavior – at the picture of prompt recognition of the data of a situation and of rational action in response to them. We know, of course, that these assumptions are very far from reality; but we hold that the logical schema of that theory is yet right 'in principle' and that deviations from it can be adequately taken care of by introducing frictions, lags and so on, and that they are, in fact, being taken care of, with increasing success, by recent work developing from traditional bases. We also hold, however, that this model covers less ground than is commonly supposed and that the whole economic process cannot be adequately described by it or in terms of (secondary) deviations from it... The reasonable thing for us to do, therefore, seems to confine the traditional analysis to the ground on which we find it useful, and to adopt other assumptions... for the purpose of describing a class of facts which lies beyond that ground. (ibid., pp. 98–9)

This opposition between two types of economic rationality is obviously related to Menger's as well as Wieser's approaches: 'We will assume that innovations are always associated with the rise to leadership of New Men' (Schumpeter, 1939, vol. I, p. 96).

Thus, some entrepreneurs are fundamentally innovators. They have the 'ability to take the lead as a part of entrepreneurial attitude' (ibid., p. 131). Whereas, 'Other entrepreneurs follow, after them still others in increasing number, in the path of innovation, which becomes progressively smoothed for successors by accumulating experience and vanishing obstacles' (ibid., p. 131).

These entrepreneurs are, therefore, imitators in the sense used by Menger and Wieser. The origin of the distinction between innovators and imitators lies in the existence or the absence of some specific skills: experience, intuition, mental freedom, ability to resist the hostility of the social environment (ibid., pp. 84–7) Entrepreneurs who have these qualities are then also to acquire what Schumpeter calls 'leadership' (ibid., p. 87). Now, 'only a few people have these qualities of leadership' (Schumpeter, 1934, p. 228). Therefore, here again, there is a kind of opposition between a small number of innovators and the main part of them who are, at best, imitators.

We can see, however, that the opposition between innovators and imitators is not used here to explain the emergence of institutions but rather the occurrence of economic evolution. This does not mean that Schumpeter was not interested at all by the problem of the emergence of social institutions. An interesting example of the attention the author paid to this type of theme is provided by an article wrote in 1918, 'The crisis of the tax state' (Schumpeter, 1918). Schumpeter tried to show that the origin of the modern state was located in its fiscal needs, starting from the European Middle Ages and ending with the contemporary organization of fiscality. A few remarks may be formulated within this context.

Firstly, it is clear that Schumpeter is interested in the original problem of Menger and Wieser, namely the study of the economic factors of emergence of institutions:

> Above all, there is the possibility, provided by the events described by fiscal history, of perceiving the laws of social being and becoming and the forces which constrain the destinies of peoples and also the way according to which *concrete* situations, especially specific forms of organisation, can emerge and disappear. (Schumpeter, 1918, p. 133)

This way of presenting the emergence of institutions has undoubtedly an evolutionary flavour. However, the term 'evolution' does not correspond here to its Lamarckian or Darwinian definitions. As Hodgson (1993, chap.10) points out, this term rather refers to 'a disturbance of existing structures and more like a series of explosions than a gentle process, through incessant transformation' (Schumpeter, 1939, vol. I, p. 102 quoted by Hodgson, 1993, p. 146). Schumpeterian evolution is more historically than biologically oriented.

Finally, history also has its limits. An outline of the main historical causes of a given situation does not mean its explanation: 'It is a prejudice to believe that the knowledge of the historical origin of an institution or of a type immediately shows us its sociological or economic nature' (Schumpeter, 1934, p. 76, see also Schumpeter, 1918, note 6, p. 173).

5   CONCLUSION

The outcome of this contribution is the highlighting of a substantial and significant continuity in three successive and prestigious versions of the Austrian tradition. However, what is more surprising is the content of this continuity. Far from being related to a kind of marginalist logic, it stresses the presence of evolutionary preoccupations within the Austrian tradition. The aspects of Menger's, Wieser's and Schumpeter's work stressed here are sometimes underestimated; the Austrian tradition is far more complex than a simple variant of marginal analysis and its evolutionary message should not be underrated. Moreover, our contribution also confirms that as early as the beginning of the 19th century, two kinds of evolutionary approaches were already present in economics: one, more related to biology and causal-genetic processes that Menger and Wieser developed; the other one, rather associated with history, that Marshall and Schumpeter illustrated. This dual situation still exists today and it might be more consistent to replace it by a more unified approach.

ACKNOWLEDGEMENT

The authors are very grateful to Geoffrey Hodgson and Pierre Garrouste for their comments and suggestions.

REFERENCES

Arena, R. (1992), 'Schumpeter after Walras: "economie pure" or "stylized facts"?', in T.S. Lowry (ed.), *Perspectives on the History of Economic Thought*, vol.VIII, Aldershot, UK and Brookfield, US: Edward Elgar.

Arena, R. (1997), 'Marshallians and Austrians on markets: uncertainty reduction, organization and institutions', Contribution to the Conference to celebrate Brian Loasby's work at Stirling University, (1967–1997), University of Stirling, Scotland, 26, 28 August.

Cahuc, P. (1993), *La Nouvelle microéconomie*, La Découverte, Paris.

Gloria-Palermo, S. (1999), *The Evolution of Austrian Economics – from Menger to Lachmann*, London: Routledge.

Hodgson, G. (1993), *Economics and Evolution – Bringing Life Back into Economics*, Cambridge: Polity Press.

Jaffé, W. (1976), 'Menger, Jevons and Walras de-homogeneized', *Economic Enquiry*, **XIV**: 511–24.

Menger, C. (1871), *Grundsätze der Volkswirtschaftslehre*, English translation: *Principles of Economics*, Glencoe, IL: Free Press (1950).

Menger, C. (1883), *Untersuchungen über die Methode der Sozialwissenschaft und der Politischen Oekonomie insbesondere*, English translation: *Problems of Economics and sociology*, Urbana: University of Illinois Press (1963).

Menger, C. (1892), 'On the origin of money', *Economic Journal*, no. 2, June.

Mitchell, W. (1917), 'Wieser's theory of social economics', *Political Science Quarterly*, **32** (1), March 104.

Schumpeter, J. (1908), *Das Wesen und der Hauprinhalt der Theoretischen Nationalökonomie*, Leipzig: Duncker und Humbolt.

Schumpeter, J. (1912), *Theorie der wirtschaftlichen Entwicklung*, Leipzig: Duncker and Humbolt

Schumpeter, J. (1918), *Die Krise de Steurstaates*, Graz and Berlin: Leuschuer and Lubensky, Italian translation: 'La crisi dello stato fiscale' in N. De Vecchi (ed.) (1983), *Stato e inflazione*, Turin: Bringhieri.

Schumpeter, J. (1934), *The Theory of Economic Development*, Cambridge, MA: Harvard University Press.

Schumpeter, J. (1939), *Business Cycles: a theoretical, historical and statistical analysis of the capitalist process*, 2 volumes, New York: MacGraw-Hill.

Schumpeter, J.A. (1986), 'Il capitolo II della teoria di Schumpeter (1912), in E. Pesciarelli, and E. Santarelli (1986 eds), *Quaderni di Storia del Economica Politica IV*, **4**: 220–43.

Seidl, C. (ed.) (1984), *Lectures on Schumpterian Economics: Schumpeter Centenary Memorial Lectures*, Berlin: Springer.

Stigler, G. (1941), *Production and Distribution Theories*, New York: Macmillan.

Streissler, E. (1972), 'To what extent was the Austrian School marginalist?', *History of Political Economy*, **4** (2), 426–41.

Wieser, von F. (1927), *Social Economics*, reedited in M.A. Kelley (ed.), 'Reprints of Economic Classics', New York: Greenberg.

8. Reading Edith Penrose's *The Theory of the Growth of the Firm* forty years on (1959–1999)

Margherita Turvani

1 INTRODUCTION

> In undertaking an analysis of the growth of the firm in the 1950s, the question I wanted to answer was whether there was something inherent in the very nature of any firm that both promoted its growth and necessarily limited its rate of growth. Clearly a definition of a firm with 'insides' was required – a definition more akin to that used by economists working on the structure of industry, such as Alfred Marshall or E.A.G. Robinson, and those from other disciplines treating the firm as an organization. (Penrose 1995, p. xi)

Thirty-five years after the first edition of *The Theory of the Growth of the Firm*, that is how Edith Penrose explained the reasons behind the research programme she had initially undertaken in the early 1950s.[1]

The book in question was published in 1959. In the years that followed there appeared other books and articles, which supplemented and developed points raised by her research – even if not all of them took her work as their starting point.[2] These works included such well-known publications as A. Chandler's *Strategy and Structure* (1962) and R. Marris's *The Economic Theory of Managerial Capitalism* (1964). In his book, Marris often makes explicit reference to Penrose's work and recognizes her influence on the direction taken by his own research. In an earlier review published in the *Economic Journal* (1961) Marris had already commented on the wealth of ideas and original analysis in Penrose's work:

> This book – which, if the evidence of last year's students' essays is any guide, is likely to prove one of the most influential of the decade – does not purport to provide an integrated analytical model of the growth of the firm. Rather it describes the why and the way, the controlling boundaries of a historical process. It is far more than an institutional description; new concepts are introduced and defined, and to some extent interactions analysed: we could say that the author is concerned with the theoretical internal biology of growth, but not, at this stage, with the logical interdependence of

the whole picture which emerges. The book is indeed so packed with ideas that it would be impossible for all of them to be consistent. (Marris 1961, p. 144)[3]

The extent and duration of the influence of Penrose's book was demonstrated even more clearly when the work was re-published twenty years later in 1980. In introducing the new edition of *The Theory of the Growth of the Firm*, Slater wrote:

> The influence of the book has been profound... Even two decades after its publication it has not lost vitality. Scarcely any economist now writing of the growth of firms can afford to ignore Edith Penrose's contribution. If you look in the index of any subsequent book on the theory of the firm or industrial organization, you cannot fail to come across her name. (Slater, 1980, p. vii)

Slater then goes on to point out how, in his opinion, the book had frequently been read in a rather careless way. Too often references to Penrose's work betrayed their superficiality. Only the general themes – such as her vision of the firm and her schematic model of a firm's growth – were referred to, and the bulk of the literature written over the intervening years had not fully appreciated and developed many important and interesting ideas in the book (such as, for example, Penrose's description of the mechanisms behind the process of growth).

Now, after another twenty years have gone by, what can be added to Slater's comments? Is Penrose's book a classic in the precise sense that it still offers useful instruments for researching the theory of the firm? In this chapter I will argue that the 1995 re-printing of *The Theory of the Growth of the Firm* primarily provides an important opportunity to explore the 'maternity' of many of the ideas that often lie behind contemporary economic studies on the firm. At the same time, we can see just where her seminal contribution is still a stimulus for deeper discussion of a set of insights which turned out to be extremely fruitful: I am referring to the crucial role of intangible resources (managerial and cognitive) in fostering and shaping the firm's capacity to grow by gradually developing a set of capabilities.

I wish to examine Penrose's work from the point of view of a young researcher in the 1990s. Having abandoned the now narrow and dated theoretical vision of the firm as a 'black box', he is attracted to pregnant images such as the 'nexus of contracts' and the firm as a 'nexus of competences', and is undecided between a 'resource-based perspective' or an 'evolutionary perspective'. Thus in a state of mental confusion in 1999 he comes across Edith Penrose's book (probably often cited but seldom read). He is surprised to find what Marris described as 'a goldmine of ideas'. Having lost none of their vitality, many of these ideas are familiar and many deserve greater recognition and further elaboration. Reading Mrs Penrose's book our researcher discovers

something that until then had received little attention and thought: growth –
that of the firm and his own mental growth – is a form of innovation. Like all
innovations, it cannot be completely anticipated *ex ante*. Although preserving
traces of the past, growth has the open-ended nature of new knowledge. As
Penrose puts it (1995, p. xiii): 'Growth is essentially an evolutionary process
and based on the cumulative growth of collective knowledge, in the context of
a purposive firm'. Our researcher thus discovers that reading a good book, a
classic, can set in motion an evolutionary process, providing the purposive
reader with the possibility of finding that, even after forty years or more,
combining elements of knowledge with fresh experience opens up new
prospects for mental growth.

The present work is organized as follows: the second section gives a general
outline of the work and deals in particular with the theme of the function and
nature of the firm and the definition of its boundaries, examining the relation
between Penrose's contribution in this field and the current debate on markets
and hierarchies. The third section outlines the characteristics of a firm's growth
and the role played by intangible resources, paying particular attention to the
role of managerial resources and the significance of the distinction Penrose
draws between productive resources and their services. It is on the basis of such
a distinction that the 'black box' of the firm can be opened up and new light cast
on its place in an economy based on the division of labour. The fourth section
looks at the mechanisms that are at the basis of a firm's distinctive capabilities, and thence sees the firm as an agent of change through its contribution to
the development of knowledge. The short final section lists some conclusions.

2   THE NATURE OF THE FIRM AND ITS BOUNDARIES

2.1   The Definition and the Nature of the Firm

In an article summarizing the state of the theory of the firm, Fritz Machlup
(1967) looked at the mainstays of the orthodox marginalist theory, comparing
them with the behaviourist and managerial approaches that were predominant
at the time. In doing so he came up with 'twenty-one concepts of the firm', and
argued that each of these different 'visions' of the firm were 'fictions', representations of a complex phenomenon that we invent according to our theoretical
or practical needs and aims. It was pointless, therefore, to discuss which concept
is the more important or more useful, given that they all serve different purposes.
Yet, the definition of the firm is the starting-point for Edith Penrose's work.[4]
She dedicates many pages to a definition and description of her 'vision' of the
firm, because that vision is the basis for her ideas about the mechanisms behind
the process of growth. The second chapter of *A Theory of the Growth of the*

Firm is entirely dedicated to a clear definition of what she means by the term 'firm' and what the function of such a firm is. The firm 'is a complex institution, impinging on economic and social life in many directions, comprising numerous decisions, influenced by miscellaneous and unpredictable human whims, yet generally directed in the light of human reason' (Penrose, 1995, p. 9).

Penrose links the definition of what constitutes a firm to the essential function it serves in the economic system: that of using productive resources to supply goods and services on the basis of plans prepared and implemented within the firm itself (p. 15). The debate on the nature of the firm (Williamson and Winter, 1993; Foss, 1993) in the 1980s, following Coase's key contribution (1937), suggests that the discriminating factor concerns the costs of using the mechanisms of price. In particular the economy of transaction costs makes this the fundamental reason for the existence of a firm in an economy which in the absence of transaction costs (that is, the costs of using the mechanisms of price), could only work through one institution: the market. But the fact that a firm is created because a coordinate set of actions must be introduced in order to achieve the productive aims is overlooked. The organization and planning provided by the firm are also the distinctive reasons and connotations shaping the firm which works in accordance with a specific design (Richardson, 1998).

When Penrose was writing in 1959, Coase's work (1937) had not been sufficiently assessed, but the 'islands of conscious power' (Robertson cited in Malmgren, 1961, p. 399) were being explored both in managerial and behavioural theories. It is not surprising, then, that there were explicit echoes of Simon (1947) and Barnard (1938) when Penrose succinctly identifies the firm with 'an autonomous administrative planning unit, the activities of which are interrelated and coordinated by policies which are framed in the light of their effect on the enterprise as a whole' (Penrose, 1995, p. 16).[5]

The autonomy and integrity of the firm, in all its variety and complexity, is the discriminating element compared to spontaneous forms of coordination: 'The essential difference between economic activity inside the firm and the economic activity in the "market" is that the former is carried on within an administrative organization, while the latter is not' (Penrose, 1995, p. 15).

Autonomy and integrity develop with the growth of the firm as it acquires new degrees of freedom for its governance, and because of this freedom productive resources can be recombined in an innovative way, even beyond the imperative of short-term profit imposed by the market: 'The larger this unit is, the smaller is the extent to which the allocation of productive resources to different uses and over time is directly governed by market forces and the greater is the scope for conscious planning of economic activities' (p. 15).

Penrose is quite clear in her insistence on the explicit intentionality of those involved in this economic activity. And she did not shift from this position during her long debate with Alchian over his claim that 'the essential point is that individual motivation and capability to predict the future may be sufficient but they are not necessary' (Alchian, 1950, p. 217) for ordered economic activity as described by the tenets of neoclassical economic theory.[6] On the contrary, in countering the viability approach proposed by Alchian, in which individuals are dispensed with by conscious rationalism, Penrose claims (1952, pp. 808–809) that firms and their fate are mainly in the hands of the people in them. Although the outcomes of intentional actions may not necessarily be deduced from the premises, as happens when a recombination of resources owned by the firm gives rise to unexpected productive services or their unforeseen use, the capacity to change the environment is one of the features of organizations. Such changes may make them winners, but can also make them losers.

So, for Penrose, the firm is not simply a theoretical construct – a fiction, as Machlup puts it – but rather a vital organization comprising agents who develop their control over productive resources, a body whose action is not limited to particular markets but essentially depends upon its own unfailing ability to carry out internal re-organization. The growth of this type of productive organization is not simply a question of self-reproduction on a larger scale (as the traditional neoclassical theory claims). Growth is not a question of increasing output but rather of expanding administrative coordination of resources. As Winter (1982) points out, in whatever field they are analysed, phenomena of growth are never simply a question of 'more of the same', but of a transformation of the form and skills of the organization or organism within which the process of growth is taking place.

2.2   The Boundaries of the Firm

The question of the boundaries of the firm is considered in terms of the size of the area of coordination – that is, the area throughout which directives are transmitted. According to Penrose, directives need to be understood as either detailed instructions or, more loosely, as the definition of policy criteria, procedures or routines governing the life of the firm and also the setting of aims that give rise to a common area of administrative coordination. Given that the aim of the firm is to use productive resources to produce and sell goods and services,

> a firm is more than an administrative unit; it is also a collection of productive resources, the disposal of which between different uses and over time is determined by administrative decision. When we regard the function of the private business firm from this point of view, the size of the firm is best gauged by some measure of the productive resources it employs. (Penrose, 1995, p. 24)

Later we are introduced to the notion of a certain vagueness in the boundaries of the firm: productive resources employed by the firm are not always under its direct control. They may belong to another firm but actively interplay with the first firm. Some resources will never be sold or acquired on the market but need to be developed inside the firm.

Clearly, if the firm is seen as a body of resources unified within a particular administrative framework, the boundaries of that framework are defined dynamically by the scale and range of administrative coordination and author- itative communication (Penrose, 1995, p. xi). If the firm so defined grows to the point that such forms of coordination are no longer available, then we will have to apply other theoretical explanations and models. According to Penrose, 'it is not clear if the theory of the growth of an industrial firm is applicable to holdings or other similar aggregations of firms' (Penrose, 1995, p. xi).

The reason for this is explained when Penrose points to and stresses the central notion of the autonomy and integrity of the firm. Highlighting the actual features of the administrative unit rather than a fictional unit based on the con- centration of the property rights over the productive resources, she reminds us that the firm is more a demonstration of the existence of mechanisms of coord- ination which are an alternative to the market than the result of a will to exercise and protect property rights.

> Suppose, for example, one giant firm buys a strong minority interest in another giant sufficient to give it partial financial control, but makes no attempt to coordinate the productive activity of the other firm with its own. It may interfere at strategic points, but its power to do so may be no greater than that attaching to other relationships, for example, to the position of a powerful customer. Is the former firm bigger than it was before? (Penrose, 1995, p. 21)[7]

A financial group cannot necessarily be understood and analysed as a 'firm', nor can its growth be understood in the same way. According to Penrose, the growth of such financial groups follows a logic that is to a large extent different from the logic of the firm (given that the latter involves the capacity to organize and manage production). She claims that the growth of a financial group should be linked directly with institutional considerations, questions of regulations, such as the definition of juridical limits and public policy criteria with regard to financial institutions (p. 22).

This failure to recognize the role played by financial mechanisms is perhaps an important limit to Penrose's model of the growth of the firm, particularly in light of the recent evolution of modern industrial systems. However, a closer examination of the implications of Penrose's approach reveals how her analysis of the firm can be applied to a study of the forms of industrial integration that are so common today and which are usually identified as quasi-firms (i.e. industrial parks, networks, company cooperation in both research and marketing). Penrose (Chap. 2) points out how, in certain cases, it is easier to recognize the boundaries of a firm (as she defines it) by looking at such organizational forms as long-term contracts, concessions and licence agreements (linking together firms which, from the point of view of ownership, are apparently independent) than by looking for financial links, which do not necessarily imply the presence of any form of administrative coordination. So control within a firm, understood as the ability to implement unified mechanisms of authoritative coordination, is a much more complex object of economic analysis than simple share-ownership.[8]

I will come back later to this idea of a firm as consisting of a cluster of resources around a centre which coordinates them, shapes their form, and, over time, establishes their structural relations. For the time being, suffice to say that such a picture is elusive enough to make the boundaries of a firm extremely flexible and malleable (independent of such institutional structures as national boundaries, for example), and well-delineated enough to make it possible to see new forms in the organization of internal coordination and authoritative communication (M-Form) for what they are: the polycentric reorganization of the resources commanded (Williamson, 1970, 1985). Such a view supplies useful ideas for the analysis of diverse phenomena such as multinationals, the spread of globalization in certain sectors of production, multidivisionalization within firms and all those phenomena which in current transaction-cost analyses are grouped together as hybrid forms in which hierarchical coordination and market coordination co-exist, supporting each other in turn (Williamson, 1991a; Croci *et al.*, 1989).[9]

2.3   Markets and Hierarchies

In discussing Penrose's definition of the firm as centred on administrative coordination and authoritative communication it is useful to briefly recall the now well-known distinction between markets and hierarchies. What we want to understand is why there are alternative institutions aimed at creating a satisfactory level of integration and coordination in an economy largely based on the division of labour. This distinction only becomes significant if it is possible to define an environment in which the various economic organizations could, one might say, reveal their relative advantages. As Knight claims:

> No one mode of organization is adequate or tolerable for all purposes in all fields. In the ultimate human society, no doubt, every conceivable type of organization machinery will find its place, and the problem takes the form of defining tasks and spheres of social endeavor for which each type is best adapted. (Knight, [1921] 1971, pp. x-xi)

Penrose's approach to the question of a firm's room for manoeuvre within the market is both original and dynamic. It is clear that while writing her theory of the growth of the firm she was unaware of the now classic dichotomy between market and hierarchy as laid down by Coase (1937). Not only does she make no reference to his work, but her own book aims to offer an innovative approach to questions raised by the neoclassical theory of the firm and the debate as to the optimal size for a firm.[10]

Penrose views the firm from inside, whilst the neoclassical theory simply saw the firm as a sort of 'black box', and showed no interest in it as an organization: 'the problem is not one of defining the best structure in the abstract, which may well be of such a kind that it can only be achieved after an infinitely long time (for example, if economies of scale are never exhausted). What is relevant, however, is an adequate definition of the forces which govern the day-to-day process of adaptation' (Di Bernardo, 1991, p. 386).

The innovative part of Penrose's approach is that she assumes

> constant returns to the firm both on the supply side and on the demand side. In the long run therefore there is no single optimum size that the firm will tend to, since any size is as profitable as any other. What then does determine the actual size of the firm at any point in time?.. The answer to this question is given by... increasing cost of growth. This is perhaps the innovation most characteristic of Mrs Penrose, so much that it has come to be known by her name as the Penrose Effect. Although there are constant returns in the long run, this constancy will be achieved only when perfect adaptation of all inputs to a particular scale has been made. This will not be possible in the short run if certain inputs are difficult to vary, and the faster the firm attempts to grow, the less well adapted will the input structure tend to be. Thus a firm is prevented from growing as fast as it may like because there is a very distinct cost of rapid growth. (Slater, 1980, p. xi)

In Penrose's model these costs of growth are linked to the difficulties of increasing and adapting managerial resources to the changing state of affairs. In such a situation, the area of administrative coordination and authoritative communication cannot be adequately expanded with respect to the market. The reason for this must be sought in those features of growth which imply that only very rarely does a firm grow according to the logic of 'more of the same'. On the contrary, growth and innovation in the use of productive resources go hand in hand. The fact that change implies innovation means that new responsibilities and new decisions are required, often in less familiar directions. The need to make a lasting revision of decision-making processes justifies the concrete and logical existence of an organizational form like the firm as an administrative unit.[11]

As others have observed, and as Penrose herself reiterates (1995), the idea that a firm has boundaries is more a logical necessity due to the assumption that there is a dichotomy between markets and hierarchies than a reflection of a clear distinction actually observable within our economic systems. Thus, she claims, there are a variety of complementary organizational responses which, thanks to mechanisms of administrative coordination, can fit together whilst remaining distinct. This point of view is in line with that recently put forward by Simon (1991), who describes the following situation. A Martian flies over the Earth and looks down at our economic systems from above: firms appear in green, the markets are red lines linking the firms. Vast areas of green can be seen all over the planet. Debriefed by his fellow Martians, he will describe his picture of the world: large areas of green linked by red lines, rather than a network of red lines interspersed with green blobs.

Penrose tends to emphasize the nuanced quality of those green areas of managerial and administrative activity which convention describes as 'firms', in contrast to 'the market'. Many of the red lines representing market coordination in fact represent fairly structured forms of coordination between firms (long-term contracts, joint ventures, networks and industrial parks), that are more properly described as forms of coordinated cooperation than simply market relations. This point of view put forward by Penrose has only recently gained a number of adherents, and it was firstly developed and expanded in G.B. Richardson (1972). His main contribution was the insistence on the need to abandon the rigid dichotomy between market and firm in favour of a tripartite division between management coordination, market coordination and forms of cooperation between firms.[12] The vast range of interrelations between firms thus creates networks in which the idea of a firm as an isolated body in a sea of market transactions loses most of its bite. This emphasis on the changing boundaries of the firm re-proposes the reasons why the firm is not simply a substitute that arises when there is a breakdown in market coordination (i.e. positive transaction costs).[13] It also focuses attention on the administrative processes within the firm and on the fact that their continual reorganization is essential if the firm is to maintain its vitality and thus redefine and extend its boundaries. The continual reorganization of the boundaries of the firm only partly depends on variations in transaction costs, for example, those connected to continuous changes in the markets, which are actually in turn the expression of reorganizations in other firms. This kind of reorganization also depends on organizational learning within the boundaries of the firm, which Penrose identifies as the administrative process defining the firm (Hodgson, 1998). Recently Demsetz has taken a similar position in criticizing those (himself included[14]) who had adopted a transactional approach to the study of the firm.

> There is much more to the problem of economic organization than is plausibly subsumed under transaction and monitoring cost. Perhaps the transaction and monitoring approaches to the theory of the firm have confined our research too much. Firms would exist in a world in which transaction and monitoring cost are zero, although their organization might be considerably different. (Demsetz, 1988, p. 154)

3 THE GROWTH OF THE FIRM AND THE ROLE OF INTANGIBLE RESOURCES

3.1 Managerial Resources

Penrose's emphasis on administrative coordination and authoritative communication as the distinctive features of the economic organization we describe as
a 'firm' defines both the nature and the limitations of such a body. A firm's
growth is the result of certain mechanisms that govern expansion, and foremost
amongst these are the managerial functions that are at the basis of the coordination and communication which hold together the resources the firm has at
its disposal.[15]

Thus the starting-point for an analysis of the process of growth is the
endogenous mechanism behind such expansion; the company's growth may
well depend on external opportunities but it also relies on a self-propelling
impetus arising out of the company's internal resources.

> But defining the problem not as one of allocative efficiency but in terms of the uses
> of, and limits to, growth of the firm, she makes a small but far-reaching move. She
> sidesteps entirely the plan versus the market dichotomy which has played a double role
> in economics: it fuelled the socialism versus capitalism debate over whether planning
> or market systems were more efficient, and it explained the boundary between admin-
> istrative and market coordination in neoclassical economic theory. Both of these
> approaches were static: Penrose moves directly to dynamics. (Best, 1990, p. 125)

As already mentioned, the firm is an administrative unit which exercises
coordination and authoritative communication. It does so by bringing resources
together in a certain cluster or structure that changes over time. Such change
is costly but also necessary if the resources available at a certain period are to
be used to best advantage. There is an endogenous mechanism – the active
search for better ways of using internal resources – which dynamically leads to
the growth of the resources the firm has at its disposal, and thus further fuels
growth. In all this, intangible resources seem to play a key role, precisely
because they are the resources behind the productive services that can be
modified and recombined over time. Managerial capabilities and human
resources in general become the focus of attention. The body of intangible
resources constitutes the body of knowledge upon which the firm can draw.

But let's start from the beginning. First of all one has to clarify exactly what
Penrose means by 'resource'. This concept is fundamental to an understanding
of the mechanisms of self-driven change, which creates the chance for a more
profitable exploitation of the intangible resources available within the firm.

Intangible resources – in particular, the managerial services a firm has at its
disposal at any one period of time – function as both a key stimulus to growth

and as a restriction upon the extent of that growth. Penrose emphasizes how managerial skills are best used as part of a team. Thus it is not individual abilities, but rather their organization within a team that creates the services a firm needs – creating what we would today call a 'company image' or 'corporate culture'.[16]

A firm works on many projects at the same time and so the coherence of the managerial team is of vital importance for growth. However, it also imposes a limit upon that growth because the acquisition of new managerial resources from the market can undermine teamwork and thus, if the firm tries to expand too rapidly, it undermines efficiency. The team is, in fact, created through working together, and individual and collective learning and training require time. So, managerial services are highly 'idiosyncratic' (Williamson, 1985) and the specialist skills acquired outside are not readily integrated within the team. The firm incurs sunk costs due to the long period of internal training required for the new resources, which also involves the diversion of internal managerial resources away from production towards the teaching process. Thus the more a firm needs new managerial resources, the greater the problem it will have in integrating those resources; and, at the same time, its existing pool of available resources will continue to limit possible growth. Therefore managerial dis-economies undoubtedly exist. But they are not a static correlative of a certain scale of production. Such phenomena are dynamic and transitory – the correlatives of expansion and growth. The self-same phenomenon that at one point hinders growth will, after due time required for training, actually create new possibilities of growth. When the new managerial resources have been integrated within the managerial group working on particular projects, they become more efficient – and at the same time they are now being under-used (given that their period of training is over), thus new resources have become available to fuel the process of growth.

Expansion, therefore, is a recurrent and unbalanced phenomenon. It occurs discontinuously and in directions that cannot be established a priori,

> with unused resources appearing from time to time, creating an incentive for the firm to find some way of using them. New resources and capabilities are being continually thrown up by the firm's experience in its current operations, as are new opportunities for expansion. This may be linked to the important concept of 'economies of growth', which are set against the better-known economies of scale. (Slater, 1980, p. xiii)

The structure of the organization is thus linked to its endowment of resources and their performance, achieved in a dynamic and – above all – non-deterministic way. But, according to Penrose,

> there is every reason to assume that the problem of fully using all resources will never be solved... because new services will become available from existing resources – services which were not anticipated when the expansion was originally planned....

The change in the service of managerial resources also changes the nature of the productive services available from other resources, as well as the significance to the firm's management of existing services. (Penrose, 1995, p. 74)

Penrose therefore claims that no firm can fully envisage the variety of services that can be derived from a particular resource, because the type of service identified is in large part limited by the management's ideas concerning possible productive associations. This claim may be read in two different ways. First, firms live in an uncertain world, in Knight's sense of the term, since management is not only fallible (that is, makes mistakes) but, most importantly, the management's world does not dispense with 'surprise' (Shackle, 1955).[17] Second, firms exist as autonomous units, characterized by their integrity insofar as there is consistency between the firm (administrative unit) and the management's ideas. Penrose thus emphasizes the connection between the 'soft side' of a firm and the 'hard side', that is, the connection between the corporate culture of the firm (its vision) and its ability to perform activities, which shape the continuous renewal of its capabilities.[18]

Thus notions such as the rigidity or flexibility of a firm's organization or of its factors of production no longer mean very much. Not only is it true that a certain endowment of resources does not rule out a flexible management of those resources, but in a certain sense it is the very rigidity (structural cohesion) of the firm's organization that makes it possible to achieve dynamic (flexible) use of resources and also new forms of internal cohesion.[19]

3.2   Resources and Services

In the previous section I often used the distinction between the pool of resources that form the supply of factors available to a firm at any given moment and the services that may arise from those resources in the future. Emphasis was also laid on the fact that the main activity of the firm is the transformation of resources into services (thanks to the action of its managerial group). Command over resources consists in precisely this activity of transformation, and administrative coordination is its most significant product.

Here it is worth recalling the distinction between the concept of productive resource and the neoclassical definition of a productive factor: a resource may be acquired in the market but, as we have seen with managerial resources, it is only within the framework of the firm using it that it acquires its distinctive character (that is, thanks to its specific place in the process of administrative coordination).

The physical resources of a firm consist of tangible things – plant, equipment, land and natural resources... and even the unsold stock of finished goods. Some of these are quickly and completely used up in the process of production... some are transformed... some that are produced within the firm, can neither be purchased nor sold outside the firm.... There are also human resources available in a firm.... For some purposes these can be treated as more or less fixed or durable resources, like plants or equipment; even though they are not owned by the firm, the firm suffers a loss akin to a capital loss when such employees leave the firm...

Strictly speaking, it is never resources that constitute themselves that are the inputs in the production process, but only the services that the resources can render. The services yielded by resources are a function of the way in which they are used... The important distinction between resources and services is not in their relative durability; rather it lies in the fact that resources consist of a bundle of potential services and can, for the most part, be defined independently of their use, while services cannot... it is largely in this distinction that we find the source of the uniqueness of each individual firm. (Penrose, 1995, pp. 24–25)

I quote at length because I believe this distinction between resources and the potential services derived from them to be the basis of one of the most innovative parts of Penrose's analysis. It lies at the root of the idea of growth being possible thanks to an endogenous mechanism at work on given resources, and also – as she herself points out – it helps to explain the distinctive character of each individual firm. Resources can be defined independently of their use, whilst services cannot. The transformation of resources into services requires some sort of collective activity and the definition of aims. In other words, services require coordination and management, whereas according to the neo-classical tenet, resources are allocated.[20] The same resource can be used for different ends, in different ways or in different combinations with other resources to give rise to different services or different systems of services.[21]

This distinction is at the base of the process which gives rise to the distinctive capabilities of an individual company – a notion that is now accepted in the literature on the theory of the firm albeit with varying emphasis. The contractual theory of the firm refers to the idiosyncratic nature of internal relationship within the organization and specifically to the processes that generate what transaction-cost economics describes as 'asset specificity' (Williamson, 1985). The evolutionary theory of the firm refers to the competence structure that in the forms of routines and capabilities differentiate individual organizations (Nelson and Winter, 1982; Dosi, Winter and Teece 1992). The resource-based approach develops within the field of strategic management, emphasizing how competitive advantage can be obtained by focusing on resource endowments of the firm, which lay the basis for distinctive competence (Mahoney and Pandian, 1992; Prahalad and Hamel, 1990).[22]

As Best (1990) points out, the distinction between resources and the open stream of services that may evolve in different circumstances and over time, highlights how the price in the market where the resource is acquired is not a sufficient measure for determining the value of the services it may generate for the firm that acquires it. Moreover, the value can vary from firm to firm, without there being any competitive mechanism in operation to even out those differences in value. The market price of a resource is an insufficient indicator of the value that a resource may have for a particular firm (given that the value can change if the resource is exploited in different contexts). So prices do not seem to contain all the information society needs for an efficient allocation of resources. From the point of view of the firm, it seems that market prices are no adequate guide when it comes to deciding the best combination of factors of production and, in fact, the combination of service resources is the result of an administrative decision-making process.[23]

3.3   More on the Nature of the Firm

Penrose often stresses that the firm is an administrative unit in which coordination is the result of management directives. But why are such directives so necessary? Penrose agrees with Coase that the market and hierarchies are distinct mechanisms for governing economic activity. But while Coase views reducing transaction costs as the fundamental reason for the existence of directives superseding repeated contracting, for Penrose the need for an administration based on command should be linked to decision-making processes in conditions of uncertainty.[24] At this point we find affinities with Knight's work ([1921] 1971).[25]

The institution of the firm arises within an economy based on the division of labour precisely because the market cannot deal with the uncertainty that is always present in human activity. In the ordered and mechanical flow of economic operations as envisaged by the idealized model of the perfect market there would be no need for particular forms of organization. When human activity takes place in a context from which a certain residual uncertainty cannot be eliminated – a context in which all the information relevant for any one decision is not available – then the problem of the management of uncertainty arises. As Knight puts it, 'centres' have to be identified which will become 'responsible' for that uncertainty. What was a self-governing society now develops a head, and what was an organism becomes an organization.

> With the introduction of uncertainty – the fact of ignorance and necessity of acting upon opinion rather than knowledge – into this Eden-like situation, its character is completely changed. With certainty present, doing things, the actual execution of activity becomes in a real sense a secondary part of life; the primary problem or function... is deciding what to do and how to do it. (Knight, [1921] 1971, p. 268)

Decision-making processes are no longer a question of pure calculation; the market itself no longer functions automatically, and specialized institutions arise to handle the decision-making processes. In fact, uncertainty means that decision-making is now a question of judgement, and in this new situation there must be a structure for the identification and attribution of responsibility. If, in conditions of perfect knowledge the interrelations between agents are known and each individual can freely assume the responsibilities for his or her actions (or be forced to do so), in conditions of Knightian uncertainty judgement replaces well-informed decisions and the boundaries of individual responsibility blur and begin to overlap.[26] Accordingly, the firm is the institutionalized site for the exercise of judgement, the site within which responsibilities are attributed. The authority that goes with the exercise of judgement is the expression of an unlimited acceptance of responsibility. Responsibility is thus concentrated. It could be said that there is a delegation of proxies centrewards, and Knight argues that it is precisely this form of uncertainty management which makes it possible to improve cooperation between individuals and constitutes the rationale for the firm. The concentration of responsibility is what makes it possible to delegate responsibility: when responsibility is concentrated it is, by definition (or, rather, mutual agreement), identifiable. Given that it is defined and identifiable, it can also be decentralized – that is, delegated as judged best: provided that the 'centre' is still responsible, however, for the residual system of agencies that has been set up. Penrose (1995, Chap. 4) elaborates this concept:

> As growth proceeds, the administrative structure of a firm changes – more and more authority becomes delegated 'down the line'.... Delegation of authority may be virtually 'final' in the sense that the decisions of subordinates in their defined fields are rarely overruled... but 'final' delegation of responsibility is impossible. Responsibility is cumulative in a firm... This progressive decentralization of authority... which leaves untouched the cumulation of ultimate responsibility is a necessary condition for continued growth. (Penrose, 1995, pp. 51–2)

The reason for this lies in the fact that, as we will see below, the conditions allowing and inducing a firm to grow are closely linked to the management's capacity to develop as a team. The gradual integration of human resources gives rise to experience, that is, the constitution of a pool of knowledge within the team. And this process, able to generate new productive services, provides the basis from which to stimulate growth.

> Individuals taking over executive functions new to them will find that many things are a problem.... As executives become more familiar with their work and succeed in integrating themselves... the effort required of them will be reduced and their capacity will therefore become less completely used, while at the same time that capacity will itself have increased through experience and the general growth of knowledge. (Penrose, 1995, p. 52)

Bearing in mind that according to Penrose 'uncertainty refers to the entrepreneur's confidence in his estimates or expectations' (p. 56), and that 'the planning of a business firm is based on expectations' (p. 56) she suggests that the firm's ability to grow relies heavily on the management's ability to develop as a team, that is on the possibility of executives having confidence in the judgement of other team members.

> Unless his own judgment has been involved, a businessman does not like to take responsibility... he may accept the judgment of people... especially if these people also share a general responsibility for the outcome. This is one of the functions of management as a team... The larger the group and the more they are willing to accept each other's judgment... the greater can be the absolute amount of activity planned. (ibid., p. 59)

Summing up, within the firm there is a process of administrative decision-making concerned with what combination of services can be derived from the productive resources. But as has been pointed out, such administrative decisions are not solely based on the evidence supplied by market prices. If prices alone are not sufficient to decide the optimal internal allocation of resources, then administrative decisions are expressions of judgement.[27] Management directives and authoritative communication are based on incomplete knowledge. Of course knowledge is partly an internal product and partly a market product (the latter being nothing other than the accumulated fruit of other administrative processes). The market thus offers only an incomplete criterion for the selection and evaluation – one might say, the certification – of information. In other words, no form of organization can totally resolve the problems posed by uncertainty, and management maintains its twofold role of authority and guarantee.[28]

4   THE DYNAMICS OF CHANGE

4.1   The Creation of Distinctive Capabilities

Penrose sees the process of the growth of the firm as being discontinuous and unbalanced. But what exactly are the mechanisms capable of producing growth, which is a form of change in the organizational structure? What drives the continual re-defining of the services to be derived from the productive resources available to the firm?

There are two mechanisms at work here: the dynamics of planning and implementation, and the implicit dynamics within that body of knowledge the firm has developed for precisely this end.

Returning to Knight's distinction between 'doing', 'what to do' and 'how to do it', in Penrose's view, there is an indissoluble link between these three elements. The firm moves from the definition of plans for expansion to their implementation, and in doing so develops a certain know-how, that is, it develops a pool of knowledge on which to build. It is this knowledge that structures the firm's distinctive skills and capabilities: they are the outcome of knowledge developed through the planning activity that gives rise to a certain know-how (which is specific to the firm and which will, in its turn, influence the direction taken by future projects).[29]

The very generation of the firm's skills thus shapes the firm as an administrative unit. In a certain sense, the bureaucratic aspect of the organization disappears behind the reality of productive processes. The firm not only ceases to be a 'black box', it is also much more complex than a mere collection of contractual links (or nexus of contracts), to use Coase's ideas (1937). Undoubtedly Coase's contribution opened up new lines of enquiry: it made it possible to force open the black box and to bring out the nature of the firm as a structure for the management of transactions. But it ignored processes of production, which only appear here and there amidst a technology that has apparently descended out of the blue. As Williamson says (1996, p. 6): 'Pin making, how to organize (more generally, how to govern) the 'eighteen distinct operations' (transactions) made famous by Adam Smith, rather than how many pins to make and at what price, becomes the object of analysis.' Paraphrasing Knight, the questions of 'what to do' and 'how to do it' are limited to the choice of the most appropriate contractual forms of 'doing': the technological and organizational problem of discovering, defining and learning 'how to do it' has been passed over in silence.[30] Similarly, the choice of 'what to do' (the problem of the market) – that is, which of the eighteen operations are best suited to the capabilities of the firm – also no longer appears to be significant. The emphasis on transaction costs may have pushed aside the core of the problem, namely, the choice between to make or to buy, assuming that all firms can produce all goods and services equally well. Other firms disappear, to be represented by the 'market', and therefore the market is treated as a perfect substitute for the firm in the area of production.[31]

As I have already stressed, Penrose's contribution today takes on new relevance precisely because it dwells on the theme of the distinctive capabilities of the individual firm and goes beyond the market-hierarchy dichotomy.[32] The development of knowledge, the progressive division and specialization of knowledge are part of the division of labour within (at the level of each individual firm) and between firms (at the level of industry). Even within the same industry, if the production of knowledge not only has a cost but that cost always depends on the specific skills and capabilities of the firm which have developed over time, then not only is the market no perfect substitute for the firm in the area of production but each firm will only exist insofar as it is capable of distinguishing itself from others – and thus reinforcing the process of the division of labour between firms. As Loasby observes, Penrose offers a modern version of the evolution of a single firm, which is at the same time a member of an industrial population. 'Firms have different experiences, and interpret them differently: thus the firms in a single industry are likely to develop different, if overlapping, sets of capabilities and to perceive different, if overlapping, sets of opportunities; and both capabilities and opportunities are changed by the very process of seeking to exploit them' (Loasby, 1991, p. 8).

At the level of each individual firm, knowledge is costly to produce, maintain and use – and thus specialization becomes a source of economies. From this point of view there is no reason to believe that organizations are any different from individuals. As von Hayek (1945) points out, knowledge is both diffused and localized, spread throughout the social fabric. A single individual cannot possibly possess all the knowledge and information available. And knowledge is non-homogeneous precisely because it is produced 'locally', given that it is the work of individuals, of separate, distinct minds. And, Hayek adds, through prices the market offers a synthetic indicator of all the information relevant at the local level, and transmits that information to all those who need it when deciding what to buy or what to produce.[33] It is through competition that the specific information possessed by individuals is compared and the shared knowledge resulting from prices is created. However, this is not a purely mechanical process. Von Hayek observes that the very local creation of information shows that individuals have an active role in the formation of the market. By combining the information in their possession with information obtained from the market, they perform a cognitive activity that can generate new knowledge and new opportunities. Thus the single individual, through his use of the institution of the market, on the one hand, spreads local knowledge and, on the other, takes advantage of a quantity of knowledge supplied by his fellows through the mechanism of price – knowledge that he could never have obtained directly. The competitive market thus appears as a procedure for discovering the new through a process exploring unused opportunities and a process diffusing information and creating new shared knowledge. This process in turn takes place within the firm. Here, too, knowledge is dispersed and here, too, the problem is what to do so that, on one hand, the information not available as a whole to anyone, becomes available to each, when relevant, and on the other, within the firm knowledge of 'time and place', to use von Hayek's phrase, is also produced and used, because the opportunities are always inextricably linked to this kind of knowledge becoming available through perception and experience.[34] What is more, the market prices to which a firm looks for information do not contain all that it needs in making its decisions: the internal allocation of resources – or, rather, the definition of productive services and their combination with each other – depends largely on 'local' knowledge produced within the firm itself by the process of administration. Firms are depositories of specialized knowledge and specialized resources (one of which is precisely the capacity to use such knowledge). So the development of knowledge through specialization becomes an advantage for all, because knowledge as a whole is not directly available to anyone.

4.2   The Development of Knowledge

We now come to the question of the role of cognitive processes within the firm. Penrose recalls the need to distinguish between 'objective' knowledge – 'knowledge about things which is, conceptually at least, independent of any particular individual or group of individuals' (1995, p. 53) – and the other forms of knowledge (experiences), 'also the result of learning, but learning in the form of personal experience' (p. 53). Thus, on the one hand, she recalls the distinction between codified and tacit forms of knowledge (Polanyi, 1967), and on the other, the distinction between the individual and collective role in the cognitive process.[35] Therefore, her treatment not only covers the question of the possibility or impossibility of transferring a body of knowledge from one context to another, it also highlights the fact that objective knowledge and tacit and personal knowledge can be uniquely combined through work in a group (an environment which re-creates the unique nature of individual experience).[36]

> The experience gained is not only of the kind... which enables a collection of individuals to become a working unit, but also of a kind which develops an increasing knowledge of the possibilities for action and the ways in which action can be taken by the group itself, that is the firm. This increase in knowledge not only causes the productive opportunity of a firm to change in ways unrelated to changes in the environment, but also contributes to the 'uniqueness' of the opportunity of each individual firm. (Penrose, 1995, p. 53)

This distinctive knowledge possessed by the firm is a form of collective knowledge, and means that the process of planning characteristic of that firm is very different from that suggested by an idea of a plan as something handed down from above and then implemented by subordinates on the basis of a set of instructions.[37] Precisely because a large part of the knowledge available is crystallized within the experience of the firm, it cannot be separated from the process of plan implementation, and the very activity of planning requires the cooperation of many individuals, each with their own knowledge. In her preface to the 1995 re-edition, Penrose writes: 'a firm's rate of growth is limited by the growth of knowledge within it' (1995, p. xvi), outlining an explicit link between the intangible resources on which the firm can draw: on the one hand, the services of human resources in the management and operative sphere, and on the other the different forms of knowledge available (tacit knowledge and transmissible objective knowledge).

Once it is recognized that the very processes of operation and of expansion are intimately associated with a process by which knowledge is increased, then it becomes immediately clear that the productive opportunity of a firm change even in the absence of any change in external circumstances or in fundamental technological knowledge. (1995, p. 56)

In producing its products the firm also produces knowledge and the conditions for its own change. Through planning and implementation new knowledge is generated and the expansion of the firm depends on the creation of an organization, an administrative unit, which models this growth in knowledge and is modelled by it:

> The administrative framework... provides an equilibrium structure of the theory and policy within which individual knowledge can evolve without threatening organizational coherence; but that equilibrium itself is the consequence of an evolutionary process during which managers learn to operate effectively together within a particular environment. It is this evolutionary process which generates the growth of managerial services – or reduction in governance costs – which is so important to her analysis, and also shapes the content and scope of those services. (Loasby, 1991, p. 61)

What takes place within the firm is a sort of diffuse form of what Schumpeter would call 'creative destruction'. By promoting the development of knowledge, the firm does not suffer the effects of a changing world, it becomes an active agent in those changes.

5   CONCLUSIONS

This chapter offers a reading of Edith Penrose's *The Theory of the Growth of the Firm*. The interpretation I have proposed here is in some ways partial[38] but nevertheless important in trying to comprehend more fully Penrose's perspective by focusing on one specific point: the determinant effect of intangible (managerial and cognitive) resources on the firm's capacity to grow. It has been shown how the dynamics of growth – necessarily linked to the development of knowledge within the firm – do not lead to a simple increase in production but rather to development along lines that tend to reinforce the heterogeneity of firms, further confirming each firm's distinctive capabilities. Thus in growing, a firm does not 'rise' like some well-baked cake, but develops in ways that reflect its previous history.

The limits on a firm's capacity for growth are temporary and are linked to its ability to draw services from productive resources over time. In this process the firm in a certain sense creates itself as an organization and, above all, develops knowledge of its environment and itself. This is why the firm cannot only grow, but also transforms itself over time – that is, it can modify the forms through which it exercises its command over knowledge, creating and defining its own distinctive capabilities.

Growth is a form of innovation – and like innovation it has all the characteristics of an uncertain activity whose results can not be foreseen. It is a form of innovation because it produces new combinations of the services drawn from productive resources – and it has an uncertain outcome because the introduction of new human resources (particularly managerial resources) is a source of novelty and discontinuity. Just like the acquisition of new knowledge, the introduction of new human resources opens potential space for future action. The implementation of plans for expansion does not end there – it lays the basis for future courses of action that were not envisaged at the time the original plan was drawn up. Reading Penrose's work thus brings us to the conclusion that if the firm is to be vital and to evolve, it must be equipped with innovative processes that are much deeper and more than mere technological innovation. Such processes attribute a new role to people within productive organizations. In writing *The Theory of the Growth of the Firm* in 1959 Penrose might not have had in mind what the reader (myself or the young researcher) could find in her book forty years later. But this is further proof of the fact that knowledge and experience combine in original ways, opening up new and unforeseen horizons.

ACKNOWLEDGEMENT

I should like to thank Brian Loasby, Nicolaj Foss, Richard Arena and an anonymous referee for reading this chapter; all errors are mine.

NOTES

1. In 1952 Penrose published an article in the *American Economic Review* on the application of biological analogies to the theory of the firm. In it she makes explicit reference to her research into the characteristics and causes of growth within a firm. Her research continued and was eventually published in 1959 as *The Theory of the Growth of the Firm.*
2. In the late 1950s and early 1960s research into the behaviour of the firm led to a gradual shift away from the traditional view of the firm as a unit for deciding such things as prices and quantities of the product to be produced. The progressive separation of control from ownership – already lucidly analysed in the 1930s by Berle and Means (1932) – and powerful processes of company growth led to attention being focused on the dynamics of growth and the internal characteristics of the firm. The firm then appeared – or, rather, reappeared (through a kind of return to Marshall's point of view) – as a vital organization capable of transformation, interaction with its environment, growth and decline. Lombardini (1973) outlines the three approaches to the analysis of the modern firm. The first focused on organizational and operational questions (Cyert and March, 1963; March and Simon, 1958; Williamson, 1970). The second started from the structural characteristics of the modern firm and modern technology, and then investigated their implications for the development of the capitalist

system at the time (Galbraith, 1967; Baran and Sweezy, 1966). The third examined the processes of growth and diversification in analysing the firm and its role in the market (Penrose, 1959; Baumol, 1959; Marris, 1964). Only in the 1970s would the rediscovery of Coase (1937) lead to the emergence of a neo-institutionalist approach, whilst a re-examination of Alchian (1950) and Penrose herself (1959) were to provide the bases for a new evolutionary theory of the firm. 'Amongst those who have taken an evolutionary point of view, Alchian's 1950 article is the most direct source of inspiration for our own work' (Nelson and Winter, 1982, p. 41).

3. In part developed before the appearance of Penrose's contribution, Marris's model is in effect an analytical discussion of this approach and brings out its macroeconomic implications in terms of managerial capitalism. Two of Penrose's innovations are incorporated in the model: the non-binding nature of demand (given the firm can diversify) and the transformation of management into a dynamic constraint. On the other hand, Marris's model explicitly introduces an autonomous objective behind management action (earnings) and the profit objective becomes one of security (through the maintenance of share prices). Thus growth, while seen as linked to the structural conditions of the firm, becomes an independent objective. Marris is thus convinced that managerial capitalism will grow and innovate faster than individual entrepreneurial capitalism. In partial conflict with the ideas of Schumpeter, this view is the core of the analysis in Lazonick (1991) – in which the visible role of management is seen as the key central component in the process enabling the USA to establish its economic supremacy over Great Britain.

4. Acknowledging that the firm is not a clear-cut entity (p. 10), Penrose believes in the importance of a definition reflecting reality in order to avoid generating ambiguity. She refuses to consider it as simply a theoretical construct or 'fiction' to use Machlup's term (1967). Incidentally, Machlup makes no mention of Penrose in this book, whereas she thanks him for having spurred her on to a rigorous drafting of the text (1995, pp. xxii).

5. It is worth noting that planning activities within the firm are organized bearing in mind the effects on the firm as an entity. Entrepreneurial choices connote the firm, and create an image of it. Starting from some ideas of Penrose, whom he explicitly thanks, Malmgren (1961) analyses the process of developing resources specific to the firm which gives rise to the capital of knowledge and information determining the specialization within the process of the division of knowledge. 'Here, then, the firm as a planning agency, rather than an instrument of coordination of transactions, becomes a tool for building possible future worlds, triggering off those processes of corporate culture production enabling the firm to recreate itself and be a reflection of its own "vision" ' (Egidi and Turvani, 1994, p. 26) .

6. In 1952 Penrose wrote: 'We have no reason whatsoever for thinking that the growth pattern of a biological organism is willed by the organism itself. On the other hand, we have every reason for thinking that the growth of a firm is willed by those who make the decisions... and the proof of this lies in the fact that no one can describe the development of any given firm or explain how it came to be the size it is except in term of decisions taken by individual men. Such decisions, to be sure, are constrained by the environment... but we know of no general laws predetermining men's choices, nor have we as yet established the basis for suspecting the existence of such laws' (1952, p. 808). Penrose here takes an extreme stance: on the one hand, her emphasis on volition and choice does not prevent her from outlining the growth of the firm as a highly evolutionary process (with the forms adopted by the growing firm being in some way determined by the previous status of each specific firm), on the other, the evolution of the firm is also read in historical terms – even though the 'distinctive capabilities' of a firm may be similar to a genetic structure. Her approach could perhaps be best seen as related to the modern theory of 'path dependent' phenomena (Arthur, 1994). For a re-examination of the evolutionary theory of the firm and the meaning of an evolutionary approach to economics, see Vromen (1995). For an in-depth discussion of Penrose's theoretical position on the appropriateness of biological analogies in economics, and for an extension of her critique of modern evolutionary theories to the firm, see Rizzello (1997).

7. For more recent interpretations of phenomena of quasi-integration between firms, we must remember that today the firm can be seen as a form of integration between stakeholders. From

this point of view, some stakeholders – such as firms that are important customers – might, in effect, exert more control than do large shareholders (Croci *et al.*, 1989).

8. Thus although the firm may benefit by combining its own resources with those of other firms through various possible agreements, this may in fact be prevented by the lack of adequate internal resources. There may not be the necessary skills (or indirect capabilities) required to create joint production services; see Foss and Loasby (1998).

9. Penrose (1956) shows a great interest in the study of international firms – as can be seen in her contribution on international investments and the growth of the firm (when such questions were attracting very little attention amongst economists), and in her numerous publications of the 1960s and 1970s. 'There are, of course, substantial differences among countries, but if we assume that certain factors of production are not only highly mobile but tend to move in packages containing different proportions and types of capital, managerial services, technology etc. bound together within the integrated framework of a firm, it is easy to envisage a process of expansion of an international firm within the theoretical framework as outlined in this book... there are naturally enough, clear differences between countries; but if we assume that certain factors of production are not very mobile and tend to move in "packages" made up of various proportions and types of capital, managerial services, technologies, etc. (held together by and integrated within that entity which we call a "firm"), one can easily foresee a process of growth in an international firm along the lines of the theory presented in this book. It is only necessary to make some subsidiary empirical assumptions to analyse the kind of opportunities for the profitable operations of foreign firms that are not available to firms confining their activities to one country' (Penrose, 1995, p. xv).

10. The aim was to get over the confusion in the neoclassical approach: if the firm is a theoretical construct defined by costs and demand curves, then there are serious problems in analysing competitive markets. In theory, the cost curve for a firm should in the long term be U-shaped – that is, show upward growth so as to make it possible to obtain an optimal size for the firm and also guarantee the survival of the competitive market (Sraffa, 1926). There had to be some dis-economies of scale 'somewhere' within the firm to justify the upward turn on the costs curve. What is more, these dis-economies did not really seem to be attributable to technological reasons. Not only did empirical evidence demonstrate the very opposite, but it was also true that such dis-economies, if they existed, could be resolved by growth to optimal size. As a result, emphasis was placed on dis-economies of management or coordination. Alternatively, there was the solution put forward by theoreticians of imperfect or monopolistic competition (Chamberlin, 1933; Robinson, 1933). In their model, a downward demand curve served as a check on the size of the firm, which would otherwise be provided by the managerial dis-economies shown in the upward costs curve. Such limits on the firm's size could be overcome if one took into consideration the firm's ability to diversify production.

11. Penrose takes up Kaldor's criticism (1934) of the theory of the optimal size for the firm. Kaldor denied that managerial costs grew too quickly with an increase in scale, and defined the firm as a productive combine endowed with a certain capability for coordination – a capability would only appear scarce in an unbalanced situation (i.e. when external conditions made adjustment necessary). In a situation of equilibrium, it could not be considered as a limiting constraint. Penrose's position seems closer to that of Coase (1937), who identifies diminishing returns on managerial activity as one of the major positive factors affecting the costs of internal organization – thus making the limit between transactions left to the market and those enclosed within the firm more liquid and mobile; see De Bernardo (1991) for further comments.

12. Langlois (1988) makes an interesting attempt to weld together the transactional approach and the approach in the work of Penrose – and Richardson's subsequent development of it (1972) – by placing great emphasis on the role played by a firm's distinctive capabilities. Taking up the work of Teece (1982, 1986) and Dosi *et al.* (1988), Langlois proposes a notion of dynamic transaction costs in order to take into account the processes of vertical integration in contexts where there is frequent and diffuse innovation (cases in which there are not only contractual costs but also all the difficulties involved in rapidly creating specific productive capabilities).

13. Commenting on the impact of his own work (1937) on theoretical and empirical studies of the firm, Coase is rather reluctant to attribute the choice between market and hierarchy only

to transaction costs. He considers the need for scholars to give due weight to the themes of management and the adaptability of organizations. See Coase (1991) and Williamson and Winter (1993).

14. Demsetz's self-criticism is particularly significant if one considers that in 1972 (in collaboration with Alchian), he published an essay on the organization of teamwork in which there is a firm denial of any specific difference in nature between the organization of the firm and the coordination within the market. He argued that the former was merely a case of centralized coordination designed to lower monitoring costs and enforce contracts. In his view, therefore, there was no difference between relations such as customer/greengrocer and employee/firm. In his later article, on the other hand, Demsetz indicates 'management' and the specialization of knowledge as two unavoidable phenomena in an economy based on the division of labour, leading to the specialized form of organization we call the firm.

15. Penrose borrows from Sargant Florence the idea that managerial resources are the key to understanding the stimulus to – and limitations upon – the growth of the firm. Florence wrote 'Business enterprise today is a corporate manifestation and its capacity to cope with larger outputs is not fixed but expands with its structure, and depends on the relation... between the governing members of the corporation... Some firms will fail with size because of management, if the immediate jump in size which they attempt is too great; or if the management is incapable of adapting its structure' (quoted in Penrose, 1995, p. 47). This idea that the top echelons of the organization are where change takes place (with the rest of the organization being relatively passive), is in turn taken from Barnard (1938, p. 35): 'Adjustments of co-operative systems are adjustments in the balance of the various types of organizational activities. The capacity for making these adjustments is a limiting factor.... These adjustment processes become management processes, and the specialized organs are executives and executive organizations. Hence, such processes and organs become in their turn the limitation of cooperation.'

16. In mainstream economics only recently the economic significance of reputation and corporate culture as a means for controlling contractual costs and establishing homogeneity of behaviour and creating stable expectations has been analysed (Kreps, 1990), whilst in other research areas, such as behavioural and management studies, the role played by corporate culture and corporate image as one of the variables that determines performance has been emphasized. For a discussion of the importance for a theory of the firm in including these concepts see Foss (1998), Fransman (1994) and Witt (1998).

17. The role of management is entrepreneurial in a precise sense: management not only provides coordination and control, it also identifies and exploits the opportunities implicit in a given structure. The idea of entrepreneurial behaviour here is similar to that found in the works of Kirzner (1979), rather than the 'heroic' view in Schumpeter's work.

18. The need for a certain correspondence between what the firm is (its whole set of resources) and what the firm does (the productive services expressing the vision or plan made by the management) helps illustrate how Penrose sees the firm not only as an economic institution but also as a social organization. And it is this nature which distinguishes the firm from other forms of organization such as the market. This point of view is shared by authors like Ghoshal and Moran (1996). In exploring the limits to the transactional approach to the study of the firm, they stress the fact that organizations provide a coherent institutional context. Taking up Penrose's vision, Goshal and Moran claim that the firm is able to do things the market cannot: 'The contribution that organizations make to the economy is not so much in doing what markets do... Rather, organizations' real contribution to economic progress is in their unique ability to create their own distinct context – not an instrumental one that mirrors the markets or responds to markets failures – but a coherent institutional context, which enables the organizations and its members to actually defy... the relentless gale of market forces' (Ghoshal and Moran 1996, p. 63) .

19. In another work (Turvani, 1998), I discuss the economic significance of a long-term work relationship with a firm. Formal rigidity goes along with a certain incompleteness in the terms of the contract: we can thus link the pairing rigidity/incompleteness not with difficulties in 'completing' all the details of the contract (due to questions of costs and available information), but rather to the fact that it is impossible at any one moment exhaustively to detail all the

potential services that might be derived from human resources. To express this concept I use the idea of 'resource liquidity', on the basis of Simon (1951). The employment contract thus implies having a sort of far-sightedness that is not present in other forms of contract (in which the parties involved try to cover the highest possible number of future contingencies).

20. The roots of this distinction between resources and services may be found in the Austrian tradition: something becomes a good insofar as it is directly or indirectly utilized, implying that agents must have capabilities available for use and that different agents may use the same thing with different capabilities, that is, giving rise to different goods. This view has very interesting implications for the economic analysis of consumer behaviour. See Bianchi and other papers in Bianchi (1998).

21. This varying efficiency in a firm's use of the resources at its disposal is focused on by Leibenstein (1966), who proposes the notion of x-efficiency. He sees the possible indeterminacy in the combination of productive services in relation to the difficulties involved in getting workers to make an adequate productive effort. This differs from the concept of 'organizational slack' introduced by March and Simon (1958) to illustrate the organizational dynamics at work due to changes in aims and expectations. Dietrich (1993) highlights the difficulty in reconstructing a univocal relation between input and services – a difficulty that opens up a whole series of problems for transaction-cost economics because the very notion of transaction is no longer independent of how that transaction is organized.

22. On the existence of and need for a common ground for comparisons and cross-fertilization between the various approaches, see Montgomery (1995) and especially the introduction by Foss, Knudsen and Montgomery.

23. Teece (1982) has noted that the economies of scope due to malleable services may be obtained from a set of resources. In the spirit of Penrose, this justifies a firm's diversification (provided the services cannot be resold because of a market failure) thus becoming the basis for generating a long-lived rent stream for the firm. Many arguments have been put forward to explain why firms diversify: for a survey, see Montgomery (1994). Best (1990) adopts a more radical approach claiming that the market cannot provide all the information necessary for the firm's choices: many services obtainable from the firm's resources may still be unknown, but will develop over time and in different circumstances. To use Arrow's terms, there are no future markets, and the firm's reorganizing and planning activities emerge as innovation.

24. In another work (Turvani, 1995) I discuss the issue of the nature of the firm in a market context by comparing the Knightian and Coasian theories of the firm. The former emphasizes the coherence of decision-making processes in conditions of uncertainty, whilst the latter stresses the costs of such processes. So whereas Knight focuses on the importance of management, Coase focuses on the forms of contract that can best share out these costs. On the same topic, see Langlois and Cosgel (1993), and Boundreaux and Holcombe (1989).

25. Even though Penrose only refers to Frank Knight in two footnotes, she elaborates the distinction between uncertainty and risk, a Knightian notion, in the context of expansion plans of the firm (Penrose, 1995, pp. 56–64), and she discusses the problem of authority delegation in a Knightian vein (p. 51). But it is primarily on the role of the firm as a cognitive agent, a collective place for the production of knowledge and progress that we find affinities between the two authors. According to Knight: 'a priori universal knowledge would not leave room for the entrepreneur. His role is to improve knowledge and bear the weight of its limits'. (Knight, introduction to the Italian translation, 1960, p. lxxiii). Penrose writes that: 'Growth... is based on the cumulative growth of collective knowledge, in the context of a purposive firm' (Penrose 1995, p. xiii).

26. It is not only a question of the problems caused by asymmetrical information (moral hazard and adverse selection). Nor is an appropriate distribution of incentive enough to re-establish individual responsibility. The problem is to develop forms for the management of uncertainty when contractual outcomes are, in fact, 'non-negotiable' – to use a definition introduced by Langlois and Cosgel (1993). These 'non-negotiable' outcomes include some that are strictly linked with the productive function of the firm – that is, they are linked to the impossibility of totally eliminating uncertainty in technological choices. Not only is the result of research unforeseeable, but there is also an element of chance at play in any introduction of new knowledge into the processes of production. See Rosenberg (1994) and Vincenti (1990).

27. In a paper devoted to Penrose's book on the growth of the firm, Foss (forthcoming) argues that some of the existing interpretations of Penrose's thought have often overlooked or suppressed her key ideas, notably the resource-base perspective. Concurring with my own reading, he identifies some of the radical innovations in Penrose's book, including the reappraisal of Knight's contribution on managerial judgement, the decision-making process within the firm and its uncertain character – both connected to the very nature of the development of knowledge.

28. Here I am dealing with some not so obvious affinities between Knight and Penrose, both of great importance for the development of a theory of the firm. For an in-depth discussion of Penrose's place in the filiation of economic ideas, see Loasby (forthcoming).

29. A firm's distinctive capabilities not only influence the direction of expansion (decided on the basis of criteria of similarity), but also affect the way that expansion takes place (the choice between new acquisitions and internal growth). The adaptability of innovative solutions not only depends on current laws or on the nature of the resources necessary for innovation (Teece, 1986). The enjoyment of quasi-rents depends essentially on the firm's previous supply of knowledge and capabilities.

30. For a revealing reconstruction of the nexus linking productive activity to innovation and the creation of knowledge, see Vincenti (1990). For an in-depth analysis of the uncertain nature of technological change, see Rosenberg (1982, 1994).

31. Loasby (1998) illustrates how the progressive development of the division of labour is always associated with a progressive division in knowledge. Every firm uses the market as a set of other firms, but to do so must develop the right (indirect) capabilities to act as an interface between its knowing how to act and gain knowledge as opposed to that dispersed in the market, that is, found in other firms.

32. On this point one should again remember the contribution made by Richardson (1972). Elaborating on Penrose's view, he highlights the fact that firms tend to grow by developing activities which are similar to each other (that is, require the same base skills), whilst they resort to other, complementary, firms for the satisfaction of other needs. Richardson (1998) has recently updated his point of view, emphasizing the clear-cut distinction between coordination by plans and spontaneous coordination, and abandoning the threefold partitioning of coordination mechanisms existing in the economic system (cooperation, directives and market): 'Firms... are needed to cause a set of actions to be carried out concurrently and in conformity with a particular design. The nature of this concurrent coordination... is such that it can never come about spontaneously as an unintended consequence of market transactions' (p. 1). He then discusses the feature of concurrent coordination which having to be continuous, requires planning and must be distinguished from the evolutionary coordination, provided by discrete adjustment though the market.

33. Other institutions as well as money perform this same function of widening the range of individual decisions and providing relevant information. Von Hayek, however, stresses that such institutions are necessarily instituted, not constituted. The market, language and money, for example, were not created by an intentional and rational collective decision; they are the historical, non-intentional result of the consolidation of inter-individual relations. He develops the distinction between organization (purposeful) and other spontaneous institutions and associates the latter with his analysis of institutional efficiency in dealing with knowledge. In another less well-known work (1952), he develops the microfoundation of his theories at the level of individuals' neurobiological endowments.

34. It thus becomes particularly important for a firm to safeguard its room for 'discretionality', areas in which to create a 'local responsiveness', a diffuse capacity to perceive opportunities that might lead to the creation of new local knowledge. Quoting von Hayek (1945, p. 520) Ghoshal, Moran and Almeida-Costa (1995) recall that one of the tasks a firm must undertake to enjoy the benefits of the continuous internal production of knowledge is that of shaping an organization which, on one hand, does not stifle individual motivation and, on the other, consciously tackles the problem raised by von Hayek: that is, 'how to expand the span of our utilization of resources beyond the span of control of any one mind'.

35. Nelson and Winter (1982) focused on how routine can consolidate knowledge. Note, in particular, that tacit knowledge is not that enclosed within an individual mind; it can also be

possessed by a group of individuals, who share non-codified (and, therefore, not easily trans-
ferable) knowledge. Routine thus covers the two aspects of the cognitive process: the tacit and
the collective. Through routine – which is a form of 'doing' – a corporate culture can be
generated, and this functions as a sort of lens through which the organization views its
environment. However, as we have previously seen, at this point there is a certain difference
between the idea of the evolving organization in Penrose's work and that outlined by Nelson
and Winter (1982) in the evolutionary theory of the firm. They note how the organization
'remembers' through routine, whilst Penrose shows how the organization produces knowledge
through 'doing'. For Nelson and Winter, routine is a sort of acquired repertoire of actions to
be carried out, whilst Penrose seems to see routine as an open and re-definable repertoire (re-
defined precisely thanks to the cognitive processes that take place within the organization).

36.　It is interesting to note how the combination of 'objective' and 'tacit' knowledge produces a
firm's distinctive capabilities which maintain, however, some features of ambiguity and
overlapping between firms. Ambiguity is especially connected to the tacit dimension of
knowledge, while overlapping capabilities may be generated, knowledge being a public good.
Criticizing the concept of 'economic resource' as used in traditional economic analysis,
Penrose observes: 'If we assume that the state of the art is not fixed and, in particular, that
the knowledge acquired by one firm is not immediately available to all firms, then the fact
that a 'goods' is freely available may encourage innovations which uses its services in
production' (1995, p. 78). If, for example, we imagine this form of 'free goods' to be
'objective' knowledge – that is publicly produced and divulged science – we can in part
understand how a tumultuous scientific development and a rapid free spread thereof are linked
to the differentiation between and break-up of firms, as well as to a strong upward turn in the
emergence of small specialized firms. The tree of shared knowledge sprouts branches, each
capable of bearing its own distinct fruit.

37.　In this context it is important to explore the function of factors such as leadership: Witt (1998)
notes that the process of developing knowledge within a firm is not only predetermined but
also ambiguous. It requires a cognitive leadership able to give it structure and coherency.
Penrose refers to similar concepts when discussing the administrative unit, stressing its
integrity and autonomy.

38.　An interpretation is always to some extent partial. Other possible interpretations are listed in
the bibliography, see in particular, the special issue of *Contribution to Political Economy*, **18**
(0), 1999 and the special issue of *Economies et Societies*, **33** (8) 1999, both dedicated to
Penrose's contribution to economics.

REFERENCES

Alchian, A. (1950), 'Uncertainty, evolution and economic theory', *Journal of Political Economy*, no. 58: 211–22.

Alchian, A. and H. Demsetz (1972), 'Production, information costs and economic organization', *American Economic Review*, no. 62: 777–95.

Arrow, K. (1962), 'The economic implications of learning by doing', *Review of Economic Studies*, no. 29: 155–73.

Arthur, B. (1994), *Increasing Returns and Path Dependence in the Economy*, Ann Arbor: University of Michigan Press.

Bain, J. (1956), *Barriers to New Competition*, Cambridge MA: Harvard University Press.

Baran, P. and P. Sweezy (1966), 'Monopoly capital', *Monthly Review Press*, New York.

Barnard, C. (1938), *The Functions of the Executive*, Cambridge MA: Harvard University Press.

Barney, G. and W. Ouchi (1984), 'Information cost and organizational governance', *Management Science*, no. 10: 155–73.

Baumol, W. (1959), *Business Behavior, Value and Growth*, New York: Harcourt.

Berle, A. and G. Means (1932), *The Modern Corporation and Private Property*, New York: Macmillan.

Best, M. (1990), *The New Competition*, Oxford: Blackwell.

Bianchi, M. (ed.) (1998), *The Active Consumer*, London: Routledge.

Boundreaux, D. and R. Holcombe (1989), 'The Coasian and Knightian theories of the firm', *Managerial and Decision Economics*, **10**: 50–61.

Chamberlin, E. (1933), *The Theory of Monopolistic Competition,* Cambridge, MA: Harvard University Press.

Chandler, A.D. (1962), *Strategy and Structure*, Cambridge, MA: MIT Press.

Coase, R. (1937), 'The nature of the firm', *Economica*, no. 4, pp. 386–405.

Coase, R. (1991), 'The institutional structure of production', Alfred Nobel Memorial Prize Lecture, Stockholm.

Croci, A. *et al.* (1989), 'Competizione dinamica, cooperazione tra imprese e strutture organizzaztive a rete', *Economia e politica industriale*, no. 64.

Cyert, R. and J. March (1963), *A Behavioral Theory of the Firm*, Englewood Cliffs: Prentice-Hall.

David, P. (1992), *Why are Institutions the Carriers of History?*, Department of Economics, Stanford University: mimeo.

Demsetz, H. (1988), 'The theory of the firm revisited', *Journal of Law, Economics, and Organization*, **4**: (1): 141–62.

Di Bernardo, B. (1991), *Le Dimensioni D'impresa: Scala, Scopo, Varietà*, Milan: Franco Angeli.

Dietrich, M. (1993), 'Transaction costs....and revenues', in C. Pitelis (ed.), *Transaction Costs, Markets and Hierarchies*, Oxford: Blackwell.

Doeringer, P. and M. Piore (1971), *Internal Labor Market and Manpower Analysis*, Lexington MA: Heath.

Dosi, G., C. Freeman, R. Nelson, G. Silverberg and L. Soete (eds) (1988), *Technical Change and Economic Theory,* London: Pinter.

Dosi, G., S. Winter and D. Teece (1992), 'Toward a theory of corporate coherence: preliminary remarks', in G.R. Dosi and P. Toninelli (eds), *Technology and Enterprise in Historical Perspective*, Oxford: Clarendon Press.

Egidi, M. (1992), 'Organizational learning and the division of labour', in H.A. Simon, M. Egidi and R. Marris (eds), *Economics, Bounded Rationality and the Cognitive Revolution*, Aldershot, UK and Brookfield, US: Edward Elgar.

Egidi, M. and M. Turrani (1994), *Le Ragioni Delle Organizzazioni Economiche*, Turin: Rosenberg and Sellier.

Eliasson, G. (1990), 'The firm as a competent team', *Journal of Economic Behavior and Organization*, no. 13: 275–98.

Foss, N.J. (1993), 'Theories of the firm: contractual and competence perspectives', *Journal of Evolutionary Economics*, no. 3: 127–44.

Foss, N.J. (ed.) (1997), *Resources, Firms and Strategies: a Reader in the Resources-based Perspective*, Oxford: Oxford University Press.

Foss, N.J. (1999), 'Edith Penrose and the Penrosians – or, why there is still so much to learn from "The Theory of the Growth of the Firm" ', *Economies et Sociétés*, **33** (8), August: 143–64.

Foss, N.J. and B. Loasby (1998), 'Introduction: capabilities and coordination', in N.J. Foss and B. Loasby (eds), *Economic Organization, Capabilities and Coordination: Essays in Honour of George B. Richardson*, London: Routledge.

Fransman, M. (1994), 'Information, knowledge, vision and theories of the firm', *Industrial and Corporate Change*, **3**: 713–57.

Fubini, L. (1997), 'Edith Penrose e la teoria della piccola impresa', *Storia del pensiero economico*, **33** (4): 149–58.

Galbraith, J. (1967), *The New Industrial State*, London: Hamish Hamilton.

Ghoshal, S., P. Moran and L. Almeida-Costa (1995), 'The essence of megacorporation: shared context, not structural hierarchy', *Journal of Institutional and Theoretical Economics*, **151** (4): 748–59.

Ghoshal, S. and P. Moran (1996), 'Theories of economic organization: the case for realism and balance', *Academy of Management Review*, **21**: 58–72.

Hannan, M. and J. Freeman (1978), 'The population ecology of organizations', in A. Meyer (ed.), *Environments and Organizations*, San Francisco: Jossey-Bass, pp. 131–71.

Hodgson, G. (1998), 'Competence and contract in the theory of the firm', *Journal of Economic Behavior and Organization*, **35**: 179–201.

Jensen M., and J. Meckling (1976), 'Theory of the firm: managerial behaviour, agency cost, and capital structure', *Journal of Financial Economics*, no. 3: 305–60.

Kaldor, N. (1934), 'The equilibrium of the firm', *Economic Journal*, **44**: 64–79.

Kirzner, I. (1979), *Perception, Opportunity, Profit*, Chicago: Chicago University Press.

Knight, F.H. (1921), *Risk, Uncertainty and Profit*, Chicago: University of Chicago Press (1971).

Knight, F.H. (1960) *Rischio, Incertezza, Profitto*, Italian translation, Florence: La Nuova Italia.

Kreps, D. (1990), 'Corporate culture and economic theory', in J. Alt and K. Shepsle (eds), *Perspectives on Positive Political Economy*, Cambridge: Cambridge University Press.

Krickx, G. (1991), 'Vertical integration: why transaction cost and resource dependence explanation cannot be easily separated', in J. Thepot and R. Thietart (eds), *Micro-economic Contributions to Strategic Management*, Elsevier Science, pp. 143–65.

Langlois, R. (1988), 'Economic change and the boundaries of the firm', *Journal of institutional and Theoretical Economics*, no. 144: 635–57.

Langlois, R.N. (1995), 'Capabilities and coherence in firms and markets', in C.A. Montgomery (ed.), *Resource-based and Evolutionary Theories of the Firm: Towards a Synthesis*, London: Kluwer Academic Publishers, pp. 71–100.

Langlois, R. and M. Cosgel (1993), 'Frank Knight on risk, uncertainty, and the firm: a new interpretation', *Economic Inquiry*, **31**: 456–65.

Langlois, R. and P. Robertson (1994), *Firms, Markets and Economic Change*, London: Routledge.

Lazonick, W. (1991), *Business Organization and the Myth of Market Economy*, New York: Cambridge University Press.

Leibenstein, H. (1966), 'Allocative efficiency vs. x-efficiency', *American Economic Review*, no. 56: 392–415.

Loasby, B.J. (1991), *'Equilibrium and Evolution*, New York: St Martin's Press.

Loasby, B.J. (1998), 'The organization of capabilities', *Journal of Economic Behavior and Organization*, **35**, pp. 139–60.

Loasby, B.J. (forthcoming), 'Edith Penrose's place in the filiation of economic ideas', *Cahiers de l'ISMEA–Serie Oeconomica*.

Lombardini, S. (ed.) (1973), *Teoria dell'impresa e struttura economica*, Bologna: Il Mulino.

Machlup, F. (1967), 'Theories of the firm: marginalist, behavioural, managerial', *American Economic Review*, **62**: 1–33.

Mahoney, J. and R. Pandian (1992), 'The resource-based view within the conversation of strategic management', *Strategic Management Journal*, **13**: 363–80.

Malmgren, H.B. (1961), 'Information, expectation and the theory of the firm', *Quarterly Journal of Economics*, no. 75: 399–421.

March, J.G. and H. Simon (1958), *Organizations*, New York: Wiley.

Marris, R. (1961), 'Review of "The Theory of the Growth of the Firm" ', *Economic Journal*, **71**: 144–8.

Marris, R. (1964), *The Economic Theory of Managerial Capitalism*, New York: Free Press.

Montgomery, C. (1994), 'Corporate diversification', *Journal of Economic Perspectives*, **8**: 163–78.

Montgomery, C.A. (ed.) (1995), *Resource-based and Evolutionary Theories of the Firm: Towards a Synthesis*, London: Kluwer Academic Publishers.

Nelson, R. (1995), 'Recent evolutionary theorizing about economic change', *Journal of Economic Literature*, **33**, March.

Nelson, R. and S. Winter (1982), *An Evolutionary Theory of Economic Change*, Cambridge MA: Belknap Press of Harvard University Press.

Penrose, E. (1952), 'Biological analogies in the theory of the firm', *American Economic Review*, no. 42: 804–19.

Penrose, E. (1956), 'Foreign investment and the growth of the firm', *Economic Journal*, **66**, June.

Penrose, E. (1959), *The Theory of the Growth of the Firm*, Oxford: Blackwell.

Penrose, E. (1980), *The Theory of the Growth of the Firm*, New York: Sharpe.

Penrose, E. (1995), *The Theory of the Growth of the Firm*, Oxford: Oxford University Press.

Peteraf, M. (1993), 'The cornerstones of competitive advantage: a resource-based view', *Strategic Management Journal*, **14**: 179–91.

Polanyi, M. (1962), *Personal Knowledge*, New York: Harper & Row.

Polanyi, M. (1966), *The Tacit Dimension*, Garden City, New York: Doubleday.

Prahalad, C. and G. Hamel (1990), 'The core competence of the corporation', *Harvard Business Review*, May–June: 78–91.

Richardson, G.B. (1972), 'The organization of industry', *Economic Journal*, **81**: 883–96.

Richardson, G.B. (1998), 'Production, planning and prices', Oxford: mimeo.

Rizzello, S. (1996), 'Mente, organizzazioni e istituzioni: i fondamenti microeconomici del neoistituzionalismo', *Economia Politica*, **13** (2): 237–75.

Rizzello, S. (1997), 'Analogie biologiche e teoria dell'impresa: la critica di Edith Penrose', *Storia del pensiero economico*, **13** (4): 97–116.

Robinson, J. (1933), *The Economics of Imperfect Competition*, London: Macmillan.

Rosenberg, N. (1982), *Inside the Black Box*, Cambridge: Cambridge University Press.

Rosenberg, N. (1994), *Uncertainty and Technological Change*, CEPR, Stanford University.

Sargant Florence, P. (1953), *The Logic of British and American Industry*, London: Routledge.

Schumpeter, J. (1946), *Theorie der wirtschaftlichen Entwicklung*, Berlin: Duncker und Humblot.

Shackle, G. (1955), *Uncertainty in Economics*, Cambridge: Cambridge University Press.

Simon, H. (1947), *Administrative Behaviour*, New York: Macmillan.

Simon, H. (1951), 'A formal theory of employment relations', *Econometrica*, no. 19, pp. 293–305.

Simon, H. (1991), 'Organization and markets', *Journal of Economic Perspectives*, no. 2: 25–42.

Slater, M. (1980), 'Foreword', in E. Penrose, *The Theory of the Growth of the Firm*, New York: Sharpe.

Spender, J. (1994), 'Organizational knowledge, collective practice and Penrose rents', *International Business Review*, **3**: 347–53.

Sraffa, P. (1926), 'The laws of returns under competitive conditions', *Economic Journal*, **36**: 535–50.

Teece, D. (1982), 'Towards an economic theory of the multiproduct firm', *Journal of Economic Behavior and Organization*, no. 3: 39–63.

Teece, D. (1986), 'Firm boundaries, technological innovation, and strategic management', in L. Thomas (ed.), *The Economics of Strategic Planning*, Lexington MA: Heath, pp. 187–99.

Turvani, M. (1995), 'The core of the firm: the issue of the employer–employee relationship', in J. Groenewegen (ed.) *Transaction Cost and Beyond*, Boston: Kluwer Academic Publishers, pp. 189–208.

Turvani, M. (1998), 'Black boxes, grey boxes: the scope of contracts in the theory of the firm', in K. Nielsen and B. Johnson (eds), *Evolution of Institutions, Organization and Technology*, Cheltenham, UK and Lyme, US: Edward Elgar.

Vincenti, W. (1990), *What Engineers Know and How they Know It*, Baltimore: Johns Hopkins Press.

von Hayek, F. (1952), *The Sensory Order*, London: Routledge.

von Hayek, F. (1945), 'The use of knowledge in society', *American Economic Review*, **35** (4): 519–30.

Vromen, J. (1995), *Economic Evolution*, London: Routledge.

Williamson, O.E. (1970), *Corporate Control and Business Behavior*, Englewood Cliffs: Prentice-Hall.

Williamson, O.E. (1985), *The Economic Institutions of Capitalism*, New York: Free Press.

Williamson, O.E. (1991a), 'Comparative economic organization: the analysis of discrete structural alternatives', *Administrative Science Quarterly*, no. 36: 269–96.

Williamson, O.E. (1991b), 'Strategizing, economizing, and economic organization', *Strategic Management Journal*, no. 12: 75–94.

Williamson, O.E. (1996), *The Mechanism of Governance*, Oxford: Oxford University Press.

Williamson, O.E. and S. Winter (1993), *The Nature of the Firm*, New York: Oxford University Press.

Winter, S. (1982), 'An essay on the theory of production', in S. Hymans (ed.), *Economics and the World Around It*, Ann Arbor: University of Michigan Press.

Witt, U. (1998), 'Imagination and leadership – The neglected dimension of an evolutionary theory of the firm', *Journal of Economic Behavior and Organization*, **35**: 161–77.

9. Economic analysis of human effort in organizations: a historical and critical perspective

Bénédicte Berthe and Michel Renault

1 INTRODUCTION

A certain number of contemporary studies have emphasized the uncertainty which characterizes the worker–employer relation, for instance the efficiency wage theory or more generally the theory of incentives. These theories address the supply of effort by the employee and the means used by firms to reduce the uncertainty concerning this effort and to encourage employees to deploy their effort.

Beneath the surface of these approaches lies a model or a conception of Man at work and/or of the individual within an organization which renders him essentially an opportunistic being, seeking to maximize his utility and so reduce his effort. Effort, or real work, is generally considered as painful, thus for W.S. Jevons: 'Work is any *painful* effort, mental or physical, that is partially or totally self-imposed in view of future pleasure' (1871, p. 248, emphasis added). The ultimate rational goal of the individual within an organization would therefore be to minimize his effort. Such a conception reveals itself to be too limited and too one-dimensional an approach to the complexity of the 'effort relationship' which links individuals (and groups) to the organization.

This chapter therefore has two objectives.

First, we will return to the origins of the modern economic conception of effort which dates, to simplify, from the 19th century and is rooted by last analysis in a physicist perception of human nature, the economics of the firm being viewed in the same perspective as machine economics. W.S. Jevons' perception of the supply of work (which is also a supply of effort) seems symptomatic of this topic and provides the 'canonical' model, which today feeds many contemporary theories on the supply of effort. We will therefore establish a non-exhaustive historical picture of these mechanistic analyses of effort, the common denominator being the 'principle of least effort' (section 2).

Second, we will outline the problematic of human effort within organizations by examining a number of contemporary models and by underlining their contributions and limitations, mainly in the case of the theory of incentives. The American radicals suggested that effort should not be considered as a consequence of an immutable human nature but partly as a function of the institutional and organizational framework. H. Leibenstein's analysis of effort seems to open up a number of perspectives which go beyond the over-strictly utilitarian framework of the usual neoclassical analysis. Conventions, cognitive frameworks and the social behaviour of the group all figure as important variables that need to be taken into account. This chapter will therefore lead logically to the opening of perspectives for redefining and enriching the notion of effort by going beyond the simplistic perception of the worker as a 'shirker' (section 3).

These two points will be approached in turn.

The scope of this chapter will of necessity be narrow. We voluntarily focus here on economic analysis and therefore we are led to neglect large parts of the motivation literature in other domains (psychology, sociology...). Nevertheless, such considerations underline our criticisms and our proposed reconstruction of the concept of effort. For example we often refer, implicitly or explicitly, to insights issued from behavioural economics which broadly introduced psychological or sociological factors in explaining human behaviour. We are of course aware that the whole question of effort requires more detailed exploration and would usefully be enhanced by more exhaustive references to extra-economic literature.

2   THE FOUNDATION IN ENERGETICS OF THE ECONOMIC ANALYSIS OF EFFORT

Broadly, the economic analysis of effort has its roots in a concept of energy, which also presided in the creation of the economic concept of rationality which determines the choices made by the individual and groups in allocating resources, and hence effort in particular. Within this framework, the principle of least action occupies a central position and we would like first to present some reminders of this physical principle, borrowed from the human sciences in the form of the principle of least effort.

2.1   The Principle of Least Action and the Energy Rationality of Nature

The modern formulation of the principle of least action goes back to Maupertuis's work (1698–1759). He was a student of D. Bernouilli's father (a pioneer in utility maximizing theory), J. Bernouilli (1667–1748). J. Bernouilli developed Leibniz's physics and was familiar with infinitesimal calculus. Maupertuis held a major place in 18th century thought: he was interested in physics, linguistics, geography, biology, morals…(Coleman, 1995, p. 42, see also Brunet, 1938) and he contributed to the introduction of Newtonian physics in continental Europe. Meanwhile Maupertuis was continuously influenced by Leibnizian metaphysics which led him to seek a rationalization for physical laws despite his mockery of Leibniz's principle of sufficient reason. The major contribution of Maupertuis to physics was one such rationalization: the hypothesis that physical laws obey a maximum/minimum principle known as the least action principle (Hamilton's principle of parsimony) first stated in the 'Accord de différentes lois de la nature' of 1744. In this work Maupertuis was dealing with problems concerning the reflection and refraction of light. In 1662 Fermat suggested the first solution in terms of a minimum: light would follow a time-minimizing path. Maupertuis criticized this conception and proposed a new solution: he made the hypothesis that the path light follows was such that the quantity of action was the least (Brunet, 1938; Coleman, 1995), action being defined as distance multiplied by speed and by the mass of the body. Despite the multiple formulation of action (see Brunet, 1938) Maupertuis successfully applied it to problems concerning the falling of bodies or levers. Meanwhile the principle obtained its full meaning from its metaphysical character. As a matter of fact Maupertuis thought his principle was giving a unity to Nature by showing that physical laws are in harmony. Leibniz's influence is clearly attested by Maupertuis' universalist claim for his principle. As Marshall noticed, the principle of least action owes much to Aristotelian physics where it can be found under the form of a principle of the rationality of Nature. This principle was then considered by scholastic thought as reflecting the wisdom of God whose purpose is the economy and conservation of Creation, as expressed by the maxim: Nature does nothing in vain. Leibniz later claimed that there is always a kind of rationality or harmony in phenomena which can be expressed in terms of a minimum or a maximum, that is to say, maximum effect and least expense (see Seris, 1987). Maupertuis' principle is at the very heart of the mechanistic conception of the universe, it allows for teleological considerations in physics (final causes in opposition to efficient causes), (Rosmorduc, 1985, pp. 39,110–11; Thuillier, 1991 p. 547). The least action principle also constitutes a first approach to conservative principles in physics, especially when it applies to equilibrium and collision of bodies. Concerning collision, Maupertuis noticed that the sum of 'forces vives' ($1/2mv^2$) is conserved in the case of elastic bodies. Later the principle of the conservation of energy will develop Maupertuis' intuition.

To mechanics the least action principle is of major importance especially for problems concerning the communication of force, wastes and efficiency (L. Carnot later underlined the importance of this principle for mechanics). As physics evolves it tends to lose its metaphysical character, at least in first analysis. J.L. Lagrange developed the principle considered as a 'simple and general result of the laws of mechanics' (1989, p. 189). Hamilton and Jacobi formulated it in terms of the variational framework and the Hamiltonian principle of least action (or parsimony) will thus be expressed in energetic terms: the integral $\int(T + U)dt$ will be called Hamiltonian action (action is a minimum for the path a particle follows: T = kinetic energy for a path going from A to B, U = potential).

The economic character of Nature governed by the principle of least action was clear in Maupertuis' mind. He wrote in his *Eloge de M. de Montesquieu* (1755): 'The problem which must therefore be resolved by the legislator is this: the body of men being assembled, the greatest possible sum of happiness must be obtained for it' (quoted by Coleman, 1995, p. 45). To Maupertuis the variety in human conduct is relative to the existence of different strategies to secure the same goal of utility maximization. As W. Coleman suggested: 'Just as action minimization was meant to show all the different physical laws were in harmony, utility maximization was going to show that all human behaviours were in harmony' (1995, p. 45). In Coleman's opinion, Maupertuis had the elements to formulate the principle of diminishing marginal utility and increasing marginal disutility (ibid., p. 45), the law of minimum pain is thus made analogous to the minimization of action. Moreover, Halevy asserted without any proof that Bentham borrowed some of his formula for 'moral calculus' from Maupertuis (ibid.).

2.1.1   Work, physics and economics

These considerations have their counterpart in economics with what we have called 'Cournot's Program' (Renault, 1991, 1992) which was to have a major role in the development of neoclassical economics. In his *Research on the mathematical principles of the theory of wealth*, Cournot compares the act of exchange with the transmission of movement by machines where losses and wastes are always to be suffered (Cournot, [1838] 1938, p. 3). He adds that, in time, the reality strains to attain the ideal state without theoretically defined losses, which corresponds to Walras, Pareto or Clark's definition of 'pure' economics (without friction). The influence of H.H. Gossen's 'Laws of human relations' should also be underlined. The economics of energy therefore plays a central role in the constitution of neoclassical economics (Mirowski, 1984, 1989; Renault, 1991). The neoclassical analysis of work thus sees itself as defined by analogy with the study of energy. As emphasized by several studies (Doray, 1981; Seris 1987, Rousseau and Vatin, 1991), the parallel emergence of the concept of work in economics and physics owes nothing to chance and the links between the 'animated engines' and the thermodynamic machine are not only metaphysical. The timing corroborates this correspondence since C.A.

Coulomb was a contemporary of A. Smith and appears as the founder of the modern problematic of the economics of effort which includes the work of L. Carnot, S. Carnot, C.L. Navier, G.G. de Coriolis and J.V. Poncelet as well as the 'energeticians' such as G. Helm or W. Ostwald. The fundamental question posed by Coulomb in *A study of man's energy* (1778) is as follows: 'to determine the quantity of action that men can provide through their daily work according to the different ways in which they can use their energy' (quoted by Rousseau and Vatin, 1991, p. 74). This bio-energetic perspective finds its methodological extension in Taylorian doctrine. Coulomb's problematic concern energy, the economics of effort, transferred to the workplace of 'human engines'. In this way, as L. Carnot states: 'The animal is like an assembly of corpuscles separated by springs of varying compression which harbor a certain quantity of life force; by stretching, these springs convert this latent force into a real and living force' (quoted by Doray, 1981, p. 71). The question of the productivity of the human machine is therefore posed. It is also an issue which questions the 'work-value' in the physical sense. This is affirmed by J.V. Poncelet:

> Animated engines can themselves be considered as a reservoir of work or of action susceptible to exhaustion after varying amounts of time and which need to be looked after and renewed frequently. However, the degree of fatigue felt by such engines (...) is, in short, one of the essential elements of the price of a working day in each country. We can therefore see that, for the entrepreneur or the factory boss, the question is not to make his men and animals produce the greatest quantity of daily work in absolute terms, thereby risking their health, but to use to best effect all of the interior action made available by food and rest. (quoted by Doray, 1981, p. 72).

The relationship between wages and the economics of effort (action) is therefore laid out, the wages of 'reproduction' correspond to an energy evaluation of action or effort in the production of movement. Work then appears as a 'mechanical currency', which is confirmed by Smith who claims that work was the 'primitive price', work being understood in the sense of effort. We also find a reference to the 'conservation' of energy. The human engine must therefore work within the law of least expense as Jules Amar affirms in *The Human Motor*.

2.1.2   From least action to least effort
'Least expense' and 'least action' constitute therefore the fundamental principle of the economic rationale of nature and is strictly analogous to the economic formulation of the principle of rationality in its two forms: the principle of maximum effect and the principle of least means as expressed by O. Lange:

the principle of greatest effect, which corresponds to the obtaining of the greatest degree of final production with a given expense of resources. The physicist Le Chatelier echoes this statement in his preface to Amar's *The Human Motor*: 'For the entrepreneur, only external work counts, and the problem of interest is to define the conditions which can maximize this external work for a worker's given state of fatigue' (quoted by Doray, 1981, p. 68).

the principle of least means, which implies employing a minimum of means in order to obtain a given final production.

These two approaches are symmetrical and strictly analogous (cf. Samuelson, 1972) in their constitution of the principles of maximum and minimum. On a semantic level, the analogy concerns the transformation of 'least action' into 'least effort' via the energy metaphor, for example by identifying utility with energy and disutility with work and effort, which we find implicitly with W.S. Jevons and explicitly with I. Fisher. This analogical process is well expressed by L. Amoroso, a disciple of V. Pareto, in the outline of his approach which becomes clear when he noticed that 'the principle of least means which is behind the behavior of all economic operators, is the same as the principle of least action' (Amoroso, 1962, p. 4). Analogies with the physical principle of least action in the human sciences are numerous: least pain, least effort... As Amoroso states, this corresponds to the general behavioural model in which 'in the process of transforming one energy to another, nature operates like a producer which, in a stationary economic establishment, is animated by the desire to produce with maximum return' (Amoroso, 1942, p. 163). The principle of least action is also fundamental to F.Y. Edgeworth (1881, p. 11) for whom the comparison between energy and pleasure is a matter of 'real and profound analogy', maximum pleasure being associated with a maximum of physical energy (ibid., p. 80) and therefore of least expense or least effort. Similarly, L. Winiarski, a friend of L. Walras and a member of the Lausanne school, made the principle of least effort the 'basis of social science' (Winiarski, 1903). For Y. Guyot:

> the entire history of human invention obeys this law: men look for least resistance; the more ingenious he is, the more he aims to reduce his effort (...) We consequently witness throughout the history of invention man's perpetual tendency to search for means to exert the least effort in order to obtain the same utility. (Guyot, 1896, pp. 32–3)

In principle, therefore, least effort is raised to the status of a rationale governing human behaviour. In every situation the individual will aim to minimize his effort, his loss or his expense and the passage to the opportunistic behaviour of agents within organizations and to the model of the 'shirker' is therefore simple to make. The pre-eminence of the mechanistic model of behaviour that we find with the behaviourists referring to G.K. Zipf's thesis (1949) entitled *Human Behavior and the Principle of Least Effort* is therefore very strong, as emphasized by J.L. Le Moigne (1997, p. 68). Zipf's goal was to find convincing arguments to support his thesis that 'every individual's entire behavior is governed by the principle of least effort' (Zipf, 1949, p. 6). In Zipf's theory the tendency to minimize effort does not mean expending as little work as possible at any moment but that a 'person's average rate of work-expenditure over time' is minimized (ibid.). It should also be noticed that Zipf, as was the case for Maupertuis, saw this principle being progressive in a process of adaptive evolution. The use of tools or technical devices participates to this orthogenesis. In Zipf's view, the principle of least effort is also correlated with the law of diminishing returns and he proposed a rationale for the mechanistic approach to effort (for more details, see Coulmas, 1992, pp. 235–8).

Thus, from its origin, the economic perspective is one of the individual aiming to avoid effort and to minimize his action within the organization. The canonical model of reference is therefore that of W.S. Jevons.

2.2 W.S. Jevons' 'Canonical' Model and the Mechanistic Conception of Effort

Jevons' analysis of the labour supply is well known, but it seems to us that one can only realistically interpret it in energy terms. Jevons' thesis, expressed by his famous curve (see Figure 9.1), is as follows:

> The painfulness of work compared to its product is represented by the curve *abcd* (...). The work is often more painful to begin with than when the body and mind are fully occupied by the job. Thus, effort is initially measured by 0*a*. At *b* there is neither pleasure nor effort. Between *b* and *c* there is an excess of pleasure due to the effort itself, but beyond c, energy begins to run out and the resulting effort is represented by the curve *cd*. At the same time we can represent the final level of the product on the curve *pq*, the quantity of product being measured on the line 0*x*. The worker will stop working at point *m*. It would be incompatible with human nature for a man to work when the effort involved in working exceeds the desire to possess, which includes all the causes of exhaustion.

For Fisher, the disutility associated with work is above all assimilated with a 'loss', an 'expense' of physical energy that should be minimized. If work procured a clear utility, the supply would become infinite. Thus from the supply point of view, we recall that work is defined by Jevons, as '*painful* effort' (Jevons, 1909, p. 245 emphasis added). Work, or productive effort, is only viewed negatively, simply as something unpleasant to be suffered, which is coherent with a physicist perception of the notion of effort. As F. Vatin emphasizes, Jevons borrows his notion of effort directly from physics, notably by putting forward its two dimensions:

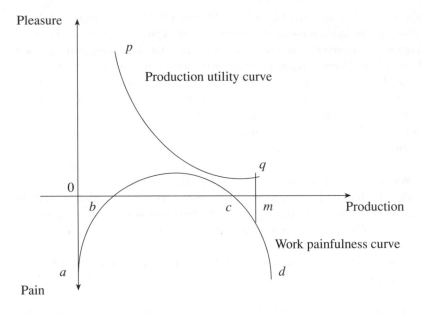

Figure 9.1   Jevons' curves

> In a given time a man can cover a variable distance, chop a variable amount of wood,
> pump a variable amount of water; in short, he can expend a variable amount of nervous
> or muscular energy. Hence the total work done will be a two-dimensional quantity,
> the product of intensity in time when the intensity is constant or the sum of the limited
> area of a curve when the intensity is variable (ibid. p. 25).

The reference to nervous energy does not invalidate the reference to energy:
in the *Principles of Science*, Jevons considered that one day it would be possible
to enter the mechanisms of the mind into the domain of physico-chemistry, the
concept of energy appearing as a unifying concept for human science. The
physical perception of work and of effort is again confirmed by Jevons:

> We can measure approximately the intensity of work by the amount of physical force
> used in a given time, although it is the effort resulting from this expenditure of energy
> that is the capital element for economics. Some interesting laws have been and could
> be discovered which will link the amount of work done to the intensity of the work
> (ibid., p. 288).

Jevons then refers to the work of Coulomb, Babbage and the physiologists
of his time as well as to his own work. On this subject, it must be remembered
that the formulation of the principle of the conservation of energy is partly due
to the work of the German physiologist H. Helmholtz; the relationship between

the physiology of effort and energy is therefore not merely accidental. The aim of this research, and in particular that undertaken by Jevons himself, is clear: to determine certain laws 'which form the physical basis of economics' (ibid., p. 292). Concerning effort, Jevons explicitly refers to R. Jennings, for example he argued, quoting Jennings, that 'The degree of toilsome sensation' increased rapidly with the work performed 'like the resistance offered by an opposing medium to the velocity of a moving body' (Jevons/Jennings quoted by White, 1994, p. 206). The object of *The Theory of Political Economy* was then to give evidence to the laws forming the physical basis of political economy, the famous work decision diagram is thus made analogous to a gravitational force field (White, 1994, p. 206). As F. Vatin emphasizes there is no break with the old perception of work effort and the 'modern' perception resulting mainly from Jevons' work: it means simply finding a common measure of physical and mental fatigue, of utility and disutility, and within this framework, energy appeared at the time as this common measure. Thus:

> From Jevons to the present day, implicitly or explicitly, economists embrace this hypothesis, just like the ergonomists when they measure a 'mental charge', according to the widely accepted mechanical metaphor. In this sense, even in contemporary neo-classical theory, work in the physical sense contributes, if only marginally, to the definition of value. The idea of 'physical' expenditure remains the prime value which allows us to include the labor supply, a frequently neglected but essential element, to complete the theory of the general equilibrium (Vatin, 1993, p. 103).

It must also be noted that, curiously, the Marxist perception of work is close to the energy perception and the *Letters concerning Science and Nature* reveal the proximity of Marx's theses to energy problematic. It is generally accepted today that Marx's ideas were in line with classical economics, in particular those of Smith in terms of his work-value theory and the definition of work as 'pain', 'the value of merchandise represents purely and simply man's work, an expenditure of human energy in general' (Le Capital I, [1867] 1975, p. 59). Marx's perception of work is essentially naturalist, even physicist, and the metaphor of the bee and the architect does not invalidate this initial base of work-expenditure or mechanical energy:

> Work is above all an act that occurs between man and nature. Man's role with regard to nature is one of natural power. The force with which his body is endowed, in his arms and legs, his head and hands, is put into movement in order to assimilate different materials to give them a form that is useful in life (ibid., p. 180).

The analyses of 'energeticians' like Podolinski (to whom Marx and Engels refer), Ostwald or Lotka, are perfectly in line with this perspective of a 'value' attributed to things by the transformation of energy. Thus as F. Vatin again emphasizes:

> In their construction as well as their objectives, the mechanical theory of work and Marx's theory of value are surprisingly similar. The objective is the same: to find a common measure of the value of the product and of the expenditure which, by comparing one with the other, allows us to identify a ratio which expresses productive efficiency. More generally, it is concerned with rendering compatible a theory of equilibrium and a theory of movement and transformation. (Vatin, 1993, p. 107)

W.S. Jevons also had the idea of the necessity of a 'reproduction' of the labour power in a physical sense, in such a way that at the end of a day's work, the worker could 'repair all his fatigue' and start again the next day 'with a full reserve of energy' (Jevons, 1909, p. 294). As M. White argues: 'Jevons (thus) appears to have been attempting to represent the labor disutilty analysis as isomorphic with a process in which potential energy was replaced with kinetic energy at work' (White, 1994, p. 208). The energy metaphor operates in a conservative context. However, what Marx seems to bring out is the 'creative' aspect of work which seems to contradict the energy paradigm in which, as S. Carnot has shown, the productivity of machines is less than one. This is doubtless what justified Engels' insistence on establishing a distinction between economic work and physical work, which does not appear in the Marxist perception.

In spite of this, the physicist and energy perception of effort remains beneath the surface of the contemporary economic perception of effort, which is essentially seen as a loss or an expense which must be minimized. In the end, only Veblen initially seems to envisage work and effort from a positive angle. For Veblen, effort is an intrinsic dimension of individual behaviour, even an instinct, 'the instinct of workmanship', and the devaluation of work and effort is linked to the advent and the domination of the 'leisure classes', rooted in the 'warring era' which saw power and wealth transferred to 'predators' (priests, warriors, and so on) who only take what is due and create no real wealth, physical or material. The devaluation of productive work and the resulting quest to minimize effort appears therefore as an essentially cultural phenomenon and not a 'natural' one as seems to have been the case in previous studies. According to Veblen, economics failed to take human behaviour into account because 'the human material with which the inquiry is concerned is conceived in hedonistic terms; that is to say, in terms of a passive and substantially inert and immutably given human nature' (1990, p. 73). Such a conception is, according to Veblen, largely outdated; to him: 'it is the characteristic of man to do something, not simply to suffer pleasures and pains though the impact of suitable forces' and therefore man is 'a coherent structure of propensities and habits which seeks realization and expression in an unfolding activity' (ibid., p. 74). Work and effort can thus no more be referred to as the 'process of saturating given desires'.

Early psychological or management literature on motivation does not escape such a mechanistic framework. The energy metaphor lies at the very heart of the 'machine metaphor in motivation' (Weiner, 1992). As B. Weiner clearly demonstrated most of the initial works exploring human motivation made explicit references to the energetic framework. H. Helmholtz, for instance, is known as a physician but also as a physiologist whose views exerted a great influence upon psychological science. W. Wundt, Weber and Fechner who were pioneers in experimental psychology, also referred to energetics. Later, Freud's theory of human motivation was also guided by Helmholtz's energetic views. As R. Holt argued:

> The concept of energy was a preoccupation of Freud's from the very beginning of his scientific work, considerably ante-dating any psychoanalytic model. When Freud was a student, energy was so much the rage, as stylish a concept as information is today, or perhaps more so. The brilliant discoveries that the apparently different forms of physical energy (heat, light, mechanical etc.) were interchangeable and interconvertible was a profoundly exciting one, and it seemed to suggest that the work done by biological organisms, in all of the many different ways they used energy, could be looked on as a further instance of these transformations. (quoted in Cofer and Appley, 1964, p. 596)

Freud's theory is illustrative of the relations between theories of human motivation and energetics. Freud conceived of human beings as closed energy systems, and energy distribution was related to happiness, this later point being reminiscent of the hedonistic framework.

Another clearly mechanistic framework in the psychology of motivation was supported by K. Lewin, who referred to field physics. Many other instances of the influence energetics exerted on motivation theories could be found, in fine they all referred to physical concepts such as work, effort, equilibrium, energy, potential...and behaviour is aimed at the attainment of a state of equilibrium or rest (the term is not neutral). Such a state can be conceived of as being determined by maximum/minimum principles (issued from the principle of least action), for example concerning the allocation of energy among various activities.

This general energetic conception of the production of effort is still present in recent theories. It is particularly apparent in the theory of incentives. Similarly, via his function of the utility of effort, H. Leibenstein's perspective seems to reiterate certain aspects of the original position, linked to 'Jevons' curve', even if its content is otherwise largely innovative, and the American Radicals analysis remains indebted to the Marxist tradition.

3   FROM RECENT ECONOMIC ANALYSIS OF EFFORT TOWARD A NEW CONCEPTION

In contemporary theories, effort is approached within the frameworks of the organization and of the employment relationship. Effort characterizes the employee's action. Effort is the object of the employment exchange and has the characteristic of being a commodity whose quantity and quality is not wholly specified and obtained when the contract is signed. It must be noticed that the problematics which surround the subject of effort are the same for all contemporary theories: the firm is not satisfied simply with buying effort in exchange for wages, the problem the organization faces is what means to employ to get the employee's effort in the course of the employment relationship.

3.1   Effort in Recent Economic Theories

Effort is taken into account in the theory of incentives, in American Radicals economics and H. Leibenstein's approach.

3.1.1   Effort in the theory of incentives

Effort and the diversity of incentives mechanisms   The theory of incentives prolongs the neoclassical tradition. The behaviour of economic agents is characterized by the rational and calculated pursuit of their own individual interests. Thus the effort produced by the employee is the result of an optimizing calculation of his utility. In consequence, the employer who wishes to obtain this effort creates some incentive mechanisms to appeal to the employee's interest to produce effort. Within a work contract, the employer can only acquire a promise of future effort. He must henceforward face what can be called a 'moral hazard': the employee has received a wage but, through opportunism, can then choose not to deploy the required effort. The employer therefore protects himself from this kind of behaviour by using incentive mechanisms. The firm will adopt the one which induces the optimum level of effort.

From a general point of view and for the entire theory of incentives, effort is the central variable. For the employee, effort fundamentally represents his entire contribution to the organization. Effort only constitutes pain for the employee and his exclusive aim is to minimize it. For the employer, effort corresponds to a new input in production, which again underlines its primordial nature. Effort is at the heart of the firm's efficiency.

From a particular point of view, and according to the incentive model considered, effort is analysed under different facets. Thus in the 'shirker model' (Shapiro and Stiglitz, 1984), effort becomes a rational means to avoid disadvantages from unemployment. In the 'gift-exchange' model (Akerlof, 1982), effort is an anthropological parameter as it constitutes a gift offered by the employee to the firm. By providing an effort which is, on average, greater than the standard norms of work fixed by the organization, a group of workers makes a gift to the firm which answers by giving to its workers a wage which is the same for all and superior to the market rate and by showing indulgence towards its least productive workers. In the equity model (Akerlof and Yellen, 1990), effort is an instrument at the service of the worker's justice. This means that the employee who receives a wage that he considers inequitable has the possibility of reducing his effort. Thus he rebalances the situation so that it appears fairer to the employee. In Casson's model (Casson, 1991) effort depends on a moral parameter. When the employee does not provide effort, he feels guilt that the firm can feed on. In the model of payment according to length of service [Lazear 1979], the young are paid beneath their marginal productivities and the longest serving are paid over and above theirs. Thus the employee continually delivers the required level of effort because if he does not, his redundancy may lead to the loss of the equivalent of a rent which he gains progressively.

Two limitations in the theory of incentives   Effort thus appears as a fundamental concept in the theory of incentives and its analysis gains ground, but at least two limitations can be exhibited.

The first limitation lies in the representation of the effort producer.

The representation of the employee which underlies these analyses of effort has evolved little since the models we previously examined. These analyses make the worker similar to a mechanism which, in the end, greatly restricts the study of the employee's contribution to the organization and does not allow us to tackle its complexity and its human aspects for two main reasons:

1. *The minimization of effort as an exclusive principle*: the incentive theory provides an over-restrictive view of effort. On the one hand, an employee's behaviour consists exclusively of producing effort; the existence of the employee is characterized only by the fact that he exerts an effort. On the other hand, the employee is supposed to minimize all his effort. However, it is difficult to conceive that all of the employee's activity consists precisely of doing as little as possible.

    The minimization of effort can be counterbalanced by various arguments (Berthe, 1998). Firstly, within the organization, the employee's activity cannot only be assimilated with suffering. Progress in ergonomics reduces the physical pain of work. What is more, the use of one's intelligence is a form of effort which cannot be only assimilated to pain. Secondly, to believe that workers are happy not to have to take decisions and that they only desire to minimize their effort is to denigrate certain human characteristics that Herzberg describes (Herzberg, 1971). Boredom and inaction are on the contrary sources of disutility. Thirdly, everything happens as if the old and famous labour economics idea of arbitration between work and leisure had simply been transposed to the organization. The employee arbitrates between more wages and less effort. Whilst in reality, within the organization, in the place and time imposed on the worker, equating the absence of effort to leisure is unsatisfactory. Inactivity at work does not correspond to a leisure activity. Considering work only as generating disutility and the worker as an effort minimizer, appears to numerous authors, especially outside economics, as an unacceptable simplification. R.E. Lane (1994) offers many empirical supports to defeat traditional economic conceptions of man at work. Most satisfaction in life is given by personal accomplishment and self-esteem obtained from work, for instance. Moreover, satisfactions obtained from work are in a large measure independent from wages, the Jevons' curve and the usual leisure/work arbitration are thus greatly outdated. These arguments are well known to management literature. What is in question is the supposed natural character of effort minimization. We earlier underlined that Veblen has shown that this conception does not rely on empirical and historical evidences. More recently K. Polanyi has also questioned this conception. To him the fact that human life is governed by the desire to obtain always greater gains, is highly contestable (1983, p. 106). The presupposed 'natural' character of human behaviour appears thus as an intellectual construct issued from the 'preconceptions of economics'. As Voltaire long ago claimed concerning the principle of least action, there is more profusion than economy in Nature, so why do economists consider maximum gain and least effort to be natural? It has largely been noticed that reciprocity, competition, game, approbation from others and so on act as much as motivation to work as wages or monetary rewards.

2. *The employee reduced to an object*: the way in which effort is analysed discredits the worker. The view of the worker has remained very mechanistic. Representations of human behaviour are very poor and remain behaviourist and mechanistic. The employee is entirely malleable by the firm. It would therefore be enough to 'push the right button' in order to obtain the level of effort required by the firm. Economic theory of incentives offers a representation of human behaviour which is a long way from post-Taylorist management theories, for instance the 'intrinsic motivation' model or McGregor's 'Y theory', where the worker is not supposed to be passive but acts by himself.[1] What is more, the worker has no separate existence. He is, in reality, relegated to the rank of potential consumer. All of the employee's action and effort has meaning only when he is considered as a consumer.

The second limitation lies in the obstacles associated with the construction of a global model of incentives within the firm.

Firms use a combination of different incentives but the approach taken by the theory of incentives does not enable the establishment of a global and unified analysis of incentives to effort. Firstly, a comparison of the mechanisms suggested by the various models is impossible because of the strength of their hypotheses and of their exclusive concentration on certain parameters to the exclusion of all others. Also, existing incentives models provide contradicting conclusions. For instance, in the 'shirker model', the threat of unemployment is an incentive to effort, whereas in the 'gift-exchange' model, in accordance with the feelings of mutual assistance and sympathy maintained between employees, to threaten one of them with unemployment may lead to a reduction of effort on the part of his colleagues. What is more, it is not easy to decide on one incentive mechanism by comparing it with the facts. The theory contains little empirical study and when there is some, the results are far from conclusive (Baker, Jensen and Murphy, 1988). Nor does it provide any precise indications of its position relative to the facts, on interpretation of the differences between the theoretic assertions and reality. Finally, the incentive theory omits the analysis of a large number of incentive mechanisms. These mechanisms are: first, low cost ones that are effective in encouraging effort (for example the importance of recognizing good work) and second, the effort incentive that springs from improving working conditions. Generally speaking man is motivated by creating something, by increasing his control over his environment. It should be added that what man creates is often considered as an extension of himself. There is, or there should be, intrinsic motivation to work, to provide effort. But as Nuttin (1991) emphasized, such motivation is dependent on the fact that the task performed corresponds to the individual's development project. When this constraint is not satisfied, the recourse to extrinsic factors of motivation is necessary. But even in this case effort and work can participate in personal development through the feeling of being useful or of participating in a collective action. Monetary rewards are thus made secondary. Yet our own empirical study conducted at a French air-postal service illustrates the importance of these two means of providing effort incentives for employees (Berthe, 1998).

3.1.2 The notion of effort for the American Radicals

The extraction of effort by power The American Radicals take up the distinction between 'labour' and 'labour power' originated by Marx. 'Labour power' is the equivalent of a capability, of a potential work held by the worker, whilst 'labour' is 'the real human effort required in the production of saleable output' (Edwards, 1976, p. 55). It clearly appears that labour power is the equivalent of the commitment to provide effort, sold in exchange of a wage by the employee to the employer in the contract theory. Also, 'labour' corresponds to the effort actually produced by the employee. The American Radicals talk as well of 'effort' to evoke the contribution of the employee (Edwards, 1976; Bowles and Gordons, 1986; Bowles and Boyer, 1988). Thus we find the same problematic with the Radicals as those encountered in the theory of incentives. At the outset of the employment relationship, the employer only buys a potential for effort (labour power) and the organizational problem raised then is to find ways of obtaining the real effort (or labour) required. This central issue in radical analysis is described as 'extracting labor from the labor power' (Bowles and Boyer, 1988).

However, although the problem raised is similar, the response to it is very different. The employer possesses a power which allows him to exert control over his employees. Thus control allows labour to be obtained from labour power (Edwards, 1979 p. 12).[2]

Thus, according to the American Radicals, with the power he holds, the employer creates a system of mechanisms which will oblige the employee to provide effort. The power is coercive and the capitalist firm is a repressive institution (Edwards, 1976, p. 64).

First, this control is expressed by supervision and discipline. Supervision provides assurance of a sufficient level of effort from the employee (Edwards, 1976). Discipline is ensured by the supervisor giving verbal orders, by the rhythm of machines or by the instructions of a computer.

Second, control is exerted by unemployment. The latter is means of emphasizing the power struggle favourable to the employer. The threat of unemployment is addressed to employees who have the audacity to let their work slip (Kohli, 1988).

Lastly, control is exerted by the firm's allocation of rewards. According to the Radicals' analysis, control and incentive are closely linked. For instance, supervision goes hand-in-hand with the bonus system (Edwards, 1979). Similarly, under the pretext that rewards bring satisfaction to the employee, this procedure masks an exploitation which is profitable in the end to the employer. The American Radicals consider that control is complex, sophisticated and sometimes invisible. Thus, even when employees participate in the creation of organization rules, they believe they are protecting their interests when they are in fact again being manipulated (Edwards, 1979).

Faced with these constraints, the employee only produces effort by submission or obedience. This behaviour can be explained in the sense that the employee is conditioned by a series of institutions that mould him to work correctly under command. The education system is an example of this (Gintis, 1990). Moreover, this behaviour is deployed in a context where the employee is dispossessed from his work and where conflict reigns in work relations. Thus, if the employee provides his effort, it is only out of submission to the absolute constraint which is exerted on him. He develops a passive resistance in the face of this pressure by using the least possible effort, and provides no extra effort of his own accord. But the employee can also exert an active resistance and become involved in sabotage (Bowles and Gordons, 1986; Edwards, 1979). However, the individual, isolated employee carries very little weight and according to the American Radicals' analysis, the only real reaction possible in the face of a firm's control is of a collective nature.

Two limitations of the American Radicals' theory   In the first instance, the American Radicals' representations of the process of the production of effort raises difficulties. Their analysis in terms of class is particularly troublesome insofar as the contours of class are difficult to identify within the modern organization.

In the second instance, this mode of extracting effort by constraint does not produce a high level of effort, but a restricted one. This second aspect does not constitute a criticism of the Radicals' approach since they share this analysis. At best, constraints produce only the effort expressly required by the firm. What is more, the production of the employer's desired level of effort is hindered by serious information difficulties (for example due to the interpretation of rules by the employee). Also, by exercising its power, the firm deprives itself of all forms of creative effort.

3.1.3   Leibenstein's view of effort

The solid foundations of effort   The theory of x-efficiency is based on the statement that a given quantity of input does not provide the same quantity of output for a single production technique, and asks what constitutes this difference, that is, this 'x'. The subject of effort is covered in detail by H. Leibenstein's various developments of this theory.

The crucial aspect of the concept of effort comes clearly out of Leibenstein's analysis. It allows us to go beyond the limitations of traditional reasoning based on input-work measured in temporal units and to introduce the uncertainty which characterizes the actions of the worker.

The premises of the definition of effort were laid down in 1966 (Leibenstein, 1966), where it appears that workers are not entirely controllable, that effort is variable and that it is not necessarily produced at its maximum level by the employee. Effort is at the discretion of the employee and it is not possible to specify it entirely in advance. Even if it were possible to do so, this would in any case be inefficient (Leibenstein, 1976).

Leibenstein's definition of effort is very precise and detailed and its configurations are very varied. They can be found in physical activity as well as in mental activity (Leibenstein, 1969). Effort is comprised of four components A, P, Q, T. The determination of each of these components by the employee establishes an 'effort bundle' APQT. 'A' represents the choice of activity, 'P' the pace, 'Q' the quality and 'T' the duration of effort (time). One 'effort point' is a single combination APQT where each component has a specific value. An 'effort position' is a range of points of effort (Leibenstein, 1976). He also notes an 'effort index' (where the 'Activity' dimension is fixed) and a 'weighted effort index' (an abstraction that provides a standardized configuration of effort) (Leibenstein, 1976). Effort is a complex entity and the notion of 'degrees of effort' reduces the four dimensions to a single one via a particular formula. Besides, effort is evaluated according to the employee's psychological appreciation (Leibenstein, 1979).

As R. Frantz (1986, p. 307) noticed, Leibenstein also introduced the concepts of 'constrained' and 'unconstrained' behaviour in the x-efficiency framework. Constrained behaviour is defined as that behaviour which is guided by the 'superego' or a desire to adhere to standards. Unconstrained behaviour is guided by an unwillingness to adhere to any obligation or standard: 'The existence of both these aspects in human personality implies at least the possibility of differential motivation or behavior, vis-a-vis single-valued motivation i.e. maximization' (Frantz, 1986, p. 307). Leibenstein also postulates that individual behaviour is influenced by norms, conventions and sanctions used at the workplace, a topic largely neglected in many other mainstream models.

Leibenstein brings up many elements concerning effort (such as the fact that effort is influenced by civilization and he refers to the cases of Japan and of the Kibbutzim). Amongst Leibenstein's numerous detailed developments of subjects, two important points should be mentioned to illustrate his analysis of the production of effort.

The function of utility and inert area: Leibenstein develops a very particular function of utility of effort. This curve, which links up utility and effort, identifies three zones. In the first, effort is appreciated for itself. The second and biggest zone presents the range of 'comfortable' effort; workers in this zone do not wish to change their situation in terms of their effort. The third zone shows that, beyond a certain level, effort becomes unsatisfactory for the individual. The employee's total utility, which corresponds to the utility of effort added to that of the wage, has the same form as the utility of effort but is simply greater (Leibenstein, 1969). The second zone of the utility function represents the 'inert area'. In fact, all workers are situated in this area. Different levels of effort make up the inert area but no employee wishes to change his situation. Leibenstein develops the idea of resistance to change. It is thus difficult for the organization to dislodge individuals who find themselves in this situation of equilibrium since cohesion within a peer-group or the conventions of the firm maintain this phenomenon.

Effort conventions: In his most recent writings, conventions have the most significant impact on the production of effort (Leibenstein, 1987). The general characteristics of a convention are as follows. A convention is a decision-making procedure which is a non-calculating procedure. It induces regularity in the behaviour of effort production. A convention is self-imposing and involves a high degree of adhesion which is not, however, absolute. The effort convention is local and stable, though flexible at its margins. The convention provides an answer to the problem of coordination but nothing guarantees that it will be optimal (Leibenstein, 1987, p. 70). An effort convention results from a firm's own history.

The employee leaves it to convention to determine the effort he must produce. A tendency to respect laws and the importance of relations with others (affiliation, approval from others) lead the individual to follow convention (Leibenstein, 1987, p. 57). Initially, the adoption of a convention requires a learning phase and an estimation of the norms of effort observed. Signs of agreement or disagreement, approbation or disapprobation from his peer-group guide the employee. Then the effort produced according to this convention becomes progressively a habit. The effort decision simply consists of complying with the direction indicated by the convention. The production of effort thus becomes the result of a stimulus–response process.

Despite the relevance of Leibenstein's analysis of effort some difficulties remain concerning the representation of human behaviour.

Criticisms of the resistance to change   Resistance to change is the essential characteristic of the employee's behaviour in his production of effort. This is found both in Leibenstein's earliest analyses where the inert area is attached to the notion of utility, and in his most recent analyses where it is governed by convention. Once in equilibrium, the employee does not modify his effort. This inertia, initially explained by an analysis in terms of the costs of change, can then be explained as a consequence of the adoption of convention. Instead of having a worker who does not like effort (the incentive theory), we have here a worker who hates change, and we can fear that this too would be restricting. An analysis of the phenomenon of inertia does have a certain appeal; however, it is the extent and predominance of the resistance to change which raises questions, as this approach neglects one important human reality: the need for change. The idea that the individual avoids all change is disturbing as we find again a mechanical image of man. This representation of human behaviour is close to that of the incentive theory insofar as they both rest on the principle of homeostasis. This is used as a metaphor to emphasize that all organisms aim for a state of stability and, should there be tension which diverts it from this state, the organism reacts in order to restore equilibrium (Weiner, 1992). Effort is the fruit of a reaction which aims to avoid any deviation from the equilibrium. However, the opposing principle to homeostasis is that of 'challenge' (Nuttin, 1991), which encourages the individual to go forward, to take risks and to discover. All these specific forms of effort that Leibenstein neglects nevertheless constitute parameters indispensable to the organization. The inventive and creative aspect of effort, even if it only constitutes a small part of a worker's activity, is no less essential from many points of view.

Despite more and more sophisticated analysis, economics often still refers to simple and mechanistic conceptions of man at work. We would try to propose some ways for taking the concept of effort further.

3.2   Suggestions for Reconstructing the Concept of Effort

3.2.1   The starting point

For every theory we previously examined, effort is the whole action used by the worker for his work within an organization. It is the object of the employment transaction. The worker is a producer of effort, and the employer attempts to obtain this production of effort by using different means. However, we have seen that the way in which effort is considered is not always fully satisfactory. Moreover, each theory approaches effort from a particular angle which restricts a global appreciation of effort itself and the procedures likely to generate one. As R.K. Filer (1986, p. 264) pointed out: 'It is somewhat surprising that effort expended on the job has not received much attention from economists'.

We consider effort as a concept which is necessary for labour economics in order to appreciate the complexity and the human aspects of the employment exchange. In order to analyse worker–employer relations thoroughly it seems to us appropriate to provide a complete and synthetic redefinition of effort. We think it appropriate to take the concept of effort as our starting point and to try to obtain a global approach of its different features, avoiding the division of the study of effort. With this in mind, we would be able to reconsider the theories previously examined in order to extract the elements relevant to the study of effort. But we also need to bring into this study certain insights from other theories that do not necessarily cover it directly. In particular we are thinking of the French economic theory of conventions as well as the recent 'theory of trust'.

We suggest constructing the foundations of this definition on the basis of the three following axes (Berthe, 1998).

3.2.2   Effort takes three forms

From the description of the nature of effort, it is appropriate to retain Leibensteins's characterization (Leibenstein, 1976). Effort has three dimensions: intensity, quality and activity. Each effort is presented in a space fixed by these three dimensions. The intensity and quality of an employee's activity are simple to appreciate. As for the activity, it corresponds more or less to the way in which the employee carries out a task, for example the movements he chooses. These three forms of effort allow us to characterize all behaviour in the workplace. In his decision to produce effort, the employee determines each of these three forms.

However, the principle of these dimensions described by Leibenstein includes implicitly a predetermined framework, a fixed state of the different possible combinations. It is therefore essential to introduce the creative aspect of work from autonomy to invention and hence to consider that creative effort is included in each of the three forms of effort. The cognitive dimensions of behaviour ought therefore to be taken into account.[3]

3.2.3 Effort is of three types

In most of the theories that discuss effort, the definition and coordination of effort originates with the firm. In order to determine the effort required, the employee refers exclusively to what the organization expects. Moreover, to some extent usual economic conception considers effort as a parameter under the control of workers. By doing so, the role of organizations is neglected or reduced to the task of finding the appropriate stimuli, mental, material…to make individuals work as much as they are able to.

However, in order to decide how much effort to use, the worker will very often rely on his colleagues. The group can easily be considered as an entity for the coordination of effort. A group of workers, for example, determines the pace of work which serves as a reference in the employee's effort production procedure. It is now well known in managerial literature that a cooperative atmosphere is 'likely to mobilize peer-group pressure against shirking and encourage "consummate co-operation" with group incentives' (Hodgson, 1988, p. 265). It should be added that worker participation, democratic decision making, a cooperative and comprehensive atmosphere…can lead to substantial increases in productivity, in the level of effort of every individual. Effort in this context can not only be seen as generating pain or disutility but instead as generating learning, skills, social relations, self-esteem…and it can be valued as such.

Moreover, in order to determine the effort he must provide, the employee can also rely on himself. The employee has personal motivations that help him to determine his level of effort. For example, keeping a tidy desk may constitute an effort of the personal kind. As Argyris pointed out: 'there is a lack of consistency between the needs of healthy individuals and the demands of the…[mechanistic] organization', mechanistic organizations require 'the agents to work in situations where they are dependent, passive, use few and unimportant abilities etc.' so that individuals are 'predisposed toward relative independence, activeness, use of their important abilities [and] control over their immediate work world' (quoted by J.F. Tomer, 1986, p. 237).

Thus we retain three types of effort: firm-type, group-type and individual-type. They depend on the source of influence which is at the origin of the effort. To determine the effort he will employ, the employee refers to one of these three sources.

This typology which distinguishes three distinct types of effort does not, however, mean that they will not be similar in certain circumstances.

3.2.4   Effort obeys three types of logic

The majority of economic theories that discuss effort are based on a single behavioural logic. These frameworks of analysis restrict both the appreciation of the phenomenon of effort production on the employee's part and the reactions on the part of the firm on the matter of mechanisms that encourage effort.

We therefore suggest that the production of effort is guided by three types of behavioural logic: the logic of interest, the logic of obedience and the logic of trust.

First, the employee can pursue his own selfish interests and carry out optimizing calculations in order to determine how much effort to deploy.

Second, the worker within an organization can conform to a certain number of conventions, rules or orders.

Third, the employee can be guided by the trust that reigns within the organization (Orléan, 1995).

This hypothesis of the plurality of behavioural logic is shared by an increasing number of French authors (Baudry, 1992; Coriat and Guennif, 1996; Mouchot, 1996; Boltanski and Thévenot, 1987).

The introduction of these three kinds of logic into the production of effort allows us to proceed with an analysis of the different means by which a firm can extract these efforts. These means are incentives, relative restraints and trust. As a result, the study and the articulation of the complementary character of these different means can be envisaged. The organization is thus considered as a complex system in which these three types of logic are intertwined, far from the simple energetic conception.

4   CONCLUSION

Despite the fact that this chapter is limited in scope, it does indicate important factors that must be taken into account by economists wishing to deal with the supply of labour effort. The mechanistic rationalist conception of human action which lies at the heart of 'mainstream' theories or models of the supply of effort by workers includes single-valued motivation, that is minimizing effort and/or maximizing leisure, gains and so on. Our criticisms should not be taken as entirely rejecting what has been called 'extrinsic motivation' (wage, consumption...). As a matter of fact, effort supply is often based on rational choices by workers and these choices can satisfactorily be described by using the usual utility maximization models. Self interest is clearly a motivation factor, but this should not be the only point of view. Other outcomes are important in determining satisfaction obtained from the production of effort, and workers cannot exclusively be considered as effort minimizers. Incorporation of psychological or sociological factors cannot be done merely by adding new parameters to usual models, this involves a reformulation of these models and sometimes of their logic. For instance the production of effort is not only guided by the logic of interest but also by the logic of trust and the logic of obedience. In addition, effort should not exclusively be taken into account from the point of view of an isolated individual. Individuals act in organizations. That is to say that effort is motivated by sociological variables, for instance rewards or punishments, approbation or disapprobation, from the group of peers. Effort appears to be context-dependent and individuals and organizations should not be considered as mere mechanisms. Effort supply models have of necessity to be more complex and interconnected than those we are used to dealing with. Our proposed reconstruction of the concept of effort is multi-dimensional.

NOTES

1. Although motivation literature is not the subject of this chapter, it must be emphasized that economic analysis of human effort corresponds only to the 'X' model of D. McGregor. Economics only considers human beings motivated by a desire to satisfy lower-level needs. But as McGregor noticed, human beings are also motivated by higher-level needs, that is to say they are self-motivated and seek self-actualization (for more details see Filer, 1986, p. 270). Like McGregor, C. Argyris postulates that 'the natural course of human development is to progress toward "maturation", defined as increased activity, independence, awareness of and control over self, aspiration for superior (or at least equal) position, and the development of long range perspective' (ibid., p. 270).
2. The employment relationship is analysed in terms of the relationship between two classes (workers and capitalists). Relations between the two classes are conflict-provoking. 'The work process becomes an arena of conflict and the workplace becomes contested terrain.' Employers belong to the dominant class which is supported by the institutions that they help create.
3. Cognitive theories of motivation focus on the expectations people have regarding what is likely to happen in the future if they follow a particular course of action in the present (Filer, 1986, p. 272); this is the basic idea of one of the most influential theories of motivation: expectancy theory. It should be noticed that expectancy theory does not entirely escape mechanistic pre-conceptions. As a matter of fact they are based on the work of K. Lewin who referred to a physical framework. One of the main authors of expectancy theory is V. Vroom (1964; see also Vroom and Deci (eds) 1970). According to Vroom, expectancy theory is aimed at predicting choices among various activities (tasks), as well as choices with respect to the amount of effort expended on those tasks undertaken. To some extent this theory led to an arbitration between rewards (for instance additional pay) and pains suffered (for instance the resentment of co-workers resulting from the higher effort produced by the individual), and to a comparison between expected utilities attributed to different courses of action. As R.K. Filer underlined, expectancy theory is 'explicitly a-historical': 'An individual's past history of choices and the consequences arising from those choices are not incorporated into current action' (Filer, 1986, p. 274). Maybe a less mechanistic approach of human motivation lies in what has been called intrinsic motivation. In this framework, satisfaction is internally generated by the worker as a result of performing the task itself. Performing a task can provide the individual with physical or cognitive stimuli that he finds pleasurable. Rewards from effort are not obtained at the end of the task as is the case, for instance, in the theory of incentives (effort and then consumption, like effect, necessarily follow cause – to parallel Veblen's opinion) but during the task. Rewards are thus rendered internal to the individual. For instance individuals can obtain pleasure from increasing one's competence or ability to bring about changes in the environment (Filer, 1986, p. 277).

REFERENCES

Akerlof, G.A. (1982), 'Labor contract as partial gift exchange', *Quarterly Journal of Economics*, **97**, November.

Akerlof, G.A. and J.L. Yellen (eds) (1986), *Efficiency Wage Models of the Labour Market*, Cambridge: Cambridge University Press.

Akerlof, G.A. and J.L. Yellen (1990), 'The fair wage effort hypothesis and unemployment', *Quarterly Journal of Economics*, **105** (2), May.

Amoroso, L. (1942), *Meccanica Economica*, Citta di Castello: Macri.

Amoroso, L. (1962), 'L'Interprétation mathématique de l'univers économique', Cahiers de L'ISEA, Series B17 no. 1, pp. 3–15, July.

Baker, G.P., M.C. Jensen and K.J. Murphy (1988), 'Compensations and incentives: practice versus theory', *The Journal of Finance*, **43** (3).

Baudry, B. (1992), *Contrat, autorité et confiance : une étude des mécanismes de coordination dans la relation de sous-traitance*, Doctoral thesis, Grenoble: Université Pierre Mendès France.

Berthe, B. (1998), *Un modèle d'analyse de l'effort du salarié dans l'organisation*, Doctoral thesis, Université de Rennes I.

Boltanski, L. and L. Thévenot (1987), *Les Economies de la grandeur*, Paris: Cahiers du Centre d'Etude de l 'Emploi, PUF.

Bowles, S. and R. Boyer (1988), 'Labor discipline and aggregate demand: a macroeconomic model', *American Economic Review*, **78** (2), May, pp. 395–400.

Bowles, S. and D.M. Gordons (1986), *L'Economie du gaspillage*, Paris: La Découverte.

Brousseau, E. (1993), *L'Economie des contrats*, Paris: PUF.

Brunet, P. (1938), *Etude historique sur le principe de moindre action*, Paris: Hermann.

Casson, M. (1991), *The Economics of Business Culture*, Oxford: Clarendon Press.

Cofer, C.N. and M.H. Appley (1964), *Motivation Theory and Research*, New York: John Wiley.

Coleman, W.O. (1995), *Rationalism and Anti-rationalism in the Origins of Economics: The Philosophical Roots of 18th Century Economic Thought*, Aldershot, UK and Brookfield, US: Edward Elgar.

Coriat, B. and S. Guennif (1996), 'Incertitude, confiance et institutions', in *La Confiance en question*, Actes du colloque de l'ADSE, Aix-en-Provence, 22–23 March.

Coulmas, F. (1992), *Language and Economy*, Oxford: B. Blackwell.

Cournot, A.A. (1838), *Recherches sur les principes mathématiques de la théorie des richesses*, Paris: Librairie des Sciences Politiques et Sociales, 1938.

Doray, B. (1981), *Le Taylorisme, une folie rationnelle?*, Paris: Dunod.

Edgeworth, F.Y. (1881), *Mathematical Psychics – An Essay on the Application of Mathematics to the Social Sciences*, London: C. Kegan Paul and Co.

Edwards, R.C. (1976), 'Individual traits and organization incentives: what makes a good worker?', *Journal of Human Resources*, **11** (1), Winter, pp. 51–68.

Edwards, R.C. (1979), *Contested Terrain*, USA: Basic Books.

Filer, R.K. (1986), 'People and productivity: effort supply as viewed by economsts and psychologists' in B. Gilad and S. Kaish (eds) *Handbook of Behavioral Economics*, Greenwich, London: JAI Press, pp. 261–87.

Frantz, R.S. (1986), 'X-efficiency in behavioral economics' in B. Gilad and S. Kaish (eds) *Handbook of Behavioral Economics*, Greenwich, London: JAI Press, pp. 307–23.

Garnier, O. (1986), 'La théorie néoclassique face au contrat de travail: de la main invisible à la poignée de main invisible', in R. Salais and L. Thevenot, *Le Travail, règles, conventions*, Paris: Economica.

Gilad, B. and S. Kaish (eds.) (1986), *Handbook of Behavioral Economics*, Greenwich, London: JAI Press.

Gintis, H. (1990), 'The nature of labor exchange and the theory of capitalist production', in S. Bowles and R. Edwards (eds), *Radical Political Economy Volume I*, Aldershot, UK and Brookfield, US: Edward Elgar, pp. 249–67.

Guyot, Y. (1896), *L'Economie de l'Effort*, Paris: A. Colin.

Herzberg, F. (1971), *Le Travail et la nature humaine*, Paris: Entreprise moderne d'édition.

Hodgson, G.M. (1988), *Economics and Institutions – A Manifesto for Modern Institutional Economics*, Cambridge: Polity Press.

Jevons, W.S. (1909), *La Théorie de l'économie politique*, Paris: Giard et Brière.

Kohli, M. (1988), 'Wages, work effort and productivity', *Review of Radical Politcal Economics*, **20** (2–3), Summer and Autumn: 190–95.

Lagrange, J.L. ([1788] 1989), 'Mecanique Analytique', J. Gabay (ed), Paris.

Lane, R.E. (1994), 'Le travail comme "désutilite" et l'argent comme mesure du bonheur?', *Half-yearly review of MAUSS*, no. 3, pp. 17–31.

Lazear, E.P. (1979), 'Why is there mandatory retirement?', *Journal of Political Economy*, **87** (6), December: 1261–84.

Leibenstein, M. (1966), 'Allocative efficiency versus "x-efficiency" ', *American Economic Review*, **56**, no. 3, June: 392–415.

Leibenstein, H. (1969), 'Organizational or frictional equilibria, x-efficiency, and the rate of innovation', *Ouartedy Journal of Economics*, **83** (4), November: 600–23.

Leibenstein, H. (1976), *Beyond Economic Man*, Cambridge, MA: Harvard University Press.

Leibenstein, H. (1985), 'On relaxing the maximization postulate', *Journal of Behavioural Economics*, **14**: 5–25.

Leibenstein, H. (1987), *Inside the Firm*, Cambridge, MA, and London: Harvard University Press.

Le Moigne, J.L. (1997), 'L'économique énergétique et pragmatique: evolution, rationalité et téléologie', *Economie Appliquée*, **50** (3): 53–69.

Marx, K. (1975 [1867]), *Le capital*, Paris: Editions Sociales.

McGregor, D. ([1966] 1975), *Leadership et motivation*, Paris: Enterprise Moderne d'Edition.

Mirowski, P. (1984), 'Physics and the marginalist revolution', *Cambridge Journal of Economics*, **8** (4), December: 361–79.

Mirowski, P. (1989), *More Heat than Light*, Cambridge: Cambridge University Press.

Mouchot, C. (1996), *Méthodologie économique*, Paris: Hachette.

Nuttin, J. (1991), *Théorie de la motivation humaine: du besoin au projet de l'action*, Paris: PUF.

Orléan, A. (1995), 'La confiance, un concept économique?', *Problèmes économiques*, no. 2422, May.

Paradeise, C. and P. Porcher (1990), 'Le contrat ou la confiance dans la relation salariale', *Travail et emploi*, no. 46.

Polanyi, K. (1944), *La Grande transformation*, Paris: Gallimard.

Renault, M., (1991), 'Du temps newtonien au temps de l'évolution dans l'analyse économique', Doctoral thesis, Université de Rennes 1.

Renault, M., (1992), 'Analogie formelle et analogie substantielle en économie: l'économique néo-classique, l'énergétique et la physique des champs', *Economie Appliquée*, **45** (3): 55–90.

Revue Economique (1989), *L'Economie des conventions*, **40** (2), March.

Reynaud, B. (1992), *Le Salaire, la règle et le marché*, Mesnil-sur-l'Estrée: Christian Bourgeois éditeur.

Rivaud-Danset, D. (1995), 'La confiance, l'action collective et les mondes possibles', in *Actes du séminaire interdisciplinaire du 23 au 26 Janvier 1995*, Compiègne: Université de Technologie.

Rosmorduc, J. (1985), *Une histoire de la physique et de la chimie*, Paris: Seuil (Point).

Rousseau, J. and F. Vatin (1991), 'C.A. Coulomb et le concept de travail', *Economie et humanisme*, no. 319: 71–80.

Samuelson, P.A. (1972), 'Maximum principles in analytical economics', *American Economic Review*, **62** (3), June: 249–62.

Seris, J.P. (1987), *Machine et Communication*, Paris: Vrin.

Shapiro, C. and J.E. Stiglitz (1984), 'Equilibrium unemployment as a worker discipline device', *American Economic Review*, **73** (3), June.

Thuillier, P. (1991), 'La revanche du Dieu Chaos', *La Recherche*, no. 232, May: 542–52.

Tomer, J.F. (1986), 'Productivity and organizational behavior: where human capital theory fails' in B. Gilad and S. Kaish (eds), *Handbook of Behavioral Economics*, Greenwich, London: JAI Press, pp. 233–55.

Vatin, F. (1993), *Le travail – economie et physique 1780–1830*, Paris: PUF.

Veblen, T.B. (1990), 'Why is economics not an evolutionary science?' in W.J. Samuels (ed.), *The Place of Science in Modern Civilization and Other Essays*, New Brunswick, NJ: Transaction Publications, pp. 56–81.

Vroom, V. (1964), *Work and Motivation*, New York: Wiley.

Vroom, V. and E.L. Deci (eds) (1970), *Management and Motivation*, Harmondsworth: Penguin.

Weiner, B. (1992), *Human Motivation*, Newbury Park, CA: Sage Publications.

White, M. (1994), 'The moment of Richard Jennings' in P. Mirowski (ed.), *Natural Images in Economic Thought*, Cambridge: Cambridge University Press.

Winiarski, L. (1903), 'Le principe de moindre effort comme base de la science sociale', *Revue philosophique*, **55** (1–2): 278–305 and 373–83.

Zipf, G.K. (1949), *Human Behavior and the Principle of Least Effort: An Introduction to Human Ecology*, New York: Hafner.

10. Path dependence in scientific evolution

Albert Jolink and Jack J. Vromen

In analogy to this [Darwinian evolution] one has to understand the development of scientific theories: not directed to an ideal (true) theory, the *one* true theory of the world, but evolution as a step to a better form, by selection of one out of several competing forms. The selection is made on the basis of preference in the community of scientists. Many factors, sociological, cultural,...., are involved. (Carnap quoted in Horwich, 1993)

1 INTRODUCTION

Few will deny that economics is currently undergoing a period of self-reflection, self-preoccupation and, perhaps, self-doubt.[1] In recent book titles the decline of economics, the end of economics and even the death of economics is proclaimed as signs of the times. In 'The End of Science' John Horgan claims that science in general has come to an end and it seems that economics may well be the first to be buried. After Fukuyama's end of history it seems we have now reach the dead-end of science and possibly the finale of economic science.

The popular issue of endings to scientific knowledge accumulation has been topical throughout the history of science and has experienced pronounced peaks after fierce debates. Economic science had been pronounced to be completed, that is, finished and done, at least three times in the last two hundred years. Others have argued that the adoption of wrong metaphors at crucial states of development of economic science have cast doubts on its durability and can only guarantee a drifting away towards its own extinction. This unidirectional presentation of the development and progress of science necessarily links the beginning to an end.

In Thomas Kuhn's presentation of the history of science, the end of what was once perceived to be a fruitful course of research marks the beginning of a revolution. New points of view replace the old ones and the latter will never be recovered. Though one may refer to the end of the old paradigm, the new paradigm will revive the science and will take it further. Kuhn's perspective thus presumes an evolving scientific endeavour, be it a discontinuous one. In this explanation of the evolution of science one would have to clarify, however, why some scientific ideas become extinct while others are selected and survive. In Kuhn's account, the conflict within the scientific community takes care of the selection of ideas, which is subsequently presented as the 'fittest' way to practise future science (Kuhn, [1962] (1996), p. 172).

In this chapter we will offer a different perspective on the evolution of science, in particular economic science, by stressing the path-dependent nature of the evolutionary process. As will be pointed out in the chapter, the evolution of science can be described in terms of a path-dependent process, in the course of which it may become locked-in to a steady state of what we shall call conventional science. We will argue that path dependence is not only related to QWERTY keyboards or to VHS video recorders, but also to the development of scientific knowledge.[2] Path dependence is understood here as a property of a particular class of stochastic *processes*. In our view, the only stochastic processes that are path-dependent are those that have their *transition probabilities* determined by the sequence of past transient states passed through in earlier phases of the processes. This sequence in turn is influenced by certain *factors* operating within a relevant previous history. On this understanding of path dependence, three aspects stand out that need further clarification and specification: process, transition probabilities and historical factors.

While philosophers and historians of science have focused on the structure of scientific research programmes and revolutions, we will focus on an articulation of its underlying *process*. We analyse science's internal social dynamics and relate it to the notion of conventional science. Conventional science, here, is a set of interrelated fundamental concepts that a majority of peers within a scientific community has agreed upon. It is in this respect that our understanding of conventional science is very close to Kuhn's 'normal science' (but see section 6 for a discussion of differences between our view and Kuhn's). We call the process preceding and leading to a conventional science, the process of conventionalization. In sections 4 and 5 we will illustrate our notions of conventional science and conventionalization in a discussion of two exemplar cases of conventionalization in economics: the conventionalization of general equilibrium theory and of game theory in economics.

A second issue to be dealt with in this process is how *transition probabilities* change in the evolution of science. To be more specific, we will define path dependence here in terms of changing transition probabilities, as opposed to constant transition probabilities. What has to be pointed out, then, is why processes of scientific development have changing rather than constant transition probabilities. It is argued here that the path-dependent characteristic of the process is largely attributable to the particular way in which selection processes in science take place. In section 3 we argue in particular that accumulated adoption of certain scientific concepts (beyond some critical threshold value) can set a self-reinforcing process in motion and that lock-in to steady states and irreversibilities may result from this.

A final issue to be addressed is which *factors* in the relevant previous history may be identified that influence which transient states a science passes through. In our analysis we distinguish between two sorts of such historical factors. The first sort of factors determine what new concepts (if any) become available for selection in a branching stage preceding the selection process. The second sort of factors determine which of the new concepts will first reach a level of adoption and use that will give it a decisive competitive edge over its rivals in the ensuing selection process. Before we turn to a more detailed discussion of the branching and selection stage, however, we first have a closer look at conventional science.

2   LOCKED-IN TO CONVENTIONAL SCIENCE

The interest of scholars in non-linear dynamics and all sorts of complexities impressively increased both the theory on, and the amount of examples of, path dependence, lock-in, increasing returns to scale and complexity. With a few exceptions, most of the endeavours in this area have focused on issues related to phenomena in a 'historical'[3] trajectory or on technological innovations of some kind.

One of the early accounts of 'lock-in' in economic science is Brian Arthur's courageous attempt to bring economics under the spell of complexity theory at the Santa Fe Institute (Arthur, 1988). In Arthur's account a dynamic (economic) system can become locked-in to a local equilibrium when self-reinforcing mechanisms first drive the system to this equilibrium and subsequently prevent it from exiting this position. These self-reinforcing mechanisms can take many forms. What they all have in common is that they provide positive feedback. Arthur's hobby-horse, in this respect, is a mechanism characterized by increasing returns to scale. One of the outcomes is that the local equilibrium may or may not be the best result when compared to a situation without these exit barriers. Another feature refers to the unpredictability of the outcomes; that is, it is not at all obvious from the start how a particular equilibrium comes to be selected, as random events act upon the system's trajectory.

Others, such as David (1985, 1988), have reinforced this positive feedback scenario with explanations and illustrations of a historical nature. Hence, less than optimal QWERTY keyboards and VHS video technology are staged to illustrate how processes can be locked-in and how other developments can be locked-out of the set of initial options. The degree of interwovenness of lock-in and a possible inefficient outcome may differ for each subject of study but can be considered separately.[4] For our purpose the possible inefficiency of the outcomes of a path-dependent process is less relevant.

It is our intention here to take the analytically derived components of the notion of being 'locked-in' to a different context, namely to a setting of inquiry, research, knowledge accumulation and scientific evolution. Our point here is that scientific knowledge and procedures that have led to this scientific knowledge are vulnerable to lock-in effects as well. Established concepts and definitions, accepted assumptions and (background) hypotheses remain, at least for longer periods, beyond dispute. The same holds to some extent for more or less standard ways to gain prestige among peers, to increase job opportunities and to have access to prestigious publication outlets. The reason for this, we contend, stems from the working of multiple self-reinforcing mechanisms. Convergence on established concepts and on standard ways of 'how to do good science' produces many different advantages for the scientists involved. It enables them to use and elaborate upon the categories employed, to engage in discussion on the basis of common definitions and accepted hypotheses and to advance research within a respecting community of peers and publication outlets. As a consequence, the more scientists accept the same concepts and standards, the more attractive it becomes for those scientists to stick to their guns and for others to join the bandwagon. By the same token, with the lion's share of the community converging on the same concepts and standards, barriers to exit conventional science are erected.

Our conventional science is very much in this locked-in position. The scientific community has reached a common understanding (most of the time a tacit one) on what 'doing good science' amounts to. This common under-standing may be exemplified in a specific text or book. We will refer to this as the 'stage of conventional science'. Adhering to conventional science has positive feedback effects for the practitioners in the field as it guarantees, to some extent, a stable and predictable point of reference. This also explains why departures from conventional science may be prohibitively costly for any member of the scientific community. Hence, once a scientific community has settled on a conventional science, there are many mutually reinforcing mechanisms working that keep it there.

The 'micro-foundation' underlying our sketch of how self-reinforcing mechanisms work in science, parallels David Hull's (1988) account of what moves individual scientists.[5] Hull argues that individual scientists engage simul-taneously in cooperation and competition. As members of the same scientific community scientists cooperate with each other not only in the sense that they have a common interest (in promoting and refining their shared concepts, standards and theories), but also in the sense that by using each other's results in their own work they build upon each other's work (Hull, 1988, p. 319). At the same time, however, individual scientists compete with one another for recognition and prestige among their peers.[6] The best way to achieve this, the best way to get credit, Hull argues, is by coming up with new results and, preferably, with new concepts (or refinements of old concepts) that colleagues subsequently use in their research. The prestige and standing of a scientist is to a large degree dependent on the extent to which her concepts are disseminated in the professional community.

This depiction of the 'micro motives' of individual scientists helps us understand why the old conventional science is perpetuated for some time, and why it eventually gives way to new variants. Conventional science does not only provide scientists with a shared vocabulary and an agenda of topics and issues to work on, it also brings with it implicit standards of what is to count as excellent science. In their attempts to practise excellent science on some of the topics on the agenda, using the conventional concepts, scientists strengthen the prominence of the concepts and standards of conventional science. Yet scientists do not merely subscribe to conventional science's concepts. They try to contribute to it. And the type of contribution that is valued the most is the introduction of a new concept that finds its way into the profession. Sooner or later different scientists will advance different conceptual innovations, all hoping that theirs will make it in the profession.

When various new concepts make their appearance, a stage of diversification (or branching) is entered. Despite the emergence of new concepts, members of the community may for some time keep using the old conventional concepts. In due time, however, new concepts will emerge that succeed in drawing the attention of scientists away from the old conventional concepts. The attention of scientists then gradually shifts from the concepts of conventional science to some of the newly proposed ones. In the event that more than one new concept pops up (which we take to be the 'normal case'), scientists may be inclined to use one of them in their own research. In this sense the newly introduced concepts can be said to compete with each other for acceptance and use in the scientific community. In the selection process that follows (and which will be discussed in greater detail in section 3) the community may converge on one of the new concepts.[7] If such is the case, the selection process is a process of conventionalization with the emergence of a new conventional science as its outcome.

Our account of scientific evolution given so far implies that new concepts are introduced in due time. In that sense our account gives an explanation of why diversification happens in science. But our account does not (and cannot) give an explanation of why new concepts pop up at the points in time they do (rather than sooner or later), of why the concepts pop up in the particular number that they do, let alone of why the concepts take the shape and content they do. Maybe an explanation could be given of these phenomena. If only we were less ignorant about the factors responsible for the data, we could perhaps explain them. Knowledge of such factors could even bring prediction of these things within reach. But our account is completely silent on such factors. It is in this sense that we call such factors historical.[8] 'Historical factors' thus are not contrasted with ahistorical or history-transcending factors in our view, but with factors that our account takes on board. The fact that we do not take these historical factors into account does not mean that we believe them to be unimportant. On the contrary, by determining what new concepts appear, they may have a lasting influence on processes of scientific evolution. Thus, far from being a plea to ignore it, our account entails that explicit notice should be taken of what exactly happens at stages of diversification (even though we do not explain it).

Putting the pieces together now, science is portrayed here as perpetually going through cycles. Stages of conventional science give way to stages of diversification that in turn are followed by a process of conventionalization followed by new stages of diversification, and so on. We have explained why and how conventional science is sustained for some time. We have also indicated how, despite its lock-in character, practising conventional science brings new variants along in a process of, what one could name, reflexive referencing. What remains to be discussed is how processes of conventionalization unfold. It is here, in these selection processes, that path dependence (in our strict understanding of it) is exhibited.

3   PATH-DEPENDENT SELECTION PROCESSES

Above, we claimed that the selection process leading to a new conventional science is path-dependent. What do we mean by this? And what reasons do we have for claiming this? Recall our definition of path dependence in terms of stochastic processes having their transition probabilities determined by the sequence of past transition states that the system under consideration went through. Now consider a situation in which a number of new concepts emerged, each of which is a candidate driving the new conventional science. To simplify matters, let us assume that only one new concept, B, emerges in a situation of conventional science in which the whole community uses concept A. A state of this system can be described in terms of the frequencies (or proportions) of users (or adherents) of A and B in the scientific community (or peer group). The frequencies f_A and f_B add up to 1, and an increase of the one frequency is matched exactly with a decrease in the other. A transition probability p signifies the probability in some state that the system will move towards $f_A = 1$ (thus having probability $1 - p$ for moving towards B).

Now to say that transition probabilities are determined by the sequence of past transient states, means that differences in sequences of past states yield different transition probabilities. By differences in sequences we not only mean differences in past states (or in the order in which they have been visited) up to some point in time t_p, but also differences between the sequence of past states a system has visited up to t_p and the sequence that system has visited up to, say, t_{p+n}. Thus in order to tell in which direction the system goes, it is not sufficient to know the present state the system is in. What has to be known in addition is what sequence of states the system has visited before. If we were able to trace the history of the system back to its initial state, and knew both the initial proportions of adherents and initial transition probability, then we could reconstruct it completely in terms of changing transition probabilities.

Path dependence is brought out most clearly by assuming that initially, at some t_o, both f_A and the transition probability p take the value 0.5. The system can then be said to be indifferent on which way to go. 'Chance events' can then be said to decide whether at some t_1, f_A is larger than, smaller than or equal to 0.5. Again we could speak of historical factors being responsible for this in the sense that these factors are not incorporated in our account in terms of transition probabilities.

What happens once the proportion of adherents to either A or B exceeds that of the other, depends on the dynamic specified. The dynamic associated with path dependence here is one related to positive feedback (or self-reinforcing mechanisms). This means that once B, for whatever reason, attracts more adherents than A, the attraction of B increases even further. Chance events may nevertheless prevent the system from fixating on B. Once B acquires critical mass, however, that is, once the adherence to B goes beyond some critical threshold value, the system inevitably converges on B (that is, $p = 0$ and, consequently, f_B goes to 1).

Now why do we believe that processes in which contending concepts are selected in science exhibit path dependence? In part, our reasons for believing this are already alluded to in the previous section. The more scientists come to accept some concept, the stronger is its attractiveness. After a concept has acquired critical mass, it shows scientists where the action is and where and how credits are to be gained in the profession. The operation of these self-reinforcing mechanisms sees to it that there is a type of positive feedback characteristic of path dependence: once a critical threshold value is reached, convergence on the concept in question can be observed.

The foregoing relates to the end stage of the selection process, one could say. But what of the early stage? The assumption that initially scientists are indifferent to which concept to accept and use does not seem to be far-fetched either, for initially many individual scientists, driven by their desire to make outstanding contributions, may be inclined to explore the potential of the new concept.

4   GETTING 'GET' RIGHT[9]

General economic equilibrium theory is a coherent body of literature in
economics, discussing issues of interrelated markets and equilibrium conditions.
The history of general equilibrium theory is fairly well documented in, for
example, Walsh and Gram, 1980, Weintraub, 1985, Ingrao and Israel, 1990
and Weintraub, 1991. The Weintraub and Ingrao and Israel accounts are
impressive Lakatosian exercises revealing the existence of different research
programmes in a pattern of accumulated historical discoveries. In Ingrao and
Israel the 'invariant paradigmatic nucleus' of this theory is identified as the aim
to demonstrate the existence, the uniqueness and the global stability of the
equilibrium in the market. Simultaneously, Ingrao and Israel lay bare a path
that runs from 'the rigorously mechanistic approach of Walras and Pareto' in
the latter part of the 19th century through 'the model theory of von Neumann
and Samuelson' in the 1930s and 1940s to 'the rigorously axiomatic treatment
of Debreu' in the late 1950s. The 'paradigmatic shifts' that these stages illustrate
are, according to Ingrao and Israel, adjustments in a process of *axiomatization*
of the theory. The presentday convention in general equilibrium theory rests
for a large part on the presentation offered by Gérard Debreu in his now classic
work of 1959,[10] *Theory of Value*.

In the scenario we have introduced in the previous section, the evolution
from one conventional science to another was made dependent on the
involvement of the practitioners, leading to new conceptual contributions (and
hence to diversification), and on the earlier 'history' leading to a critical mass
of adherents of one of the new contributions. The earlier 'history', here, and
the transition probabilities dependent on it, was made synonymous with path
dependence. This diverges slightly from Weintraub's deliberate 'canon
creation' in the history of general equilibrium theory (Weintraub, 1991).
Weintraub argues that economic knowledge and the history of economic
knowledge is constructed by, for example, a selected group of articles in an
authoritative survey (hence leaving out certain articles). On the other hand, our
set-up need not exclude Weintraub's 'constructed knowledge' contraption
either: in Weintraub's account the 'interpretive community'[11] may reinforce the
work by members of their community, hence creating a feedback-mechanism.
In this context, we would rather speak of a 'conventional science' to emphasize
the boundaries of the relevant community and to stress the environment of the
construction of knowledge. Hence, we would rather emphasize the conventional aspect of the construction of concepts. As such, the scientific community
will review, evaluate and judge the work of its peers, with a convention
emerging from this process. As new concepts are introduced and become part
of the shared vocabulary, the agenda of topical issues may be complemented

and adjusted. This may, gradually, lead to adjustments of standards of what good science is.

Following Ingrao and Israel's work it is obvious that the concepts of 'conventionalization', 'diversification' and 'selection' may be read into their account of the history of general equilibrium theory. In their history Walras is branded, for obvious reasons, as the convention following a conventionalization process of general equilibrium theory during the 18th and 19th century. Ingrao and Israel identify a path that runs from A.N. Isnard (1749–1803), through N.F. Canard (1750–1833) and J. Dupuit (1804–1866) to A. Cournot (1801–1877) and, finally, L. Walras (1834–1910). Although one may question whether Walras' work was the conventional science *strictu sensu*, as agreed upon by the scientific community at the time, his *Eléments d'économie politique pure* is certainly accepted by later general equilibrium theorists as the materialization of relevant and determining factors of general economic equilibrium theory. Likewise the work of Wald, Hicks, von Neumann and Morgenstern, Arrow and Debreu, and so on are recorded as part of this body of literature. Later authors contributing to the fine-tuning of the equilibrium conditions further shaped the evolution of general equilibrium theory.

The question remains, of course, as to how this process of evolution did take place. Although we tend to agree with Ingrao and Israel that axiomatization may have been one of the options along with which the process took place, it remains an open question for us, as it is for them, why it took this option instead of another. In fact, in their book, Ingrao and Israel acknowledge that from each stage (Walras, von Neumann, Samuelson, Debreu) many possible diversifications may, and do, depart.

It is a historical fact that the potentiality of Walras' work attracted several adherents who could see the benefits of this innovative, conceptual framework. Economists have attributed several contributions to Walras' work: some have emphasized the 'socialist' content and implications of Walras' economics; others tend to see his contribution to the 'marginal utility revolution' as the prime issue; still others the 'theorizing interdependent markets', or 'the mathematization of economics'. It becomes obvious from Ingrao and Israel that for the evolution of general equilibrium theory the mathematization or axiomatization of market equilibria has been important as an introduction of new concepts, or presentation of new concepts, and as the elaboration of a vocabulary. In this respect one may argue both ways: the introduction of mathematics has not altered the concepts involved and has only translated them into Greek symbols; on the other hand, one may argue that the introduction of mathematics has forced the conceptual framework in a domain limited by the requirements of the mathematics.

Once locked-in the positive feedback (theoretically, intellectually, academically) to proceed along these lines contributed to the line of research, as early econometric works exhibit.[12] Within this quest for equilibrium in interrelated markets the issue of the mathematical proof of existence-, uniqueness- and stability-conditions of equilibria becomes a topic which is added to the agenda. This topic is still a minor issue in Walras' work. The existence-, uniqueness- and stability-conditions become the criteria for theory appraisal along the path. As 'diversifications' such as the theories of von Neumann and of Samuelson in the 1930s attract their adherents, the existence-, uniqueness- and stability-conditions are mainly elaborated along the shared vocabulary-terms (mathematical concepts) set out by Walras and elaborated upon by later practitioners. The issues of existence-, uniqueness- and stability-conditions gain even greater importance in the distinct, though derivative account of general equilibrium theory in the work of Debreu in 1959.

The 'paradigmatic shifts' observed by Ingrao and Israel may well be interpreted as the diversification and conventionalization process described in the sections above: the diverging contributions leading to a change in the agenda of topics. Both the historical circumstances during the first part of the 20th century as well as the scientific developments in, for example, logical positivism have led to a change in standards of (good) science. The evolution of general equilibrium theory, from Walras to Debreu, is a clear case in which the conventions have been replaced by new conventions; the shared vocabulary has been extended and altered, the agenda of topics has been adjusted and the criteria and standards of science have evolved.

5 CONVENTIONALIZING GAME THEORY

In the history of game theory two events stand out as landmark events, events that are unsurpassed in importance by any other event. The first event is the appearance in 1944 of John von Neumann and Oskar Morgenstern's *The Theory of Games and Economic Behavior*. The second event comprises a sequence of papers that John Nash published in the early 1950s. The two events delineate pretty much what we call game theory nowadays. Von Neumann and Morgenstern started the whole thing and John Nash is primarily responsible for the shape that game theory subsequently took. Nash's work is sometimes seen as a natural outgrowth of ideas that, albeit in embryonic form, were already there in von Neumann and Morgenstern's pioneering classic.[13] This view has been voiced in several versions. One version is that the Nash equilibrium, the solution concept that Nash put forward for non-cooperative games, is a generalization of von Neumann and Morgenstern's minimax solution, that was applicable only to non-cooperative zero-sum games.[14] Others praise Nash for having freed game theory from the straitjacket that von Neumann and

Morgenstern forced upon it.[15] What both versions have in common is the idea that Nash resolved theoretical issues in game theory that von Neumann and Morgenstern put on the research agenda but did not resolve themselves.

Contrary to what some commentators suggest,[16] von Neumann and Morgenstern did not create game theory *ex nihilo* (see also Leonard, 1995). In mathematics, important preparatory work was done by Waldegrave, Zermelo and, especially, Borel and Ville.[17] And economists such as Cournot, Bertrand and Edgeworth can be regarded as forerunners of game theory, even though the mathematics that von Neumann introduced was of course not already there. Moreover, Morgenstern's discussion of the Sherlock Holmes–Moriarty problem indicates that Morgenstern hoped that game theory could come to grips with the vexing problem of the interdependence of agents' mutual expectations in situations of strategic interaction. As Schotter (1992) points out, Morgenstern also expected game theory to be able to shed some light on the typical Mengerian theme of the organic origin of institutions. For the purposes of our chapter, however, we can forget about these antecedents of von Neumann and Morgenstern's book and simply take 1944 as the birth date of game theory.

It is 'common knowledge' among present-day game theorists that in their *Theory of Games*, von Neumann and Morgenstern basically obtained two theoretical results. They proved the so-called minimax theorem: in two-person, zero-sum, non-cooperative games the pair of minimax choices is the solution. They also showed that in n-person cooperative games a set of patterns of coalition formation exists (which they called the stable set) which is consistent with rational behaviour. It is clear that neither von Neumann nor Morgenstern considered game theory to be finished and exhausted with their *Theory of Games*. It is also clear that their *Theory of Games* opened up several different avenues for further research, if only because of the fact that game theorists could concentrate on either non-cooperative or cooperative game theory. There is some evidence, however, that von Neumann and Morgenstern held that game theory could make most headway by further work on n-person cooperative games. Thus they assigned priority to cooperative game theory (rather than non-cooperative game theory) on the research agenda for the next generation of game theorists to work on.

Initially in the late 1940s and early 1950s most work of game theorists focused on cooperative games. Several game theorists, among them Robert Aumann, worked on further elaborations of 'the stable set', the solution concept that von Neumann and Morgenstern had put forward for cooperative game theory. At about the same time, several new solution concepts were proposed. Martin Shubik, Lloyd Shapley, Howard Raiffa and John Harsanyi all came up with new solution concepts of their own.

The contributions that eventually would come to mould game theory into its subsequent shape came from John Nash, however. In fact, Nash proposed several things. First he also offered a solution concept for cooperative games of his own, the so-called Nash bargaining solution. But, second and even more importantly, he launched what later was to be called the Nash programme. The leading idea in the Nash programme is that cooperative games can and should be analysed as non-cooperative games by including the possibility of making binding agreements as a possible first move for the players in the enlarged corresponding non-cooperative games. In a sense, non-cooperative game theory was hereby elevated to the status of the more fundamental or basic theory within game theory. Finally, Nash introduced the solution concept that came to dominate virtually all subsequent work on non-cooperative games, the Nash equilibrium. In short, Nash proposed not only to redirect the focus of game theorists from cooperative games to non-cooperative games, but also to analyse the latter in terms of his own Nash equilibrium.

We suggest that what thus happened in the 1950s, in this exciting episode in the history of game theory, when 'giants walked the earth' (Aumann, 1989, p. 18), can be considered as a stage of diversification. No doubt all persons working on game theory believed that they were pursuing the same project that von Neumann and Morgenstern had started. And there surely are continuities. As Aumann (1989, p. 16) notes, for example, von Neumann and Morgenstern introduced a new method of modelling that has remained the archetype of game-theoretic modelling for subsequent generations. The distinction that von Neumann and Morgenstern made between normal form games and extended form games is still widely used by game theorists. Yet in their attempts to contribute to von Neumannn and Morgenstern's project, game theorists put forward new solution concepts of their own. Gradually the attention of game theorists shifted from von Neumann and Morgenstern's solution concepts to the new ones.

Interestingly, von Neumann and Morgenstern did not appear to be particularly pleased with the direction in which Nash, in particular, took the project.[18] Those who argue that the Nash equilibrium is a generalization of von Neumann and Morgenstern's minimax solution also draw attention to the fact that the essentials of the Nash equilibrium can already be found in Cournot's study of oligopoly. But Schotter (1992, p. 106) argues that Morgenstern consciously rejected a revival of Cournot's ideas in the context of his joint endeavour with von Neumann. Von Neumann and Morgenstern were looking for a solution concept, Schotter argues, that unlike Cournot's and Nash's notions was independent of the players' expectations about the behaviour of others. A similar critical attitude towards Nash's ideas can be found in Luce and Raiffa's influential (1957) book. After a critical discussion of the Nash programme,

Luce and Raiffa (1957, p. 153) concluded, 'a reduction of the cooperative game to a non-cooperative one [...] is completely *ad hoc*'.

We now know that the resistance and strong reservations of several pioneers of game theory against Nash's ideas did not prevent these ideas from eventually dominating game theory. It was far from obvious for these early pioneers that the potential of Nash's proposals exceeded those that other game theorists advanced. Neither was it obvious to all involved that the proposals competed for hegemony with each other (see Luce and Raiffa, 1957). For some, the different proposals could and did co-persist peacefully as complements rather than rivals, each having its own purpose and scope of application.[19] At the same time, the few studies of this period that have seen the light so far[20] stress the internal competition within the community of game theorists. It cannot be denied that in the end Nash's proposals survived the selection process. They attracted by far the most adherents.

This is not to say that other proposals disappeared altogether. In particular Edgeworth's notion of the core that Shubik reintroduced has found many applications in economics. Indeed, it can even be argued that it is via this notion that game theory first gained a real foothold in economics. Debreu and Scarf (1963) showed that in perfect competition, when the number of market participants goes to infinity, the core equals the set of equilibrium prices. Only after this theoretical contact was made with convention general equilibrium theory, did game theory start finding its way into economics.

Why then did not the core become as popular as Nash's proposals? What 'historical factors' made Nash's proposals first acquire critical mass? We certainly do not claim to be able to pinpoint all relevant factors here. But at least some of them, we venture, relate to the fact that Nash's proposals allowed for even closer contact with conventional general equilibrium theory than the core or any of the other contenders. Nash's proposals were better attuned to the familiar standards for theory appraisal that conventional general equilibrium theory exemplifies than any of its rivals. For one thing, the core has relatively bad *existence* properties. The core's main fault is that it is often empty, as Aumann (1985, p. 53) puts it succinctly. The solution concept that Nash put forward for non-cooperative games fares better in this respect. The better existence properties of the Nash equilibrium indeed seem to be one of the reasons behind its current centrality in economics.

Moreover, the Nash equilibrium can be said to be the embodiment of the fundamental behavioural assumption in conventional economics that agents are utility maximizers (see Aumann, 1985, p. 43). Also, for quite some time game theorists seem to have thought that Nash equilibria are self-enforcing.[21] Given that conventional economists are preoccupied with the search for *stable* equilibria, this idea made the Nash equilibrium all the more attractive for them. Factors like these, we contend, that all relate to the continuity of the Nash equilibrium with economic theory of the time, explain at least to some extent why it has been the Nash equilibrium rather than any of the other solution concepts that first built up a critical frequency of adopters in the community of game theorists.

What about the third standard that was established in the course of the conventionalization of GET, that of *uniqueness*? In many games, von Neumann and Morgenstern's solution concept for cooperative game theory, the stable set, does not single out just one *unique* pattern of coalition formation (but allows for many different ones). There is some evidence that von Neumann and Morgenstern were not bothered by this non-uniqueness.[22] After the community of game theorists massively adopted both Nash's programme and the Nash equilibrium, it soon turned out that the Nash equilibrium also has bad uniqueness properties. Many games have multiple Nash equilibria. But game theorists working in the Nash tradition tended to treat the non-uniqueness of Nash equilibria as a shortcoming that had to be overcome. Recognition of this property led many game theorists to look for refinements of the Nash equilibrium concept. The proliferation of the Nash equilibrium refinement literature after Selten's pioneering work in the mid-1970s demonstrates how firmly the standard of uniqueness was already entrenched by then.

In sum, we showed that the processes of the conventionalization of game theory and its inroad in economics display the cyclical pattern that we discussed above. Von Neumann and Morgenstern's 1944 book was the standard reference point of all those who contributed to the further development of game theory in the 1950s and 1960s. The contributions, which mainly existed in proposals of different new solution concepts, can be analysed in our terms of diversification. Although its superiority was far from obvious to several pioneers of game theory, Nash's work eventually best survived the selection process that followed. One of the reasons for this, we ventured, is that in several respects Nash's work fitted conventional economics better than any of its contenders. If we are right on this, the remarkable thing is that some of the standards for theory appraisal that were established with the conventionalization of general equilibrium theory can account at least partly for the present popularity of Nash type game theory in economics. The preoccupation with the existence and stability of equilibria exemplified in general equilibrium theory can also be found in Nash type conventional game theory. In a sense, then, the path that game theory took is dependent on the path that economics took with the conventionalization of general equilibrium theory.

Along with the conventionalization of Nash type game theory came a shift in the research agenda of game theorists. Cooperative game theory, which attracted most of the attention of von Neumann and Morgenstern and their early followers, gave way to non-cooperative game theory. After Nash type game theory established itself as the conventional science, the increased importance of the standard of uniqueness was evinced by the proliferation of the Nash refinement literature. Contrary to the standards of existence and stability, the standard of uniqueness did not contribute to the early adoption of Nash's ideas, for the Nash equilibrium was quickly found to have bad uniqueness properties. It was this discovery that stirred game theorists to come up with several refinements of the Nash equilibrium and thus to enter a new stage of diversification (as the first stage of a new cycle).

6 WHAT'S NEW?

Prima facie, our analysis of theoretical developments in economics resembles Thomas Kuhn's (1962) well-known account of scientific revolutions. In his *Structure of Scientific Revolutions* Kuhn also argued that scientific development characteristically follows a recurrent cyclical pattern. The elements in Kuhn's account of the cycle that seem to resemble our analysis most closely are the following. Relatively long periods of 'normal science' alternate with relatively short periods of 'revolutionary science'. The stage of normal science is characterized by the existence of a shared paradigm. The prevailing paradigm provides researchers with a common stock of presuppositions, approaches and definitions and focuses their research efforts on a restricted set of problems and puzzles. Sooner or later the paradigm breaks down and in its wake, during the stage of revolutionary science, a diversification of new competing theories can typically be observed. Next an opaque process of competition ensues in which all kinds of social factors are inextricably interwoven. The outcome of this process cannot be predicted in advance. After some time one of the competing theories wins out and a new paradigm is established.

In our analysis of the various stages in the path-dependent structure of scientific evolution we likewise distinguish between conventional science, the diversification of new approaches, and the selection of one of these as the new conventional science. In characterizing the stage of conventional science, we also stress the importance and impact of shared, established categories and definitions. We also include social factors (such as prestige among peers) in our account both of the conventionalization of science and of the selection process following the diversification of new approaches. And, finally by analysing the selection process as a path-dependent process we also call attention to the pervasive impact of at first seemingly unimportant historical 'accidents'. Is not our analysis merely a reformulation of Kuhn's account then? Is it not just old wine in new bottles?

For various reasons we do not think that this is the case. First of all our primary concern is somewhat different from Kuhn's, that is, on the stage that takes a centre place in our analysis, Kuhn is relatively silent: that stage in 'revolutionary science' in which one of the competing new theories is selected; Kuhn does not give us much more here than some vague references to a process of competition (Kuhn, 1996, pp. 17 and 23), to a 'Darwinian natural selection analogy' (ibid., pp. 171–2) and to an 'evolutionary view on science' (ibid., p. 173). Kuhn is silent on how, exactly, this process of competition or process of selection works. He does not specify which factors and structures steer this process. Although we certainly do not claim that we have identified these factors and processes completely and exactly, we have shed some light on them by analysing the selection process in terms of path dependence and by suggesting what kind of historical factors impinge on this process.

Second, we disagree with some of Kuhn's more controversial claims when they are related to economics.[23] We refer here to claims that are deliberately left out in our condensed presentation of Kuhn's account. Kuhn does not only claim that old paradigms give way to new ones, but also that the new ones are radically different from the old ones. Paradigm shifts are compared with *Gestalt switches*. In one of the most contested passages in the book, Kuhn seems to suggest that scientists who are raised and trained in the old paradigm inhabit a different world than scientists who have acquainted themselves with the new paradigm (see Kuhn, 1996, p. 112). It is precisely because of these deep-cutting discontinuities that Kuhn speaks of scientific revolutions. By contrast, we believe that as far as economics is concerned, the transition from the one conventional economics to the new one does not cut so deep. There is at least as much continuity as there is discontinuity. That is why we prefer to speak of scientific evolution. In the case of the conventionalization of general equilibrium theory, for example, we do not go as far as to deny that the existence, stability and uniqueness issue preoccupying general equilibrium theory were totally absent in Walras. These issues were there in Walras all right. But it is just that they gained more, if not exclusive attention in present-day general equilibrium theory. Likewise, Nash succeeded in shifting the research efforts of game theorists in the direction of non-cooperative game theory. Von Neumann and Morgenstern may not have liked either this redirection or Nash's solution concept for non-cooperative games. But it is equally true that von Neumann and Morgenstern's own minimax solution for non-cooperative games can be seen as a special case of the general notion of a Nash equilibrium.

Does Lakatos' methodology of scientific research programmes fit our account here better? The reasons we have given for discarding application of the Kuhnian notion of paradigm shifts can also be invoked, we think, to discard the applicability of the Lakatosian idea of research programmes superseding each other. In order to warrant speaking about different research programmes there should be more discontinuity in the development of concepts, issues and standards in GET and game theory than we think has been the case. But can we not therefore speak of changes within one and the same research programme?

Unlike Kuhn, Lakatos allows for the possibility of evolutionary changes within one and the same research programme. Scientists can tinker with their 'protective belt propositions', Lakatos argues; they continue to work in the same research programme as long as they retain their 'hard core propositions'. The terms in which we have analysed evolution in economics, however, are somewhat orthogonal to Lakatos' concerns. Instead of propositions, we identified (solution) concepts, issues and standards as the entities that are evolving in economics. Furthermore, the type of evolution we see is more in terms of additions, refinements (with respect to concepts) and shifts in emphasis (with respect to issues) than replacements (as Lakatos sees it).

A third major difference between Kuhn's account and ours concerns the issue of what prompts diversification of new theories. Kuhn holds that diversification of new theories occurs only when the old paradigm is in a state of crisis.[24] Only after anomalies accumulate, when expectations of researchers are repeatedly frustrated that certain puzzles can be solved in the old paradigm, Kuhn argues, does the process of diversification of new, competing theories start. In our view a shared feeling of crisis is not a necessary condition for the diversification of new approaches and concepts. Typically, the diversification springs from a shared feeling of excitement and conviction that conventional science can fully exploit its perceived potential. True, proponents of new concepts must believe that there is something in conventional science that can be improved upon. Otherwise they would not even consider making a contribution. But this is a far cry from a Kuhnian crisis. Proponents of new approaches and concepts typically hold that by putting forward their proposals they take conventional science one step further. Our account suggests that by doing so scientists do not simply add something to the existing stock of knowledge, but also withdraw attention from conventional science. What typically occurs is that different researchers come up with different proposals. What we suggest is that a shared sense of dissatisfaction permeates science only after the diversification of new concepts has already taken place. Multiple persisting new concepts are typically not taken as complements or supplements, but as rivals. The general feeling is that such a situation is to be overcome. Ideally, all scientists need to reach an agreement on which approach and set of concepts to converge.

In short, our approach differs from that of Kuhn in that we stress and study the evolutionary rather than revolutionary features of theoretical developments in economics. In this, our approach much more resembles Hull's treatment of theoretical developments than Kuhn's (and Lakatos', it might be added). We do not deny that there are major changes to be observed in these developments. But we do not believe that these changes are so dramatic as to make it appropriate to speak of incommensurable worlds after and before the changes. Traces from the old are always recognizably visible in the new. We also do not believe that major changes occur because those responsible for the changes feel that the potential of the old conventional theory is exhausted. Quite the contrary, new theories proliferate because their proponents believe that there is plenty of potential in the old conventional theory that has not yet been exploited. Finally, we agree with Kuhn that the process following this diversification can be regarded as a selection process. Kuhn does not indicate what this amounts to, however. We have argued that this process can be fruitfully analysed in terms of path-dependent processes.

7   TO SUMMARIZE

In this chapter we have offered a perspective on the evolution of science, in particular economic science, by stressing the path-dependent nature of it. While philosophers and historians of science have focused on the structure of scientific research *programmes* and *revolutions*, we have focused on an articulation of its underlying *process*. Our description of the self-reinforcing mechanism underlying science parallels David Hull's (1988) account of what moves individual scientists; as such we argue that individual scientists engage simultaneously in cooperation and competition. Hence, science is portrayed as perpetually going through cycles. Stages of conventional science give way to stages of diversification that in turn are followed by a process of selection and conventionalization, followed by new stages of diversification. We have argued that the path-dependent characteristic of the process is largely attributable to the particular way in which selection processes in science take place. In two case studies we have illustrated the evolution of these branches of economic science.

NOTES

1. See, for example, Kreps (1997).
2. Intricate issues, such as whether such a process is rational or whether it leads to a growth of knowledge, are not discussed here.
3. On the notion of 'history' in path dependence literature see Jolink (1996).
4. Some of the recent discussions on lock-in and path dependence have focused primarily on the inefficiency of the outcome property, thereby fogging the distinction (see Liebowitz and Margolis, 1995).
5. This is not to say that we fully agree with everything that Hull puts forward on these matters. Hull seems to be quite confident, for example, that some community-transcendent standard of careful (empirical) scrutiny sees to it that in science individual 'vices' are turned into public 'virtues'. Especially in the case of economics, we tend to be less confident on this. For further discussions and elaborations of Hull, see, for example, Kitcher (1993) and Wilkins (1998).
6. Hull does not believe that this is the sole motivation of scientists. As a matter of fact, we think that one of the interesting aspects of his view is that he believes that scientists are also driven by curiosity.
7. In our evolutionary framework, two different interpretations can be given of such a process of convergence. Either each member uses one set of concepts in each period of time only, and all members converge on the same set of concepts as time proceeds. Or each member

uses his or her own fixed mix of sets of concepts in each period of time and these individual mixes eventually all give way to the same set of concepts.

8. We believe that our use of 'history' here is perfectly in line with Arthur (1988).
9. This section draws heavily on Ingrao and Israel's impressive account of the notion of equilibrium in the history of science (Ingrao and Israel, 1990).
10. Ingrao and Israel, 1990, p. 4.
11. 'Interpretive communities are made up of those who share interpretive strategies not for reading but for writing texts, for constituting their properties.' Fish 1980, quoted in Weintraub 1991, p. 6.
12. The lock-in effect seems to be observable nowadays in US economic graduate programmes as well, where students believe that mathematics is the quintessential prerequisite in economics (see Colander and Klamer, 1990).
13. See, for example, Hargreaves Heap and Varoufakis, 1995, pp. 49–50.
14. See, for example, Ingrao and Israel, 1990, p. 271.
15. See, for example, Binmore, 1992, p. 12.
16. See, for example, Schotter, 1992.
17. See Dimand and Dimand, 1996, chapters 6 and 7, for a detailed discussion.
18. On von Neumann, Shubik (1992, p. 155) recalls a conversation in which von Neumann made clear that he did not share Shubik's enthusiasm for the potential of Nash's work for economic applications.
19. See Aumann, 1985.
20. See O'Rand, 1992 and Aumann, 1989.
21. See Aumann, 1985, p. 48.
22. This seems to have been related to von Neumann and (especially) Morgenstern's belief that several different institutions can originate organically from some problem situation. As mentioned earlier, the (Menger-inspired) study of the organic origin of institutions was one of the target fields of the application of game theory for von Neumann and Morgenstern.
23. Kuhn may have held that economics never transcended the pre-paradigmatic stage. But this is irrelevant for our present purposes. What we are investigating here is in what respects, if any, the Kuhnian account *if applied to economics*, differs from ours.
24. The same holds for Lakatos. Lakatos agrees with Kuhn that there should be some kind of crisis – a research programme should be theoretically and empirically degenerating, to use Lakatos' own terminology – for scientists to consider new (hard core) propositions. Hence, we also depart from Lakatos on this point.

REFERENCES

Arthur, B.W. (1988), 'Self-reinforcing mechanisms in economics', in Philip Anderson, Kenneth Arrow and David Pines (eds), *The Economy as an Evolving, Complex System*, Reading, MA: Addison-Wesley, pp. 9–31.

Aumann, R.J. (1985), 'What is game theory trying to accomplish?', in K.J. Arrow and S. Honkapohja (eds), *Frontiers in Economics*, Oxford: Basil Blackwell, pp. 28–76.

Aumann, R.J. (1989), 'Game theory', in J. Eatwell, M. Milgate and P. Newman (eds), *The New Palgrave: Game Theory*, London: Macmillan, pp. 1–53.

Binmore, K. (1992), *Fun and Games: a Text on Game Theory*, Lexington, MA: Heath.

Colander, D. and A. Klamer (1990), *The Making of an Economist*, Boulder, CO: Westview Press.

David, P.A. (1985), 'Clio and the economics of QWERTY', *American Economic Review Proceedings*, **75**: 332–7.

David, P.A. (1988), 'Path-dependence: putting the past into the future of economics', IMSSS Tech Report no. 533, November, Stanford University.

Debreu, G. (1959), *Theory of Value*, New York: Wiley.

Debreu, G. and H. Scarf (1963), 'A limit theorem on the core of an economy', *International Economic Review*, **4**: 236–46.

Dimand, M.A. and R.W. Dimand (1996), *The History of Game Theory, Volume I; From the Beginnings to1945*, London: Routledge.

Hargreaves Heap, S.P. and Y. Varoufakis (1995), *Game Theory: A Critical Introduction*, London: Routledge.

Horgan, T. (1997), *The End of Science: Facing the Limits of Knowledge in the Twilight of the Scientific Age*, Reading: Helix Books.

Horwich, P. (ed.) (1993), *World Changes: Thomas Kuhn and the Nature of Science*, Cambridge MA: MIT Press.

Hull, D. (1988), *Science as a Process : an Evolutionary Account of the Social and Conceptual Development of Science*, Chicago: University of Chicago Press.

Ingrao, B. and G. Israel (1990), *The Invisible Hand: Economic Equilibrium in the History of Science*, Cambridge, MA: MIT Press.

Jolink, A. (1996), 'If history matters then what is history?', mimeo EIPE, Erasmus University Rotterdam.

Kitcher, Ph. (1993), *The advancement of science: science without legend, objectivity without illusions*, Oxford: Oxford University Press.

Kreps, D.M. (1997), 'Economics – the current position', *Daedalus*, 126, pp. 59–86.

Kuhn, T.S. ([1962] 1996), *The Structure of Scientific Revolutions* (third edition), Chicago: University of Chicago Press.

Leonard, R.J. (1995), 'From parlor games to social science: von Neumann, Morgenstern, and the creation of game theory 1928–1944', *Journal of Economic Literature*, **33**, pp. 730–61.

Liebowitz, S. and S. Margolis (1995), 'Path dependence, lock-in, and history', *Journal of Law, Economics and Organization*, **11** (1), April: 205–26.

Luce, R.D. and H. Raiffa (1957), *Games and Decisions: Introduction and Critical Survey,* New York: John Wiley and Sons.

O'Rand, A.M. (1992), 'Mathematizing social science in the 1950s: the early development and diffusion of game theory', in R.E. Weintraub (ed.), *Toward a History of Game Theory*, Durham, NC: Duke University Press, pp. 177–205.

Schotter, A. (1992), 'Oskar Morgenstern's contribution to the development of the theory of games', in R.E. Weintraub (ed.), *Toward a History of Game Theory*, Durham, NC: Duke University Press, pp. 95–112.

Shubik, M. (1992), 'Game Theory at Princeton, 1949–1955: a personal reminiscence', in R.E. Weintraub (ed.), *Toward a History of Game Theory*, Durham, NC: Duke University Press, pp. 151–63.

von Neumann, J. and O. Morgenstern (1944), *A Theory of Games and Economic Behavior*, Princeton: Princeton University Press.

Walras, L. (1926), *Eléments d' économie politique pure*, Paris: Pichon & Durand-Auzias.

Walsh, V. and H. Gram (1980), *Classical and Neoclassical Theories of General Equilibrium: Historical Origins and Mathematical Structure*, Oxford: Oxford University Press.

Weintraub, E.R. (1985), *General Equilibrium Analysis: Studies in Appraisal*, Cambridge: Cambridge University Press.

Weintraub, E.R. (1991), *Stabilizing Dynamics: Constructing Economic Knowledge*, Cambridge: Cambridge University Press.

Weintraub, E.R. (ed.) (1992), *Toward a History of Game Theory*, Durham, NC: Duke University Press.

Wilkins, J. (1998), 'The evolutionary structure of scientific theories', *Biology & Philosophy*, **13** (4): 479–504.

11. Reflections on the progress of heterodox economics

A.W. Coats

1   INTRODUCTION

Keynote speeches, especially those scheduled to be delivered at the end of a gathering of the faithful, are liable to become partisan exercises designed to reiterate and reemphasize the main themes and objectives of the proceedings, rally supporters, perhaps damn the opposition, and send forth the true believers – and hopefully also some of the waverers – as missionaries, to spread the gospel and bring in new converts.

This is, of course, a caricature, influenced by the recent British party conferences, for I do not seriously believe the organizing committee had this scenario in mind when they invited me to appear. For one thing, given the sheer number and miscellaneous character of the conference sessions and papers presented during the past two days, no single individual could hope to summarize, let alone synthesize the proceedings. Moreover, after a lifetime of scholarly caution I am certainly not the kind of person to proclaim a new paradigm, propose a novel, all-embracing theory or framework for evolutionary/institutional political economy, or publish a new manifesto designed to advertise and proselytize this Association's message. What I can offer, however, are some general reflections and perspectives on the current heterodox scene, drawing on my study of Anglo-American economics over the past five decades. The fact that the Steering Committee, and some of the more active members of the Association, have been engaged in a process of comprehensive self-examination with respect to the organization's name and purpose, may make this intervention more timely and appropriate, coming as it does from an inveterate economist-watcher and hitherto undeclared fellow-traveller among the evolutionary/institutionalist proponents of economic heterodoxy.

In the ensuing account I shall not attempt to cover all the many forms of economic heterodoxy. For the sake of terminological convenience, I shall follow Brian Loasby's lead when he remarked, at last year's conference, that

Institutional economics must be evolutionary economics...because institutions are a response to incomplete knowledge...they may have unexpected consequences, both beneficial and harmful and are likely to change over time...and *evolutionary economics must be institutional economics*, for in a world of imperfect knowledge and of bounded rationality processes must be structured by institutions. (Loasby, 1996, pp. 18–19. Emphasis supplied.)

It would obviously be inappropriate for me, as an outsider, to comment on the current deliberations concerning this Association's title. But I can fully appreciate the difficulties involved, for they resemble those encountered by some other heterodox economic organizations.

For example, the principal body representing American institutionalists – the American Association for Evolutionary Economics (AFEE), originating in 1958, but formally established in 1966 – was, fifteen years later, struggling with such serious divisions among its members, that Allan Gruchy, a leading founder member, declared 'I have come to wonder whether or not there can be enough agreement among our members to make a viable organization with a well-defined image. It may have been a mistake on my part to believe that institutional economists are organizable.' (From his remarks on receiving the Veblen–Commons award, the AFEE's highest accolade. (Gruchy, 1974, p. 207).

Gruchy was soon proved right, for a rival organization, the Association for Institutional Thought (AFIT), was formed by a group of the AFEE's more purist hardcore or doctrinaire members who wished to work entirely within the confines of a 'particular intellectual lineage' stemming from Veblen, Dewey, Ayres, Commons, Mitchell and others (Ranson, 1981, p. 522). AFIT's founder-members believed the existing organization (AFEE) was too tolerant of economic orthodoxy, and the resulting eclecticism undoubtedly reflected the beliefs of the Journal of Economic Issues' editor, Warren Samuels, who was working towards a reconciliation, maybe even a synthesis, of orthodox and heterodox economics. This has not in fact occurred. The AFEE and its Journal have continued to thrive and enjoy substantial support. (The AFIT also survives, but on a significantly smaller scale than the AFEE.)

Another, broadly comparable, example of the organizational problems in economic heterodoxy is the so-called 'uprising' of behavioural economics, an ill-defined category that includes contributors from mainstream economics as well as a wide variety of other social sciences and disciplines. At their first annual conference, in May 1984, the behavioural economists expressed criticisms of orthodox economic theory that many, if not most members of this Association would heartily endorse. They objected to the mainstreamers'

1. reliance on positivism as the methodological foundation for economic research; their
2. reliance on deductive reasoning as a sufficient basis of a (social) science; their

3. preference for static analysis of equilibrium outcomes rather than disequilibrium processes; and, especially, their
4. adherence to a simplistic model of rational agents exhibiting optimizing behaviour.

(Gilad, Kaish and Loeb, 1984, p. 42. Original wording modified)

In discussing the organization's objectives and strategy, the Behavioral Economists' Conference posed three questions similar to those currently facing the European Association for Evolutionary Political Economy)

a) What should be the organization's title?
b) Is it wise to chip away at mainstream economics, or should Behavioral Economics (or Evolutionary Political Economy) aim to achieve a *rapprochement* or add on to it?
c) Is there a justification for an additional journal?

(ibid. p. 16. Original formulation modified.)

The second question – whether to chip away at mainstream economics or work constructively towards a *rapprochement* – has both historical antecedents and implications for the future. It recalls the basic difference between the institutionalism of Veblen and Ayres, who were seeking an alternative to orthodox economics, and that of Commons (and Mitchell), who believed the two were complementary. Unlike the old institutionalism, however, behavioural economics was not designed as a doctrinal movement with ideological significance, but simply (and perhaps naively) as 'an approach to doing economic research'. It could therefore appeal to researchers in many different disciplines and fields, for it is not substance-specific. The behavioural economists sought consistency with the accumulated body of knowledge in the behavioural sciences (most institutionalists would surely approve of this). They welcomed support from those disciplines; required economic theory to 'concentrate on and be able to explain real observed behavior'; and to be 'empirically verifiable with field, laboratory, survey, and other microdata generating techniques'.[1]

They were not concerned by the wide range of their members' specialities – however incongruously lumped together under a catch-all title, and they drew comfort from Baumol's claim, on behalf of his contestable markets theory, that 'No uprising by a tiny band of rebels can hope to change an established order, and when the time is ripe for rebellion it seems to break out simultaneously in a variety of disconnected centers, each offering its own programme for the future' (ibid., quoting Baumol, 1982, p. 1). Something of this kind seems to be happening now in European evolutionary political economy. Is this Association in the vanguard? Its membership, though interdisciplinary, is surely less heterogeneous than that of the behavioural economists; and the latter's confident faith in 'empirically verifiable' economic theory now seems somewhat dated – apart from the limited, though promising, work in experimental economics.

Before turning to the broader issues implied in my title, let me raise some further questions. Why have the heterodox European economists been so slow, by comparison with their American counterparts, in forming their own association? Was there no continental European dissenting body of ideas?[2] If not, why not? What were the precise motives and aims of this Association's founders; and what is the organization's place in the intellectual and professional development of European economics? Indeed, given recent doubts, is there such a phenomenon as a European economics? (Frey and Frey, 1995).

2   PROBLEMS OF DEFINITION AND FOCUS: HETERODOXY, ORTHODOXY, PROGRESS

You will not be surprised to learn that I have had some misgivings about my title: 'Reflections on the progress of economic heterodoxy', given the problems of defining the key terms: heterodoxy, progress and, by implication, orthodoxy. The variety of views and approaches encompassed under the umbrella of institutional economics has long been acknowledged, and repeatedly debated. Moreover – as with Mark Twain's obituary – the movement's decease has repeatedly been announced prematurely.

If Institutionalism is difficult to define, the task is not much easier with economic orthodoxy. As far back as 1885, Marshall's colleague, Henry Sidgwick, commented wryly that orthodox political economy has 'the characteristic unusual in orthodox doctrines of being repudiated by the majority of accredited teachers of the subject'.[3] However, to quote Mandy Rice Davis, a notorious English lady of dubious morals: 'Well: they would say that, wouldn't they?'

Any attempt to define the characteristics and demarcate the boundaries of heterodox and orthodox economics, which are constantly shifting, would require a whole monograph, for the task becomes more difficult the more pervasive the heterodox or dissenting influences. For those who are undeterred I recommend that you start with a deconstruction of the eight admirable 'theoretical perspectives' listed in this Association's constitution. In each case, the Association's affirmative heterodox assertion is followed by the orthodox alternative. For the present purpose I shall focus on some of the major trends in economics over the past two or three decades, and define 'progress' inclusively as a movement in the general direction desired by heterodox economists, *whether or not it derives from heterodox or orthodox sources.*

Dissatisfaction with orthodox or mainstream economics can, of course, be traced back at least to the early 19th century. More recently, as Nicholas Georgescu-Roegen remarked a quarter of a century ago: 'No science has been criticized by its own servants as openly and constantly as economics' (1971, p. 1, cited by Hodgson, 1992, p. 122). Evidence for this claim can be found in the official lectures delivered by successive Nobel laureates in economics, many of which contain severe strictures on the discipline's condition and/or past development. In recent years the dissenting chorus has been increasingly insistent; more varied in its sources and substance; and organized in a growing number of scholarly bodies. Of special interest in the present context are the criticisms of 'neoclassical' economics expressed by thoughtful leading mainstream economists who have sought to remedy the discipline's deficiencies. In so doing, they have been (wittingly or unwittingly) undermining its orthodox foundations and contributing to the convergence between the orthodox and heterodox approaches.

One of the most telling examples of what might be termed 'subversive orthodoxy' is the path-breaking book by Richard Nelson and Sidney Winter: *An Evolutionary Theory of Economic Change* (1982), which significantly advanced the theory of the firm in an evolutionary/institutionalist direction. Yet it contains only a passing mention of institutionalism as such (in a footnote on p. 404) where they observe that: 'On questions of the larger system [as contrasted with their specific focus], we converge substantially with the older tradition of evolutionary thinking in economics that has institutional evolution as its principal concern'. Nevertheless, while emphasizing the revolutionary implications of their work, 'which involves a major reconstruction of the theoretical foundations of our discipline' (p. 4), the authors attack the theoretical orthodoxy in economics which provides 'a narrow set of criteria that are used as a cheap and simple test for whether an expressed point of view is worthy of respect'. This orthodoxy, they add, is 'quite widely enforced'. It appears especially in the leading textbooks used in 'Relatively standardized undergraduate intermediate macroeconomics courses designed to provide background for more advanced applied work...essentially the same ideas also appear at more advanced level courses, although with more mathematical tools' (ibid, pp. 6–7).

Unfortunately, heterodox critics often fail to appreciate the variety of levels at which the theoretical orthodoxy is manifested, or how varied and flexible it is. Many of the heterodox objections:

Can be accommodated with slight changes of meaning, treated and accommodated as special case models, or absorbed by broadening the theory somewhat, all with very few ripples. The fact that prevailing theory itself defines what are reasonable and sophisticated exceptions to prevailing theory and what distinguishes appropriate or inappropriate proposals for amendment or reform is another defence. Beyond this, parochial attitudes and intellectual vested interests resist change, so that it is difficult to abandon the established way of looking at things given the existing power structure within the profession.[4]

Although many, perhaps the majority of orthodox economists acknowledge the limitations of the discipline's basic theoretical apparatus – for example, the preoccupation with equilibrium; the definition of competition; the strict version of the concept of economic rationality, with its accompaniments of perfect information, optimization, ability to calculate a wide range of options etc.; and the discipline's inability to handle long run and progressive change – this does not lead to a generalized agnosticism or eclecticism, and search for an alternative framework. Moreover:

> The logical structure of the intermediate texts [which constitutes the basis of economic orthodoxy] underlies much of the informal discussion of economic events and policies engaged in by economists and others with substantial economics background...[thus, in a sense] the conclusions of intermediate analysis seem much more indicative of where the discipline stands than do appraisals that are theoretically more sophisticated, but also more difficult and less familiar to nontheorists...[Indeed] the strong simplifying assumptions of the intermediate texts often have close analogies in advanced work, right out to the theoretical frontiers. (ibid. pp. 7–8)

The orthodox theoretical apparatus enshrined in standardized textbooks widely used in American universities and colleges (and, to a lesser extent, worldwide) constitutes the core training and education of American economists. A careful reading of the 1991 Report of the American Economic Association's Commission on Graduate Education in Economics (known colloquially as Cogee) (Krueger *et al.*, 1991) reveals how entrenched is the orthodox conception of economic ideas and methods but also, unwittingly, how that orthodoxy threatens the reputation and effectiveness of the entire profession. The Cogee report is the outcome of the largest and most thorough investigation of American economics ever undertaken,[5] but its results are disappointing to all those who seek far-reaching and effective proposals for the reform of the economics curriculum and the training process. The Commissioners seemed complacent in dealing with the widely recognized problems resulting from the curriculum's excessive formalization, mathematization, and narrowness;[6] and they made no effort to assess its consequences for the economics profession and the general public.[7] The Report by the Executive Secretary of Cogee (Hansen, 1991) revealed the sharp decline in the percentage of American students taking doctoral degrees in economics. But for the marked increase in the number of foreign students taking these degrees, there would already have been a severe crisis in the demand for economics faculty in American colleges and universities.[8]

The related, but separate, Kasper Report, prepared by nine Chairmen of Economics Departments in elite liberal arts colleges, voiced its members' concern at the indirect deterrent effects of graduate training in economics on recent cohorts of undergraduate seniors, many of whom decided to enlist in other graduate programmes (Kasper *et al.*, 1991). Additional, as yet unpublished, papers prepared for the Commission focused on the tendency for increasing numbers of graduate students to enter other, more applied, programmes, such as business, public policy, law and economics, health economics, etc. These trends are compatible with data from Britain and Australia on the relatively declining demand for undergraduate and graduate economics courses, and in Britain, also, on the numbers taking economics at A level (pre-university). Evidently economics' increasingly technocratic character is leading to a widespread loss of enthusiasm for the subject at several different levels. As one gloomy, but well-qualified respondent said in one of the unpublished reports: 'Economics is going the way of the classics'. No doubt the public's widely reported loss of confidence in economics also helps to make the discipline seem less attractive to potential recruits.

A question for this Association's researchers is: How far is the situation in Europe changing as in the USA? And how far does the relative decline in the attractiveness of orthodox neoclassical economics provide an opportunity for heterodox economists to extend their influence?

Turning to economics research, whether in academic or non-academic institutions, the prevailing diversity of topics, methods and approaches is remarkable. Undoubtedly the shortcomings and limitations of graduate education leave their mark, for example by inhibiting creativity and deviance from the established norms. But fortunately its effects are often only temporary. In this connection I recall with pleasure a conversation with a new assistant professor at an American university where I was a visitor. When I asked him about his dissertation subject he responded that he did not want to discuss it. Once the dissertation was completed and he had his Ph.D., he was determined to switch to research on a more interesting and worthwhile topic! He had earned his professional union card, and did not intend to be inhibited by his training. This was perhaps an extreme case; but many newly minted Ph.D.s move into applied research, whether in academia or beyond;[9] and this is one process whereby the boundaries between orthodoxy and heterodoxy are becoming increasingly blurred. Thus some obstacles to the progress of economic heterodoxy are being eliminated, or at least reduced.

3   PROGRESS IN OR TOWARDS ECONOMIC HETERODOXY

As already noted, progress in economic heterodoxy can come about as the result either of changes in heterodox or orthodox ideas and practices, or by a combination and/or convergence between the two. At the risk of oversimplifying, it seems clear that during the past two or three decades the pace and extent of conceptual change have been much greater among orthodox than among heterodox economists, for many of the more thoughtful neoclassical economists nowadays acknowledge the validity of the profound and widespread criticisms of their theoretical apparatus and methods – especially their basic assumptions, the problems of applying and testing the theory, and the frequency of policy failures. Their creative responses have been gradually converting mainstream economics into a broader, more flexible, diverse, doubtless less coherent, interdisciplinary and realistic subject far removed from the rigid stereotype featured in earlier heterodox critiques.

The most striking single example of a convergent movement between economic orthodoxy and heterodoxy has been the rise of the so-called 'new institutional economics' (NIE) in the USA since the mid-1970s. Various attempts have been made to explain the origins and assess the significance of the movement, which hardly constitutes a 'school'; but it has undoubtedly emerged from within the orthodox camp, and it reflects the long-expressed desire to somehow 'take institutions into account'.

During the past decade there has been a lively and, on the whole constructive debate between the NIE and its rival, the old institutional economics (OIE), which has attracted historians and methodologists, as well as the protagonists. Fortunately for my purpose there is an invaluable, thoughtful and balanced review of the issues in Malcolm Rutherford's excellent book: *Institutions and Economics. The Old and the New Institutionalism* (1994).[10] Rutherford is fully aware of the differences *within* the two camps, and rejects the familiar but hackneyed and exaggerated contrast between the supposed 'descriptive, anti-formalist, holist, behaviorist and collectivist' OIE, and the 'more formalist, individualist, reductionist, oriented towards rational choice and economizing models, and generally anti-interventionist' NIE (ibid., p. 4). Within each movement there are two distinct streams of thought – the Veblen/Ayres' and the Commons' approaches in the OIE, and the neoclassical and Austrian wings in the NIE; and there are conflicts and complementarities within and between them. Yet they face 'a common set of problems' and 'can learn from each other' (ibid., p. 173). Both sides acknowledge the importance of norms, conventions, habits and routines in economic life as influences on individual behaviour; and both admit that once information costs and bounded rationality are recognized, choice can no longer be presented in terms of global optimizing. The two movements face the same problems with respect to the various species of rationality; and while the OIEs strongly resist the concept of rational maximization, 'the alternative adaptive concept of rationality is gaining ground among the NIE' (ibid., p. 79).

According to Rutherford, a broader concept of rationality is needed, one that can encompass both narrow self-interest and other psychological needs or ideals. This is why mainstream economics is gradually taking account of the role of altruism, trust, envy, fairness, empathy, equality, and other aspects of human action previously ignored by orthodox writers. While some orthodox economists are 'infuriated' by the OIE tendency to take social norms as given, the NIE have 'failed to provide an alternative satisfactory explanation of norms'.[11]

The OIE/NIE relationships are more complementary in respect of the distinction between evolutionary (spontaneous) and design (intentional) processes; and the supposedly fundamental dichotomy between the OIE's methodological holism and the NIE's methodological individualism has been demonstrated to be false. Provided the two approaches are not expressed in extreme terms they can be reconciled via Joseph Agassi's concept of 'institutional individualism'.[12]

As noted earlier, the behavioural economists objected to the mainstream economists' reliance on positivism as the methodological foundation for economic research, although by that time (1984) positivism, as variously interpreted, had long been discredited by philosophers of science. Since the 1970s there has been a remarkable anti-positivist 'uprising' in the English language economic methodology literature, and this has continued to be vigorous well into the 1990s. I have recently counted almost thirty current methodological positions (Coats, 1997b, p. 42), all of which undermine in varying degrees the 'official' positive approach enshrined in Milton Friedman's notorious 1953 methodological essay. Needless to say, to your relief, I do not propose to discuss all the alternative approaches now being advocated, although some undoubtedly represent a significant advance on earlier views both in philosophical sophistication and in understanding of the working economist's practical problems. Admittedly not all readers welcome the current buzzing, blooming confusion. Indeed, one leading figure has complained that the barbarians are at the gates: anarchy is nigh. And there is no consensus with regard to institutionalist or evolutionary methodology – though pattern-modelling, holism, storytelling, orientation theories, pattern predictions, and appreciative theory are current contenders (ibid., p. 43).

One of the most familiar and persistent criticisms of orthodox economics is its narrowness, and there have been innumerable calls for a more interdisciplinary approach to social and economic affairs. Recently, however, there has been within neoclassical economics an unprecedented widening of the range of topics considered by economists in a movement known by its exponents as economic imperialism. (In fact, economics imperialism would be a preferable term, since it would avoid confusion with the writings of J.A. Hobson, V.I. Lenin, and the many historians concerned with the development of late capitalism.) The economics imperialists claim that economics is the only genuine social science, and that its central corpus of analysis, especially the concept of utility maximization, can explain human behaviour in effect universally – for example crime, marriage, smoking, law, medicine, even brushing teeth! The crucial weakness, apart from its inherent arrogance, is that its exponents rarely take the trouble to study in depth, with due respect for evidence, the subjects to which they apply their theories and techniques. There is, however, increasing evidence of genuine interaction, even collaboration between economists and other social scientists – sociologists, political scientists, psychologists and anthropologists.[13]

The links between economics and psychology are especially strong, with specialists on both sides making serious efforts to learn, and to learn from, the knowledge and expertise of specialists in the other field. Political science may be roughly described as at a half-way stage, in which public choice theorists impose the orthodox economists' theories on political affairs while taking into account the nature and complexity of political processes. A particularly fruitful example of the combination of economic analysis and political science is the so-called political economy of economic policy reform, a body of research that is theoretically informed, empirically grounded, and sensitive to actual historical circumstances.[14]

Among OIEs, one of the most enduring complaints was that orthodox economic theory was static and mechanistic whereas evolution, process and change were considered to be essential requirements of a viable institutional economics. Nowadays these and related concepts such as path dependency, hysteresis, and the irreversibility of historical time are the subject of fruitful discussion and analysis among economists of many different doctrinal persuasions. Also the inescapable historicity of economics is now generally conceded, even by otherwise conventional neoclassical economists. In all these matters, there are unmistakable heterodox elements.

Viewed as a whole, notwithstanding the obvious continuing dominance of mainstream economists in teaching and in the academic reward system – but somewhat less so in non-academic employment and in the discipline's public reputation – it is still reasonable to speak of the 'progress' of heterodox economics, even though there are no grounds for complacency. As Ulrich Witt has observed:

> Neoclassical economics has caught up with many of its critics in recent years. Besides the countless formal attempts to get to grips with the non-static character of economic problems, there are now neoclassical theories of technical progress and innovation ...of differential economic growth and development...of long-term institutional change...and so on. The success rate with which neoclassical economics attacks new problems once they have been identified and addressed by its critics may even take much of the momentum out of the critical heterodox movement of evolutionary economics some day. Symptomatically, efforts are already being made to develop elements of a neoclassical interpretation of economic evolution. (Witt, 1991, p. 101)

These developments may be viewed with satisfaction by heterodox economists as evidence that they have been working in the right direction, for many decades. However, Malcolm Rutherford paints a much less flattering portrait.

> The significant developments in the theories of transactions costs, the internal organisation of firms, corporate finance, business cycles, environmental externalities, public goods, common property problems, common law, public choice and even social conventions and norms have not come from the recent generations of old institutionalists, a failure of such magnitude as to surely raise serious questions in the minds of even the most ardent supporters of the [OIE] tradition. (Rutherford, 1994, p. 177)

4   CONCLUDING REFLECTIONS

Certain broad conclusions emerge from this manifestly incomplete survey. The old institutional economics is by no means dead, and the rise of the new institutional economics is a clear and significant example of the recent tendency towards the convergence of orthodoxy and heterodoxy. While at present the momentum for change seems to come mainly from the orthodox camp, interpreted broadly, many of the new and valuable research initiatives on both sides reflect concerns that had no counterpart in earlier orthodox economic literature. The likelihood of a new grand synthesis or revolutionary paradigm seems less now than it did two decades ago, when there was much talk (not all of it loose) of a crisis in the discipline. However, the bewildering diversity of current views ensures that there will continue to be many intellectual niches for heterodox economists to occupy, and innumerable paths open to a more fruitful exploration of economic and social life.

5   POSTCRIPT

The Progress of Heterdox Economics was the subject of a Roundtable Discussion at the History of Economics Society's Greensborough Conference, in June 1999. The proceedings have been published in *The Journal of the History of Economic Thought*, Vol. 22 (3) 2000, pp. 145–90.

NOTES

1. This has been strongly argued by Herbert Simon, who maintains that 'the progress of economics, and especially the prospects for adequate empirical testing of economic theories, would seem to depend on finding new kinds of data to supplement the kind of aggregate evidence now typically employed', such as case studies, survey research, and laboratory experiments. He has long been a severe critic of the way economists treat the auxiliary

assumptions needed to make their general theories or concepts applicable in practice. These assumptions of the limits on rationality or the accuracy of information, 'are generally made in a casually empirical armchair way' (Simon, 1987, p. 225).

2. Apart from this Association there have been other recently formed dissenting organizations, for example the Association pour la Critique des Sciences Economiques et Sociales inaugurated in France in the mid-1970s, with the aim of regrouping 'the labourers in the social sciences who question the political neutrality and objectivity of these sciences and who are conscious of a rupture between themselves and the dominant economic tradition' (Jalladieu,1975, p. 11). Another interesting body is the International Confederation of Associations for the Reform of Economics (ICARE) founded in 1993. The constituent Associations had 5000 members at the end of 1996 (copies of vol. III of its Newsletter were available at the Athens conference).

3. Quoted by Smyth, 1961, p. 74. At the opposite pole from Sidgwick's mild demurrer is the banner at one time displayed by the monks of the Athos monastery Esfigmenou, which read 'Orthodoxy or Death'. (Ellingham *et al.*, 1996, p. 379). As Philip Mirowski has observed, although its opponents often treat it as a monolithic doctrine, the currently ruling orthodoxy, neoclassical economics 'is best described as a sequence of distinct orthodoxies, surrounded by a penumbra of quasi-rivals; and it is this, more than any deductive or inductive successes, which accounts for its longevity' (Mirowski, 1994, p. 68; quoted by Lawson, 1997, p. 105).

4. Ibid pp. 47–8. Sentence order modified. O'Driscoll and Rizzo make a similar point (1985, p. 231) 'There is a "sponginess" to neoclassical economics that enables it to absorb divergent elements without ever emphasizing their main points. These fringe ideas become footnotes to which theorists can refer as evidence that they have taken the ideas into account.' See also Lawson, 1997, pp. 87–8.

5. The Commission examined the 94 separate graduate programmes in economics in American institutions of higher education, classifying them into five 'quality tiers'. These programmes were not essentially different from one another, and according to a leading Commissioner, those in the lower tiers were doing the same things as those in the higher tiers, but doing them less well (personal communication).

6. There is a vivid depiction of the experience of American graduate education in economics by D.L. Strassman, in which economic theory means mathematical models and 'the legitimate way to argue is with models and econometrically constructed forms of evidence'. The 'verbal and geometric masterpieces produced' by earlier generations of economists are dismissed, because 'major scientific triumphs call for a better theory with a better model in recognizable form' (presentation in equations with mathematically expressed definitions, assumptions and theoretical developments clearly laid out) '...students learn that it is bad manners to engage in excessive questioning of simplifying assumptions'. It is thought to be too easy to find fault with existing models (1994 p. 154), sentence order changed; quoted by Lawson (1997, pp. 333–4).

7. In this respect, and some others, Cogee was inferior to the first, much more modest (but still substantial) survey of graduate economics in the USA conducted by Howard Bowen, and published in the *American Economic Review* in 1953 (cf. Coats, 1992).

8. While the total number of economics doctorates remained approximately constant, the percentage of American Ph.D.s fell from 67.3 to 47.2 in the period.

9. As the distinguished econometrician, Ed Leamer, discovered when he was a graduate student at the University of Michigan, there was a large physical and intellectual gap between the econometric courses taught on the third floor and the econometric modelling going on in the basement. 'Even more amazing was the transmogrification of particular individuals who wantonly sinned in the basement and metamorphosed into the highest of high priests as they ascended to the third floor' (Leamer, 1978, p. vi; quoted in Lawson, 1997, p. 7).

10. See also the symposium in the *Review of Political Economy* Vol. 3, 1989, pp. 249–380; Vol. 2, 1990, pp. 83–93, with contributions by Warren Samuels, A.W. Coats, G. Hodgson, R. Langlois, M. Rutherford, A. Mayhew, V. Vanberg, C. Leathers.

11. Ibid., pp. 79–80. For a stimulating discussion of norms, conventions, rules, routines and status, see, for example, Vanberg, 1994 and Choi, 1993.

12. Agassi aimed 'neither to assume the existence of all coordinations nor to explain them, but rather to assume the existence of some coordination in order to explain the existence of some other coordinations. It is an error to assume the only satisfactory explanation of institutions is by assumptions which say nothing about institutions' (Agassi, 1960, p. 263; cited by Rutherford, 1994, p. 37). There is, of course, a huge social science literature on the relationship between the individual and social change. For a striking example see Lloyd, 1986, *passim*.

13. There have been a number of valuable recent surveys of the interactions between economics and the other social sciences. However, space considerations preclude a discussion of this growing literature.

14. There is a recent survey of this subject in Coats, 1977a.

REFERENCES

Agassi, J. (1960), 'Methodological individualism', *British Journal of Sociology*, 11 September: 244–70.

Agassi, J. (1975), 'Institutional individualism', *British Journal of Sociology*, 26 June: 144–55.

Baumol, William J. (1982), 'Contestable markets: an uprising in the theory of industry structure', *American Economic Review*, **72** (1), March, 1–13.

Bowen, Howard (1953), 'Graduate education in economics', *American Economic Review Supplement*.

Choi, Young Back (1993), *Paradigms and Conventions. Uncertainty, Decision-Making and Entrepreneurship*, Ann Arbor: University of Michigan.

Coats, A.W. (1992), 'Changing perspectives in American graduate education in economics', 1953–1991', *Journal of Economic Education*, **23**(4), Autumn: 341–52.

Coats, A.W. (1997a), 'The internationalization of economic policy reform: some recent literature', in A.W. Coats (ed.), *The Post 1945 Internationalization of Economics*, Annual Supplement to Vol. 28, *History of Political Economy*, Durham, NC: Duke University Press, pp. 337–54.

Coats, A.W. (1997b), 'Fusfeld and Methodology', in Nahid Aslanbeigui and Young Back Choi (eds), *Borderlands of Economics. Essays in Honor of Daniel R. Fusfeld*, London: Routledge, pp. 32–46.

Ellingham, Mark *et al.* (1996), *Greece, The Rough Guide*, London: Penguin Books.

Frey, Bruno S. and R.L. Frey (eds) (1995), 'Is there a European economics?', *Kyklos*, **48**: 185–311.

Georgescu-Roegen, N. (1971), *The Entropy Law and the Economic Process*, Cambridge, MA: Harvard University Press.

Gilad B., S. Kaish and P.D. Loeb (1984), 'From economic behavior to behavioral economics: the behavioral uprising in economics', *Journal of Behavioral Economics*, **13**: 1–22.

Gruchy, Allen G. (1974), Remarks on the receipt of the Veblen-Commons Award, *Journal of Economic Issues*, **8**(2), June: 205–7.

Hansen, W. Lee (1991), 'The education and training of economics doctorates: major findings of the American Economic Association's commission on graduate education in economics', *Journal of Economic Literature*, **29**(3), September: 1054–87.

Hodgson, Geoffrey M. and Ernesto Screpanti (eds) (1991), *Rethinking Economics: Markets, Technology and Economic Evolution*, Aldershot, UK and Brookfield, US: Edward Elgar.

Hodgson, Geoffrey M. (1993), *Economics and Evolution. Bringing Life back into Economics*, Cambridge: Polity Press.

Jalladieu, Joel (1975), 'Restrained or enlarged scope of political economy: a few observations', *Journal of Economic Issues*, **9**, March: 1–13.

Kasper, Hirschel *et al.* (1991), 'The education of economists: from undergraduate to graduate study', *Journal of Economic Literature*, **29**(3), September, 1088–1109.

Krueger, Anne O. *et al.* (1991), 'Report of the commission on graduate education in economics', *Journal of Economic Literature*, **29**(3), September, 1035–53.

Lawson, Tony (1997), *Economics and Reality. Economics as Social Theory*, London: Routledge.

Lloyd, Christopher (1986), *Explanation in Social History*, Oxford: Blackwell.

Loasby, Brian (1996), 'Uncertainty, intelligence and imagination: George Shackle's guide to human progress', Address to European Association for Evolutionary Political Economy Conference, Antwerp, November 1996 (unpublished).

Mirowski, P. (1994), *More Heat than Light: Economics as Social Physics, Physics as Nature's Economics*, Cambridge: Cambridge University Press.

Nelson, Richard R. and Sydney G. Winter (1982), *An Evolutionary Theory of Economic Change*, Cambridge, MA: Belknap Press of Harvard University.

O'Driscoll, Gerald P. and Mario J. Rizzo ([1985] 1996), *The Economics of Time and Ignorance*, London: Routledge.

Ranson, Baldwin (1981), 'AFEE or AFIT: which represents institutional economics?', *Journal of Economic Issues*, **15**: 521–9.

Rutherford, Malcolm (1994), *Institutions in Economics: The Old and the New Institutionalism*, Cambridge: Cambridge University Press.

Sidgwick, Henry (1885), 'The scope and method of economic science', Presidential Address to Section F of the British Association for the Advancement of Science, reprinted in R.L. Smyth, *Essays in Economic Method*, London 1961, pp. 73–97.

Simon, Herbert (1987), 'Behavioral Economics' in J. Eatwell, M. Milgate and P. Newman (eds) *The New Palgrave. A Dictionary of Economics*, London: Macmillan Press, Vol. I, pp. 221–5.

Vanberg, Viktor J. (1994), *Rules and Choice in Economics*, London: Routledge.

Witt, Ulrich (1991), 'Reflections on the present state of evolutionary economic theory', in G.M. Hodgson and E. Screpanti (eds), *Rethinking Economics: Markets, Technology and Economic Evolution*, Aldershot, UK and Brookfield, US: Edward Elgar, pp. 83–102.

Index

Ackerman 75, 78
action, principle of least 180–82, 183–5
AFEE (American Association for Evolutionary Economics) 226
AFIT (Association for Institutional Thought) 226
Aftalion 89
Agassi, J. 65, 233, 237
ahistoricism 22, 32–4
Akerlof, G.A. 190, 191
Alchian, A.A. 4, 119, 121, 122, 129, 168–9, 170
  competitive selection 116–17
  debate with E. Penrose 151–2
Almeida-Costa, L. 173
Amar, J. 183, 184
America, economics education 230, 236
American Association for Evolutionary Economics (AFEE) 226
American Economic Association Commission on Graduate Education in Economics 230
American Historical School 45
American Radicals, theory of effort 193–5
Amoroso, L. 184
Andvig, C. 89
Arena, R. 9–10, 137
Argyris, C. 199, 201
Aristotle 32
Arrow, K.J. 213
Arthur, W.B. 2, 3, 25–6, 35, 169, 207
Ashton, T.S. 17
Association for Institutional Thought (AFIT) 226
Association pour la Critique des Sciences Economiques et Sociales 236
atemporal equilibrium 46–50
Aumann, R.J. 215, 216, 217
Australia, competition policy 108

Austrian school 6–7, 10, 41–66, 57–9, 129, 133–46
  competition 113–14
  origins of economic evolution 123
Ayres 104, 226, 227

Baba, Y. 36
Backhouse, R.E. 129
Baker, G.P. 193
Baran, P. 168
barbarian era 95, 98, 99
Barnard, C. 151, 171
barter economy 136
Baudry, B. 200
Baumol, W.J. 3, 168, 227
Bazzoli, L. 53
Becker 52
Beginnings of Ownership, The 98
behavioural economics 226–7
behavioural logic 200
Benhabib, J. 3
Bentham 182
Benthamite calculus 64
Berle, A. 168
Bernado, B. Di 155, 170
Bernouilli, J. 180–81
Berthe, B. 11, 191, 193, 198
Bertrand 215
Best, M. 157, 160, 172
Bianchi, M. 172
Binmore, K. 223
biological analogies 43, 123–4, 169
  competition 9, 108, 115–29
  evolution 43
  mutation 79–80, 85
  organic growth 169
Boettke, P. 41, 45, 46, 47, 48, 51, 55, 64, 65
Böhm Bawerk 64
Boltanski, L. 200
Borel 215

Boundreaux, D. 172
Bowen, H. 236
Bowles, S. 193, 194
Boyer, R. 193, 194
British economic policy 109
Broda, P. 8, 104
Brunet, P. 181
Buchanan, J.M. 129
Bunn, J.A. 35, 36
Bush, P.D. 104
Businario, U. 121
business cycles 7–8, 71–90
Business Cycles 72, 78, 86, 88, 143

Cahuc, P. 133
Canard, N.F. 213
capitalism 102, 103
    development of 115–16
Capitalism, Socialism and Democracy 72
Carlsson, B. 41
Carnap 205
Carnot, L. 181, 183
Carnot, S. 188
Casson's incentive model 191
causality, sequential 54
Chamberlin, E. 170
Chandler, A. 148
chaos theory 20–21
Choi, Y.B. 236
Clark, J.B. 76, 116
Coase, R. 151, 155, 161, 164, 168, 170,
    172
Coats, A.W. 12–13, 233, 236, 237
Cogee (AEA Commission on Graduate
    Education in Economics) 230, 236
Colander, D. 223
Coleman, W.O. 181, 182
Commons, J.R. 8, 43, 44, 55, 60, 64,
    226, 232
    change 48, 50
    institutions 41, 42, 60, 227
    legal order 61–2
    private property 91–106
    transactions 53, 66
competition 9, 107–130
competitive general equilibrium model
    111, 113, 116
competitive selection 9, 107–30
contingency 20–21, 35
Contribution to Political Economy 174

conventions, effort 196–7
coordination equilibria 26
Corei, T. 104
Coriat, B. 200
Coriolis, G.G. de 183
Cosgel, M. 172
Coulmas, F. 185
Coulomb, C.A. 182–3, 186
Cournot, A. 213, 182, 215, 216
Cournot's Program 182
Cowan, R. 35
Cowen, T. 64
Croci, A. 154, 169
cultural evolution 95–6
cultural models 102
cumulative causation 3–4, 49
Currie, M. 54
Cusumano, M.A. 36
cycle analysis 7–8, 71–90
Cyert, R. 168

Darwin, Charles 35, 114, 118–19, 129
Darwinism 33, 35, 43, 115
    see also neo-Darwinism
David, P.A. 2, 3, 5–6, 13, 54, 207
Dawkins, R. 118, 121
Debreu, G. 12, 212, 213, 214, 217
Deci, E.L. 201
decision-making processes 161–3
Demsetz, H. 156, 170–71
Depew, D.J. 126, 128–9, 130
Dewey 52, 226
Di Bernado, B. 155, 170
Dietrich, M. 172
Dimand, M.A. 223
Dimand, R.W. 223
Distribution of Wealth, The 76
Dobzhansky, T. 126
Doray, B. 182
Dorfman, J. 104
Dosi, G. 129, 160, 170
Dowd, D.F. 104
Dulbecco, P. 6–7
Dupuit, J. 213
Durlauf, S. 35
Dutraive, V 6–7, 53

Econometrica 72
economic equilibrium theory 212–14,
    220

economic evolution 9, 107–30
Economic Journal 148
'economic man' 65
economic policy, British 109
Economic Theory of Managerial Capitalism, The 148
economics imperialism 233–4
Economies et Societies 174
economy, isolated household 137–8
Edgeworth, F.Y. 184, 215, 217
education, economics 230–31
    American 236
Edwards, R.C. 193, 194
effort, human 179–201
effort, principle of least 183–5
Egidi, M. 3, 169
egoism, energic 142–3
egoism, hedonistic 143–4
Eldredge, N. 49, 130
Ellingham, Mark 236
Eloge de M. de Montesquieu 182
Ely 116
emergence of institutions 3–5
employees
    effort 189–95
    incentives 190–93
    resistance to change 197
employers, control over employees 194
Encyclopedic Dictionary of Mathematics 34
End of Science, The 205
endogeneity 7
Endres, A.M. 129
energic egoism 143–4
energic rationality 134
energy 180–89
energy rationality 180–82
Engels F. 187, 188
entrepreneurs 142–6
entrepreneurship, effect on markets 51
equilibrium 28, 29
    atemporal 46–50
    market 46–50
    model, competitive general 111, 113, 116
    Nash 26
    theory, general 12, 212–14, 220
equity incentive model 191
ergodic systems 18–19

evolution
    biological *see* Darwinism, neo-Darwinism
    cultural 95–6
    economic 107–30
    of institutions 3–5, 42–3, 133–46
    of science 205–10, 219–22
evolutionary game theory 118
Evolutionary Theory of Economic Change, An 229
expectancy theory 201

Fechner 189
Fermat, P. de 181
Filer, R.K. 198, 201
Fink, R. 64
firms 150–52, 161–3
    boundaries 152–6
    growth 148–74
    international 170
    optimal size 170
Fish 223
Fisher, F.M. 23
Fisher, I. 79, 184, 185
Fisher, R.A. 117, 122, 124
flexibility of institutions 57–61
Florence, P. Sargant 171
Foray, D. 36
Foss, N. J. 151, 169, 171 ,172–3
Foster, J. 9, 115, 123, 128
Fransman, M. 171
Frantz, R. 196
Freud, S. 189
Frey, B. S. 228
Frey, R.L. 228
Friedman, M. 107, 110, 113, 119, 120, 233
Frisch, R. 7–8, 71–90

Galbraith, J. 168
game theory 5, 12, 118, 214–19, 220
Garrison, R. 46, 65
Garrouste, P. 4, 55, 58, 63, 64, 65
general equilibrium theory (GET) 12, 111, 113, 116–18, 212–14, 220
Georgescu-Roegen, N. 228–9
German Historical School 43
Ghoshal, S. 171, 173
gift-exchange incentive model 190, 193
Gilad, B. 227

Gloria-Palermo, S. 9–10, 135
Gloria, S. 51
Gonce, R.A. 104
Gordon, W. 45
Gordons, D.M. 193, 194
Gossen, H.H. 182
Gould, S.J. 35, 49
Gram, H. 212
Greenstein, S. 35, 36
Greif, A. 34
Grindley, P. 36
growth of the firm 148–74
Gruchy, A.G. 104, 226
Grundsätze der Volkswirtschaftslehre 135
Guennif, S. 200
Gunning, J.P. 63
Guyot, Y. 184

Haavelmo 75
habits, human, effect on market 52–4
Hadley 116
Hahn, F. 34, 41
Halevy 182
Hamel, G. 160
Hamilton, W. 48
Hamilton's principle of parcimony 181, 182
handicraft era 95, 104
Hansen, W.L. 230
Hargreaves Heap, S.P. 223
Harsanyi, John 215
Harter (Jr) 104, 105
Hayek, F. von 107, 109–10, 114, 120, 124, 129
  institutional economics 43, 58, 64, 173
  knowledge in organisations 165, 173
  market equilibrium 47, 57, 111
Heap, S.P. Hargreaves 223
hedonistic egoism 142–3
hedonistic rationality 134
Hegel, F.G.W. 98
Helm, G. 183
Helmholtz, H. 186, 189
Herzberg, F. 191
heterodox economics 12–13, 228–35
Hicks, J.R. 54, 213
hierarchies
  dichotomy with markets 154–6
  in economic organisations 127

High, J. 51
historical economics 15–18
historicity 5, 22
History of Economic Analysis 72, 88
Hodgson, G.M. 3–4, 41, 42, 48, 49, 52, 53, 61, 104, 107, 118, 123, 146, 156, 199, 236
Holcombe, R. 172
Holt, R. 189
Horgan, J. 205
Horwitz, S. 47, 48, 51
household economy, isolated 137–8
Hull, D. 208–9, 221, 222
human action, effect on market 50–54, 61
Human behavior and the principle of least effort 184–5
human effort 11, 179–201
Human Motor, The 183, 184
human resources of a firm 157, 160

ICARE (International Confederation of Associations for the Reform of Economics) 236
Imai, K. 36
imitators 138, 141, 145
imperialism, economics 233–4
incentives, theory of 190–93
individualism 139–43
individuals, role in market formation 165
Industrial Dynamics 41
information in institutions 56–7
Ingrao, B. 212, 213, 214, 223
innovation, Schumpeter's theory 72–90
innovators 138, 141, 145
Instinct of Workmanship, The 97
institutional economics 6–7, 41–66, 232–5
Institutional Economics 100–101
institutions *see also* firms
  coordinating role 100–102
  definitions 60
  evolution of 3–5, 55–63, 133–46
  flexibility 57–9
  knowledge in 56–7
  permanency 57–9
Institutions and Economics. The Old and the New Institutionalism 232

International Confederation of Associations for the Reform of Economics (ICARE) 236
international firms 170
Ioannides, S. 34, 46, 57
Isnard, A.N. 213
isolated household economy 137–8
Israel, G. 212, 213, 214, 223

Jacobi 182
Jaffé, W. 64, 138–9
Jalladieu, J. 236
James 52
Jennings, R. 187
Jensen, M.C. 193
Jevons' model 11, 185–6
Jevons, W.S. 43, 64, 179, 184, 185–9
Jolink, A. 12
Jones, L.B. 129

Kaish, S. 227
Kaldor, N. 4, 170
Kalecki, M. 87, 109
Kasper, H. 230
Kasper Report 230
Kauffman, S. 130
Kelm 121
Kennedy, W.F. 104
Kirat, T. 104
Kirzner, I.M. 47, 51, 64, 111, 171
Kitcher, Ph. 222
Klamer, A. 223
Knight, F.H. 154, 159, 161–2, 163, 164, 172, 173
knowledge
    as firm's resource 157, 163–7, 173–4
    in institutions 56–7
Knudsen 172
Kohli, M. 194
Kreps, D.M. 171, 222
Krueger, A. 230
Krugman, P. 35
Kuhn, Thomas 12, 205–6, 219–21, 223

labour 193–4
Lachmann, L.
    on entrepreneurial behaviour 51
    on institutional dynamics 42, 57–63, 65, 66

on market economy 46–7, 48, 55–6, 64
Lagrange, J.L. 182
Lakatos 220–21, 223
Lamarkian analogy 120–21
Lane, R.E. 192
Lange, O. 116,183–4
Langlois, R.N. 41, 42, 43, 54, 56, 65, 170, 172, 236
Lassert 34
Lazear, E.P. 191
Lazonick, W. 169
Le Chatelier 184
Le Moigne, J.L. 185
leadership
    function of 174
    relationship to masses 139–42
Leamer, E. 236
least action, principle of 180–82, 183–5
least effort, principle of 183–5
Leathers, C.G. 42, 43, 63, 64, 236
Legal Foundations of Capitalism 101
legal order 61–2
Leibenstein, H. 172, 180, 189, 190, 195–9
Leibniz 181
leisure class 93
Leonard, R.J. 215
Letters concerning Science and Nature 187
Lewin, K. 189, 201
Liebowitz, S.J. 20, 21, 22, 23–4, 34–5, 222
Lloyd, C. 237
Loasby, Brian J. 50, 111, 165, 167, 169, 173, 225–6
lock-in effect 2–3, 207–8, 223
Locke 92
Loeb, P.D. 227
logic, behavioural 200
Lombardini, S. 168
Lotka 187
Louçã, F. 7–8, 76, 88, 89
Luce, R.D. 216–17

machine era 95–6
Machlup, F. 150, 152, 169
Mahoney, J. 160
Malmgren, H.B. 169
Malthus, T. 118–19, 122, 123, 129

managerial resources 157–9
managers 142–6
March, J.G. 168, 172
Marginalism 43
Margolis, S.E. 13, 20–21, 22, 23–4,
   34–5, 222
Market as an Economic Process, The 46
markets
  dichotomy with hierarchies 154–6
  effects of human action 23–4
  failure 23–4
  metaphor for institutions 44
  theories 6–7, 41–66
Markov chains 19–20
Marris, R. 148–9, 168, 169
Marshall A. 1, 10, 115, 146, 168, 181
Marx, Karl
  evolution 114, 118–19, 122
  ownership 92, 96–7, 104
  work 187–8
masses, relation to leadership 139–42
Maupertuis 180–82, 185
Mayhew, A. 236
Maynard Smith, J. 118, 120, 129
McGregor, D. 192, 201
McNulty, P.J. 111
Means, G. 168
mechanical analogies 71–90
melioration 28–9
Menger, C. 1, 3, 5, 10, 43, 44, 55, 58, 65,
   133–9, 141–2, 145–6
Metcalfe, J.S., model of competitive
   selection 122–8
Methodenstreit 43
Micromotives and Macrobehaviour 3
Mill, J.S. 123
Miller, E. 44, 45
minimax theorem 215
Mirowski, Philip 182, 236
Mises, L. von 47, 54, 64, 113–14
Mitchell, W.C. 52, 64, 140–41, 226, 227
Moigne, J.L. Le 18
Mokyr, J. 34, 120
money
  evolution of 3, 135–8
  significance in social economy 141–2
Monopolies Commission (UK) 112
Montgomery, C. 172
Moran, P. 171, 173
Morgan, M.S. 114, 116

Morgenstern, O. 5, 12, 213, 214–15, 216,
   218, 220, 223
motivation, human 188–9, 201
Mouchot, C. 200
Murphy, K.J. 193
Mylonadis, Y. 36

Narduzzo, A. 3
Nash, J. 214–15, 216–19, 220
Nash equilibria 26, 214–15, 216–19
Nash programme 216–19
Natural Value 140
nature, energy rationality of 180–82
Navier, C.L. 183
negotiational psychology 53
Nelson, R.R. 56, 120, 121, 122, 160,
   169, 173–4, 229
neoclassical economics 116, 120, 233,
   234, 236
neoclassical growth model 117
neo-Darwinism 9, 116–20
  see also Darwinism
Neumann, J. von 5, 12, 214–16, 218,
   220, 223
New Institutional Economics (NIE)
   41–2, 232–3
Newtonian systems 9, 119–20
Niehans, J. 13
non-ergodic systems 18–19
Nuttin, J. 193, 197

O'Driscoll, G.P. 41, 47, 48, 54, 55, 56–7,
   58, 64, 65, 236
Old Institutional Economics (OIE) 11,
   42–66, 232–5
O'Rand, A.M. 223
organic institutions, emergence of 135–9
organised market economy 137–8
Origin of the Species, The 114
Orléan, A 200
Orsenigo, L. 129
orthodox economics 12–13, 228–35
Ostwald, W. 183, 187
ownership 91–105

Pandian, R. 160
parcimony 180–5
Pareto, V. 182, 184, 212
Pareto dominated equilibria 28
Pareto optimality 23

path-constrained melioration 28–9
path dependence 2–12, 15–36, 205–23
pattern coordination 48
Peirces 52
pendulum metaphor 71, 73, 79–87
Penrose, E.T. 10–11, 112, 121, 148–78
Penrose Effect 155
Perlman, M. 64
permanency of institutions 57–61
Petander, K. 89
pin-making (Adam Smith) 115, 164
Podolinski 187
Polanyi, K. 45, 192
Polanyi, M. 166
Poncelet, J.V. 183
possession 91–105
Prahalad, C. 160
Principles 137
Principles of Science 186
private property 8–9, 91–105
Prychitko, D. 41, 46, 47, 48, 51, 65
psychology, social 53
punctuated equilibria 3, 49

QWERTY keyboard adoption 2, 30–31, 34

Raiffa, H. 215, 216–17
Ramstad, Y. 49, 61, 62, 64, 66
Ranson, B. 226
Regulation 22
Reindustrialization and Technology 172
Renault, M. 11, 182
Research on the mathematical principles of the theory of wealth 182
resources of a firm 157–61
Ricardo 92
Richardson, G.B. 111, 151, 156, 170, 173
Rizzello, S. 169
Rizzo, M.J. 41, 47, 48, 54, 55, 56–7, 58, 64, 65, 236
Robinson, J. 4, 54, 55, 170
rocking horse metaphor 73–5, 78–9, 87, 89
Rosenberg, N. 172, 173
Rosenbloom, R.S. 36
Rosmorduc, J. 181
Rothbard, M.N. 65
Rousseau, J. 182

routine 173–4
rule-following behaviour 56–7
Ruse, M. 120
Ruth, M. 121
Rutherford, M. 42, 55, 65, 105, 232, 235, 236
Ruttan, V.W. 34

Samuels, W.J. 43, 44, 45, 63, 226, 236
Samuelson, P.A. 184, 212, 213
Sanderson, W. 36
Sargant Florence, P. 171
savage era 95, 98–9
Scarf, H. 217
Schelling, T.C. 3
Schotter, A. 5, 56, 65, 215, 216, 223
Schumpeter, J. 13, 71–90, 133–4
    correspondence with Frisch 73–89
    creative destruction 127, 128, 167
    economic analysis 142–6
    economic evolution 10, 121–4, 126, 127
    pendulum metaphor 71, 73, 79–87
Schumpeterian shocks 73, 79, 85
science, evolution of 205–10, 219–22
selection, competitive 9, 107–30
selection mechanism analogies 118
selection processes, path-dependent 210–11
Selfish Gene, The 118
self-organization 9, 123–31, 137
self-reinforcing mechanisms 207
Selten 218
sequential causality 54
Seris, J.P. 181, 182
services 159–61, 171–2
Setterfield, M. 54
Shackle, G. 159
Shapiro, C. 190
Shapley, L. 215
shirker incentive model 190, 193
shocks, Slutsky 73, 79, 83
Shubik, M. 215, 217, 223
Sidgwick, H. 228
Silverberg, G. 129
Simon, H. 151, 156, 168, 171, 172, 235–6
Slater, M. 149, 155, 158
Slutsky 87
Slutsky shocks 73, 79, 83

Smith, Adam 9, 115, 117, 119, 129, 164, 183
  market model 113–14
Smith, J. Maynard 118, 120, 129
Social Economics 64, 139, 140
social psychology 53
Solow, R. 34
Spencer, H. 107, 114, 122
Sraffa, P. 4, 170
static general equilibrium 117
Statistical Evidence as to the Causes of Business Fluctuations 77
Statistical Methods for Biological Research 117
Steedman, I. 54
Steinmuller, E. 34
Stigler, G. 135
Stiglitz, J.E. 190
stochastic processes 21, 206
stochastic systems 18
Stolper, W. 89
Strassman, D.L. 236
Strategy and Structure 148
Strauss, L. 104
Streissler, E. 135
Structure of Scientific Revolutions 219–20
Study of man's energy, A 183
Sumner 116
sunk cost hysteresis 32–4
Sweezy, P. 168
Swoboda 144
Szathmary, E. 129

Teece, D. 160, 170, 172, 173
Thalberg, B. 89
Theory of Business Enterprise, The 105
Theory of Economic Development, The 76, 134, 143
Theory of Games and Economic Behavior, The 214–15
Theory of the Growth of the Firm 10–11, 148–68
Theory of the Leisure Class, The 93
Theory of Political Economy, The 187
Theory of the Simple Economy 140
Theory of Value 212
Thévenot, L. 200
Thullier, P. 181
Tilman, R. 105

time framework of market 54–5
Tinbergen 89
trade unions 96
transactions
  as unit of economic analysis 53
  characteristics 66
  working rules 49–50
Turvani, M. 10–11, 169, 171, 172

UK economic policy 109
Untersuchungen 135, 141–2
utility of effort 196

Vanberg, V. J. 42, 55, 63, 236
Varoufakis, Y. 223
Vatin, F. 182, 185, 187–8
Veblen, T.B. 1, 5, 32, 64, 226, 227
  competition 115–16
  cumulative causation 3
  economic man 52, 65
  evolutionary economics 48–50, 115–16, 123
  institutions 55, 60–61
  private property 8, 91–106
  work 188
Veblenian evolution 121–2
vested interests 95–7
Ville 215
Vincenti, W. 172, 173
violin metaphor 87
Voltaire, F. 192
von Hayek, F. *see* Hayek, F. von
von Mises, L. 47, 54, 64, 113–14
von Neumann, J. 5, 12, 212, 213, 214–16, 218, 220, 223
Vromen, J. 12, 169
Vroom, V. 201

Wald 213
Waldegrave 215
Waller, W.T. 52
Wallis, Professor 117
Walras, Leon 43, 64, 76, 116, 182, 212
  entrepreneurs 144
  general equilibrium theory 213, 214, 220
  rational behaviour 143
Walsh, V. 212
Weber, B.H. 126, 128–9, 130, 189
Weiner, B. 189, 197

Weintraub, E.R. 212
White, M. 187, 188
Wicksell 75, 78, 87, 89
Wieser, F. von 133–4
  analysis of institutions 10, 139–42,
    146
  entrepreneurs 145
Wilkins, J. 222
Wilkinson, F. 129
Williamson, O.E. 24, 53, 107, 151, 154,
    158, 160, 164, 168, 170
Winiarski, L. 184
Winter, S. 56, 120, 121, 122, 151, 152,
    160, 169, 170, 173–4, 229
Witt, U. 123, 171, 174, 234

women, capture of 94, 99
Wonderful Life 35
work 179, 182–9
working rules for transactions 49–50, 62
Wright, G. 34
Wundt, W. 189
Wynarczyk, P. 41, 63, 64

Yellen, J.L. 191
You, J-B. 129
Young, H.P. 3, 5
Yule 79

Zermelo 215
Zipf, G.K. 184–5